Globalization and the Politics of Pay

Globalization and the Politics of Pay

Policy Choices in the American States

SUSAN B. HANSEN

Georgetown University Press
Washington, D.C.

As of January 1, 2007, 13-digit ISBN numbers will replace the current 10-digit system.
Paperback: 978-1-58901-088-8

Georgetown University Press, Washington, D.C.
©2006 by Georgetown University Press. All rights reserved. No part of this book may be reproduced or utilized in any form or by any means, electronic or mechanical, including photocopying and recording, or by any information storage and retrieval system, without permission in writing from the publisher.

Library of Congress Cataloging-in-Publication Data

Hansen, Susan B.
    Globalization and the politics of pay : policy choices in the American states / Susan B. Hansen.
        p. cm. — (American governance and public policy series)
    Includes bibliographical references and index.
    ISBN-13: 978-1-58901-088-8 (pbk. : alk. paper)
    ISBN-10: 1-58901-088-4 (pbk. : alk. paper)
    1. Wages—United States. 2. Wages—Government policy—United States—States. 3. Labor policy—United States—States. 4. Working class—United States—Economic conditions. 5. Globalization—Economic aspects—United States. I. Title. II. American governance and public policy.
HD4975.H315 2006
331.2′10973—dc22   2005027242

This book is printed on acid-free paper meeting the requirements of the American National Standard for Permanence in Paper for Printed Library Materials.
13 12 11 10 09 08 07 06 9 8 7 6 5 4 3 2
First printing

Printed in the United States of America

For my husband Fred,
with all my love

Contents

List of Tables and Figures

Preface

THIS BOOK HAS HAD a long gestation. During research on my 1983 book *The Politics of Taxation*, I discovered that most economists doubted that state tax rates or incentives had much effect on business location or investment decisions. But most politicians, the media, and the business community believed otherwise. This puzzling discrepancy pointed to the ways in which ideas and evidence (or lack thereof) influence public discourse and public policy decisions.

During the 1980s, the impact of deindustrialization was painfully evident in the Pittsburgh region and elsewhere in the United States. Was international competition to blame? Lack of innovation? Greedy labor unions? Why was Japan so successful? Policymakers seeking alternatives to the loss of jobs, incomes, and tax revenues needed answers. But the general response from the Ronald Reagan administration was that the federal government should keep its hands off and let competitive markets adjust to the new economic realities. The Reagan tax cuts were supposed to spur business investment, and the firing of the striking air traffic controllers sent a strong message that the days of union power were numbered. Via trickle-down economics, unemployed workers would supposedly benefit from opportunities in emerging industries.

For state and local politicians, however, the plight of the unemployed in their jurisdictions demanded a more activist response to deindustrialization and international competition. Though creating jobs through patronage had a long (if less than honorable) history, job creation through active intervention in private markets was a new departure for subnational governments. Cutting taxes was not a viable option either, because most states and localities faced deficit budgets caused by the 1981–82 recession, declining revenues, and cutbacks in federal aid. So many states and localities began to experiment with a variety of new methods to transform their economies: venture capital programs, high-technology initiatives, promotion of exports, enterprise zones. The goal was job creation; the new catchword was "economic development." Dozens of new agencies and programs were initiated, and economic development became a growth industry, with its own practitioners, professional conferences, reports, and books.

All this activity attracted the attention of political scientists like myself who were students of state politics. My initial research on state economic development was a 1984 American Political Science Association conference paper examining the impact of tax subsidies, right-to-work laws, and industrial policies on economic trends in the American states. And throughout the 1980s, I and several others in the comparative state politics field (including Paul Brace, Peter Eisinger, Virginia Gray, and David Lowery) continued to track state economic initiatives, their political rationales, and their impact. In this era of devolution, many significant policy innovations emerged at the state level; the states were developing far stronger institutions and capacity for governance than in an earlier era, when "states' rights" was a thinly disguised euphemism for racism. But critics of devolution feared that the loss of federal standards and mandates would lead to a "race to the bottom" in areas such as environmental regulation, welfare, and higher education. And few of the initiatives in economic development, entrepreneurship, or industrial policy showed much short-term impact in states such as Pennsylvania and Michigan, which continued to shed jobs and population.

The severe recession of the early 1990s led to soaring budget deficits in most states and cutbacks in many programs, including investment in higher education as well as in economic development policies. Aided in part by the Republican takeover of Congress in 1994 and a corresponding increase in state offices held by Republicans, tax subsidies and regulation of labor costs were resurrected from an earlier era. The debates over the effectiveness of such programs continued as well, but they offered a significant political advantage in an era of tax revolts and budgetary constraints: Direct appropriations were not required. However, the focus of voters and state elected officials remained on unemployment and the loss of jobs, allegedly to foreign competition. Governors continued to campaign with promises to "create jobs" and "get this state moving again," and in a 1999 article I found that their popularity ratings while in office were increasingly tied to trends in state unemployment.

Still the question remained: Could state governments actually create jobs or boost their economies? Paul Peterson's seminal 1995 book had argued that economic development was precisely what subnational governments *should* be doing, while redistributive policies were likely to fail because of interstate competition. But as the American and the global economies became increasingly interdependent, many doubted whether even the national government could withstand pressures to control labor costs and limit government spending on education or other social policies. In the United States, many politicians at local, state, and national levels insisted that high labor costs were driving jobs to the Sunbelt or overseas. A 1995 study by the Organization for Economic Cooperation and Development argued that the United States was in fact doing far better in terms of job creation than most European countries, which were advised to emulate the United States and reduce the "social wage" and restrictions on employers' ability to hire and fire, because these added to their labor costs.

In the late 1990s, I developed an indicator of trends over time in state labor costs. I had initially intended this to serve as a control variable in my ongoing analysis of the impact of state/local taxes and other policies on economic growth. But I was struck, first, by the considerable decline in state labor costs since 1970; and second, by the large range of variation across the states in both levels and trends. I also noted that "controlling labor costs" was seldom part of the rhetoric of state elected officials or economic development professionals. Campaign speeches might discuss "competitiveness" or the merits of a "good business climate," but telling working people that they should be paid less did not seem to be a viable electoral strategy. In a 2001 article, I argued that, despite rhetoric about human capital investment and the need to create more "good" jobs, the states were in fact moving toward a low-wage strategy for economic development.

How had most states managed to show such drastic declines in labor costs since 1970? And what were the economic and social consequences? My index of state labor costs proved to be a robust tool for the analysis of these questions. Given the differences in labor costs between the United States and Europe, the index would also enable me to consider questions about the relative impact of globalization, a topic much in dispute within both political science and economics. My research into the history of the role of the American states in regulating labor costs led to a greater understanding of the reasons why the United States and Europe differed, as well as curiosity about alternative policies to create jobs while maintaining a good quality of life.

Along the way, I have become indebted to many individuals for their ideas and support. First of all, the National Science Foundation provided financial support for an early stage of this research. This enabled me to collect data and to interview economic development officials and policy-makers in several states; I am grateful to all of them for their critical insights. Second, many others in the field of comparative state politics have offered methodological advice, shared their data with me, and provided valuable feedback at various points in the process. Third, the Pennsylvania Institute on Public Policy and the University of Pittsburgh's Institute of Politics provided contacts with state representatives, union officials, and lobbyists in the Commonwealth, as well as invigorating arguments about the ideal versus the feasible. Fourth, Pittsburgh and Allegheny County have been at the fulcrum of many ongoing debates about deindustrialization, the role of labor, and human capital. I have learned a great deal from observations of local efforts (some successful, others less so) at economic transformation.

Finally, the University of Pittsburgh has provided a collegial environment for doing research, developing theories, and testing out my ideas on colleagues and students. I am especially grateful to my colleagues Carolyn Ban, Ralph Bangs, Moe Coleman, Ray Owen, Guy Peters, and Alberta Sbragia. Many graduate students, including Katharine Floros, Agustin Grijalva, John Hoornbeek, Adam Lawrence, Stephanie McLean, Sawa Omori, and Maria Qing Yang provided invaluable research assistance.

This book is dedicated to my husband Fred. I am very grateful for his unfailing love and support, his patience with the lengthy process of researching and writing a book, and his superb computer skills. Discussions with him about both substance and format have helped to sharpen my own arguments and (hopefully) improve the writing and data presentation. However, all errors of interpretation and omission are my own responsibility.

CHAPTER ONE

Globalization, Interstate Competition, and Labor

IN THE AMERICAN FEDERAL system, the fifty states actively compete for jobs, business investment, and factory locations. Labor costs have played a role in this interstate competition since the days of slavery and the pre–Civil War plantation economy. In recent years, however, global economic trends have put additional pressures on businesses to reduce labor costs. As Levi (2003, 51) notes, "The movement of jobs to locations with low-wage and nonunionized workers, and the consequent race to the bottom, is worldwide."

How have the fifty states responded to an increasingly integrated global economy? Has there indeed been a "race to the bottom" in wages and benefits? If so, what have been the economic and social consequences? Has reducing labor costs led to more jobs, even if these are low paid? Or have some states been able to thrive in the international economy without reducing the living standards of their citizens?

Consider examples of workers in three very different states: Ohio, Arkansas, and Washington. In 1970 a machinist's wife from Dayton, Ohio was the prototypical American voter, according to Wattenberg and Scammon's influential book *The Real Majority* (1970). How has life in Ohio changed for this "typical" woman and her family between 1970 and today? And how do trends in labor costs in Ohio compare with other states?

First, the global context. From World War II until 1970, the United States enjoyed a trade surplus, exporting more than it imported. By 2000, however, the trade deficit was a record $651 billion. Imports from China are cheap and readily available at the local Wal-Mart, now the largest employer in the United States (Slater 2003). But in 1970, the year its stock first went public, Wal-Mart had only thirty-eight stores, mostly in rural areas of the South, and it was committed to a "Buy America" policy (*Frontline* 2004).

In 1970, the typical Ohio voter's husband most likely worked for an automobile company and was a member of the United Auto Workers (UAW). At that time, the automobile industry employed 811,000 Americans and the UAW had 1.5 million members; only a few thousand foreign cars were sold. But by 2000, more than 40 percent of cars purchased in America were either imported or assembled by foreign-owned companies such as Honda, which built a huge (nonunion) factory in Ohio in 1982 (Yanarella and Green 1990). Also by 2000, UAW membership had fallen to only 640,000 members, and the proportion of American workers belonging to labor unions had declined to 12 percent, compared with 28 percent in 1970. Labor union membership used to be a good predictor of voting Democratic. In 1970, Ohio was a competitive state: The governor and one U.S. senator were Democrats, while the state legislature and the other senator were Republican. But by 2004, more than 50 percent of white male union members voted Republican. Ohio's governor and state legislature were in Republican hands, and Ohio's well-mobilized Republican voter turnout in 2004 gave the presidency to George W. Bush.[1]

In 1970, our machinist's wife was unlikely to work outside the home; only 41 percent of married women with children were in the labor force. Nor did she need to, because her husband's job paid well enough to place them solidly in the middle class, and his employer's health insurance covered the whole family. They owned their own home (although with a mortgage), owned an American-made car, and without too much difficulty could send their children to college; tuition at Ohio State University was only $1,500 a year.

By 2000, however, the proportion of married women in the labor force had risen to 63 percent. In part, this occurred because of gains by the women's movement, falling birthrates, and a much higher proportion of women attending college. But it was also a matter of economic necessity, because men's wages had stagnated since the 1970s. So our machinist's wife was likely to be working at least part time, perhaps at Wal-Mart (which now has eight supercenters in the Dayton area), or at another retail or service job, in order to be able to afford the mortgage, car payments, and college tuition. Ohio State University tuition had risen to $7,500, at a rate far faster than the overall inflation rate or the actual cost of instruction. Access to college has thus become much more difficult for working-class families.[2]

The machinist's wife might also be working today because her husband has been laid off. Manufacturing employment has declined sharply in Ohio since 1970, and several major factories in Ohio (Rubbermaid, Goodyear, Big Three automobile factories and suppliers) have closed. Her husband might have received unemployment benefits for a time, but if he did find work it was probably with lower wages and fewer benefits; in 2005 nonunion Wal-Mart employees in Dayton averaged $8.50 per hour and worked an average of twenty-eight hours per week. Also, the family is less likely to have health coverage; 45 million Americans (many of them Wal-Mart employees or other adults working full time) lacked health insurance in 2005.

Because the jobs available for both husband or wife pay so little, either or both may now be working two jobs to make ends meet. This of course means less time for the children, vacation, and recreation, or for social or political activities (Schor 1991; Warren and Tyagi 2003). Two-income families may still be able to approximate a middle-class lifestyle on credit; average credit-card debt in the United States today is more than $7,500 a person, and many owe thousands more for home mortgages, car leases, or student loans. Total credit charges increased by 350 percent between 1990 and 2003, but total personal income over that time span increased only 188 percent (Walker 2004). Consequently, rates of personal bankruptcy and mortgage foreclosure are at record levels, and many working families are only one paycheck (or one medical crisis) away from these unfortunate outcomes.

Though Ohio may have been typical in 1970, its workers were not faring well in 2005. In fact, Ohio lost more manufacturing jobs than any other state between 2000 and 2004 (AFL-CIO 2004), and it has been losing population to faster-growing Sunbelt states. But what of workers in other states? Consider an employee of a poultry-processing plant in Arkansas. These jobs have high injury rates but are not unionized, and wages are well below the national average (in 2000, $11.98 an hour, compared with $16.32 in Ohio). These factors have encouraged major producers like Tyson Foods to expand operations in northeastern Arkansas.

A recent surge in Hispanic immigration has added to competition for employment; Arkansas ranks second only to North Carolina in its percent increase in immigration since 1990. Also, Arkansas (unlike Ohio) is a right-to-work state. This means that even if workers at a plant vote to join a union, they cannot be required to pay union dues; such states tend to have much lower levels of union membership. Union membership in Arkansas in 2000 was only 5.8 percent, compared with 24 percent in Ohio. However, despite its right-to-work law, low wages, and low taxes, Arkansas has been losing manufacturing jobs overall.

Furthermore, Arkansas ranks thirty-sixth among the fifty states in the value of its exports. Although foreign investment has quadrupled in the

United States since 1978, little of this has gone to Arkansas. Wal-Mart's headquarters is located in Bentonville, and members of founder Sam Walton's family still live here. Several of them are now billionaires. But per capita income in Arkansas still ranks among the lowest in the United States (forty-seventh out of fifty in 2004), and a high proportion of its families and children live below the official federal poverty line. As in most other southern states, voter turnout is low. Once solidly Democratic, Arkansas has been electing more Republicans to the state legislature. Although Bill Clinton served as governor of Arkansas for more than twelve years, the state now has a Republican governor, Mike Huckabee.

But the states include winners as well as losers in the global economy. Our third example is an aircraft worker in Washington State, which in 2000 led the United States in manufacturing employment as a percent of the labor force. Washington has benefited from commercial purchases of Boeing jets as well as from exports of military aircraft, and it is one of the leading states for prime contracts from the Defense Department. Our skilled aircraft worker is likely to be a union member and to earn even more than manufacturing workers in Ohio. Washington has a high proportion of its manufacturing workforce unionized (23 percent in 2000), and it pays high wages in manufacturing. Although the state has no income tax, its tax burden is the highest in the United States, and it provides generous benefits for workers' compensation, welfare, and unemployment. But clearly neither high wages nor high taxes constitute barriers to a strong position in exports. Unlike Ohio and Arkansas, both "red states" that supported George W. Bush in 2000 and 2004, Washington is a "blue state" and reliably Democratic, with two Democratic senators and a Democratic governor (all female) in 2005, as well as a Democratic state legislature. Its voter turnout is also among the highest in the United States.

The United States as a whole has become much more closely linked to the global economy since 1970. International trade (exports plus imports) now accounts for 20 percent of gross domestic product, compared with only 8 percent in 1970. As of 1990, 20 percent of American workers were employed in export-related industries, although that proportion has declined considerably since then because of the growing trade deficit.[3] Yet as these three examples illustrate, the American states differ considerably in wages, levels of unionization, and the impact of the international economy. Though few Americans today are immune to global influences, workers in some states are far more vulnerable than others to competition from abroad.

The purpose of this book is to explore these state differences. The states have gained increased responsibility in a number of policy areas since the

1970s, including health, the environment, welfare, corrections, and education. Most observers credit the states with increased capacity for governance and administration.[4] But do the states have the capacity to foster economic growth in an increasingly global economy? According to many observers in academia and the media, no nation, region, state, or municipality is immune from the impact of the increased mobility of global capital. Multinational corporations can readily shift investments, production, jobs, plants, or research and development to locations that offer lower wages, lower taxes, or weaker environmental or safety regulations.

Social science research, however, has found marked differences in how countries have responded to the predations of global capitalism. Some argue that the United States, with its liberal free-market tradition, open economy, and small welfare state, has been much more vulnerable than most European countries to pressures to reduce taxes and lower labor costs (Wilensky 2002; Kollmeyer 2003). But as this book shows, data on economic trends for the United States as a whole mask considerable differences among the states. Unlike in more centralized European countries, in America taxes, government spending, and labor costs are shared responsibilities of the state and federal governments. Yet as the examples just given show, the states doing well in the global economy are not the low-tax, low-wage states like Arkansas but the states with better-paid, better-educated, more productive workers like Washington.

The states have indeed reduced taxes and the cost of labor since the 1970s, but some far more than others. Is globalization responsible? As this book argues, domestic political factors are a more proximate explanation; the states (and nation-states as well) can choose how to respond to international economic trends. In an era of declining voter turnout, weak labor unions, and increasing Republican dominance of both state and federal elective offices, the "global economy" has provided a compelling rationale for policies designed to benefit business interests and weaken the bargaining power of labor. The promise of "creating jobs" has persuaded Americans of all political and social backgrounds that lower taxes and lower labor costs are necessary to enhance competitiveness. But do state efforts to cut taxes and labor costs actually create jobs? If so, what kinds of jobs are attributable to these policies? And what are the social and political consequences of Americans working longer but earning less?

This book attempts to answer these questions by examining trends in state labor costs since 1970. I first describe the multiple ways in which the fifty American states influence the cost of labor. I argue that state latitude in labor policy has been an important reason why labor costs in the United

States have tended to be far lower than those in other industrial democracies. I develop a comprehensive measure of state labor costs for the period 1970 to 2000, and I use this measure to explore reasons why some states have reduced labor costs far more than others. I also use this measure to assess the economic and social consequences of the overall decline in state labor costs since 1970. The results highlight the difficult choices American states must make in response to global economic trends, and they suggest some policy alternatives to the low-wage strategy.

In this chapter, I first review the historical and theoretical rationales for an analysis of state labor costs. I then consider six explanations for low and declining labor costs in the United States: globalization, the weakness of the American labor movement, demographic trends, the role of state and federal courts, the size of the welfare state, and the lack of institutions to coordinate business, labor, and public policy. I next describe how interstate competition in a federal system has exacerbated each of these factors. The chapter concludes with an outline of the argument to be set forth in subsequent chapters.

LABOR COSTS AND STATE COMPETITIVENESS

Labor constitutes a large proportion of the factor costs of most business enterprises. In addition to wages and salaries, government taxes and regulations (payroll taxes for health or pension benefits, minimum-wage and overtime laws, workplace safety and environmental policies) constitute the "social wage" that increases labor costs. Of course, employers have generally been critical of any public policies that might increase the cost of labor and thus threaten their profits. And they have often put pressure on governments to help them reduce the cost of labor.

Globalization has added new urgency to business concerns. A standard neoliberal argument in economic theory holds that as the cost of labor increases, fewer workers will be hired, unemployment will rise, and businesses will relocate to low-wage regions.[5] Benería (2003, 2) describes the "Washington consensus" articulated in the 1980s by the World Bank, the International Monetary Fund, and the Ronald Reagan and the George H. W. Bush administrations: critiques of government intervention in the economy and hostility to labor unions, combined with support for market deregulation, dismantling of the welfare state, privatizing state-owned enterprises, trade liberalization, and open doors to international investment and corporate mergers.

In theory, advanced industrial countries will be constrained to reduce labor costs to keep jobs and capital from flowing to low-wage developing countries. In practice, however, countries differ considerably in their responses to the global economy; political and social institutions mediate the effects of international competition for capital.[6] Porter (1985, 2002) argues that advanced industrial economies have a competitive edge in the international economy. Low-wage, low-skill jobs may indeed move elsewhere, but gains in productivity and technology should be compensated with high wages and rising living standards. Volgy, Schwarz, and Imwalle (1996) found that countries where workers had greater political power were able to maintain wages despite ties to the international economy. But in weak-labor countries, workers have failed to reap wage gains commensurate with productivity increases. In the United States, labor unions' strong resistance to the North American Free Trade Agreement (NAFTA) and to most-favored-nation trading status for China reflects their concerns with job losses and stagnant wages.

The American states provide an ideal laboratory in which to test these competing findings concerning the impact of globalization. In the United States, the federal government collects payroll taxes for Social Security and Medicare. But other policies that influence the social cost of labor (unemployment insurance, workers' compensation, union regulation, minimum-wage laws, workplace safety) are affected by state as well as federal political choices, and vary considerably across the states. As I show in this book, state policies have an independent effect on both labor costs and on economic outcomes, even when the impact of federal government policies is taken into account. And interstate competition over labor costs may be a major reason why labor costs and the "social wage" (taxes and regulations that affect the cost of labor) have risen so much more slowly in the United States than in Europe since the 1970s.

The states vary considerably in policies affecting the cost of labor. Though states actively compete for investment and factory locations by means of tax subsidies, regulatory relief, and other incentives for business, labor costs continue to play a major role in interstate competition. Even after the Civil War put an end to slavery, the South remained a low-wage region. Most southern states have been hostile to unions and have kept employee and welfare benefits low in order to give employers more control over the labor force (McCrate 1997). The federal minimum wage adopted during the New Deal represented an effort to raise southern wages and improve living conditions in the South (Paulsen 1996). This was strongly resisted by low-wage states, which felt they would lose an important comparative advantage. Personal income in the South did rise relative to the rest of the country, particularly after the New Deal (Bernat 2001). But considerable differences in wages and unionization remain between North and South.

Several eastern and midwestern states, however, have a long history of efforts to improve workplace conditions and job security. Populists, Socialists, and Progressives in states such as Wisconsin advocated policies designed to enhance union strength, invest in human capital, limit child labor, and protect workers' health, pensions, organizing rights, and job security.[7] Many states have also adopted minimum wages above the federal minimum and provided generous benefits for unemployment and workers' compensation. In states such as Michigan and Pennsylvania, union density is nearly as high as in the "strong worker power" states identified by Volgy, Schwarz, and Imwalle (1996), who otherwise rank the United States low in worker power. Yet many other states (especially in the South) come closer to the liberal-market economy norms attributed by Swank and Wilensky to the United Kingdom and to the United States as a whole. The American states thus provide an ideal laboratory for examining the economic and social effects of labor costs.

The fifty American states also vary greatly in their links to the global economy. Of course the states are not fully independent international actors, as are the sovereign states of Europe, Asia, and Latin America. Yet in recent years, state policies have played an increasingly active role in setting the terms of trade between their local or regional economies and the international marketplace.[8] Still, some state economies are far more dependent than others on exports, immigration, and foreign investment. These include large industrial states with high concentrations of foreign investment and immigrant populations (California, New York, New Jersey) as well as several southern or midwestern states in "automobile alley," where major Japanese or German automobile plants have located since the 1970s. A few states also account for the bulk of American exports in manufacturing or agricultural products, whereas states bordering Canada or Mexico have experienced increased trade since the passage of NAFTA in 1993. But in many states, only a small proportion of employment or commerce can be directly linked to international trade or foreign investment.

Given this wide variation, we can use data on the American states to explore the relationship between links to the global economy and trends in state labor costs. Do low or declining labor costs convey a competitive advantage in exports or foreign investment? Have the states most closely connected to international trade experienced the greatest pressure to reduce labor costs and constrain union power, or do these policy trends reflect domestic political factors? The answers to these questions can not only contribute to the ongoing debate over the impact of globalization but can also suggest state or national policy measures that might enhance state economic growth or employment trends, and thus mitigate the impact of the international economy.

In this book, I examine trends in state labor costs since 1970, and I assess the economic and social impact of the decline in manufacturing wages, labor union density, and social policies benefiting workers. I consider a range of state economic outcomes (growth in gross state product, personal income, productivity, exports, and foreign investment) in addition to trends in job creation and unemployment. Many U.S. government policies influence labor costs as well, including the payroll tax used to finance Social Security and Medicare, federal minimum-wage laws, and federal regulations that affect workers' rights and labor union activity. Democratic and Republican presidential administrations also differ considerably in their labor policies. In addition, federal defense spending has a profound impact on state economies; the geography of defense contracts and military base closings can influence state economic trends, and military goods constitute a significant proportion of American exports. My results will demonstrate, however, that state labor costs have an independent impact on state economic and social trends even when these federal policies are taken into account.

The evidence presented here challenges the theory that cutting the cost of labor will enhance competitiveness; states with high labor costs are in fact doing better with respect to economic growth, exports, and foreign direct investment. The strong link between high labor costs and productivity growth provides a competitive advantage in the increasingly specialized global economy. But reducing labor costs has had adverse social consequences in the states: slower rates of job creation, slower declines in poverty rates, stagnant growth in personal income, rising inequality, lower voter turnout, higher crime and suicide rates, and instability in family life. Many states are indeed pursuing a "race to the bottom" in terms of labor costs and social policies. However, these trends are not justified by either globalization or economic benefits.

THEORETICAL FOUNDATIONS

Several theoretical frameworks have been used to guide this analysis. The first is drawn from the literature on globalization. Its theories predict policy convergence across political units and a race to the bottom as states compete for highly mobile capital by reducing the size and costs of the public sector, enhancing productivity, and limiting labor costs. As already noted, considerable research has been done in economics and political science to examine the impact of globalization, with highly divergent results.

The second framework is provided by analysts of American federalism. The logic of interstate competition within the federal system functions (and, it can be argued, was designed to function) as a major constraint on labor costs long before the pressures of globalization entered the political equation. According to Tiebout's Law (Tiebout 1956), the creation and maintenance of subnational jurisdictions permit people and businesses to "vote with their feet" and to locate in areas that provide their optimal mix of taxes and services. Following this logic, Peterson (1995) argues that because of interstate competition for business and population, state and local governments are unlikely to be able to pursue policies to redistribute income (progressive taxes, generous welfare benefits) because businesses and wealthy individuals would simply move to lower-tax areas. He further argues that states should invest in policies likely to foster economic development, especially infrastructure and education (although he does not consider labor costs).

The third framework is drawn from analyses of national and subnational differences in economic trends, particularly the role of governments in fostering or constraining growth in income, productivity, and employment. Much political and economic research in this area has been based on nation-states (both industrialized countries and developing nations), but the literature on comparative state politics has also considered the economic trajectories of the American states. Since the stagflation era of the 1970s, states have taken a far more active role in economic development. Debate continues over the role of state/local taxes in economic growth, but newer strategies (industrial and entrepreneurial policies, the states' role in the international economy, investments in human capital) have attracted critical attention to both their political rationale and their economic effects.[9]

The fourth framework derives from studies of the emerging European Union (EU). Beginning in the years after World War II, many Western European countries took steps to diminish barriers to trade, culminating in a common currency (the euro) and the creation of a supranational parliament, judiciary, and executive. There are obvious parallels to the creation of the United States from the original thirteen colonies and to the historic debates over the relative powers of the central government versus the member states (Sbragia 2005). Proponents of the EU hope to foster growth and productivity by reducing barriers to trade and competition among member states for business, investment, and population. The EU includes high-wage as well as low-wage areas (especially since its recent expansion into Southern and Eastern Europe). But unlike the United States, the EU has made conscious efforts to restrain competition among member states and to minimize any race to the bottom in terms of labor costs or social policies.

These four frameworks are used here to address two core political questions: Why have labor costs *declined* in most states since the 1970s? And why have they declined in some states far more than others? Proposals to reduce wages or benefits are unlikely to be winning campaign issues in state elections. Survey data show that public support for labor unions and for a higher minimum wage has remained high, even as union membership has dropped and wages have stagnated. So we must find explanations for widely shared policies that have been adopted without much evidence of popular support.

Clearly, the influence of business interests in the states cannot be discounted. And the logic of interstate competition may force governors and legislators to adopt policies even if they (and the voters) would prefer otherwise. We must also consider how policies to reduce labor costs have been packaged and "sold" to legislators or voters. As I will show, the rhetoric of globalization has frequently been used to justify reductions in labor costs, even though states with higher labor costs actually perform better in terms of international trade. The "jobs" mantra has proven to be a potent political symbol to gain public acceptance for (or at least acquiescence with) a number of social and fiscal policies with little popular support.

LABOR COSTS: WHY SO LOW IN THE UNITED STATES?

The Organization for Economic Cooperation and Development (OECD) has compiled an index of labor costs in advanced industrial societies.[10] This index includes not only wages paid by employers to employees but also the "social wage": the cost of various welfare state benefits, such as pensions, health care, mandated vacations, unemployment, and paid parental leave, which are imposed on employers through taxes and regulations (costs such as pension contributions are sometimes shared by employees as well). According to the OECD's indicator, labor costs since 1970 have tended to be far lower in the United States than in most European countries (figure 1.1). This reflects the smaller size of the American welfare state, particularly the absence of comprehensive health benefits, and the corresponding lower tax burden on both businesses and their employees (Wilson 1998).

The OECD also charts trends in employment for its member countries. John Schwarz (1988) cited high job-creation rates as a major indicator of America's "hidden success," and Wilensky (2002) considers the "great American job machine" to be a prominent example of American exceptionalism among the nineteen "rich democracies" he analyzes. As figure 1.2 shows, the United States has indeed outperformed Europe in

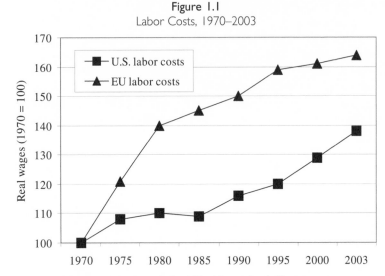

Figure 1.1
Labor Costs, 1970–2003

Note: Labor costs have been lower in the United States than in Europe.
Source: Organization for Economic Cooperation and Development databank, 2004.

creating new jobs, at least before 2000.[11] Economists (Siebert 1997) and the OECD's own analyses (OECD 1995, 1999) have blamed such "Eurosclerosis" on high taxes, too-generous welfare state benefits, and restrictions on the ability of employers to fire workers without advance notice and generous severance pay.

A comparison of figures 1.1 and 1.2 might suggest a direct causal relationship between labor costs and trends in job creation. As scholars have observed, however, other factors, including a larger internal market, faster population growth, and high levels of in-migration, also account for the faster growth in the U.S. labor market (Wilensky 2002). In chapter 4, I will examine the empirical relationship between labor costs and job growth in the American states. Job creation is indeed slower in states with high labor costs. However, as Wilensky (2002, 504) argues, "If employment expands because of a rapid creation of low-paid service jobs, an increasing number of them part-time or taken by people looking for full-time work; because of stagnant or declining real wages; and because of increases in the rate of family breakup, while productivity increases fade and trade balances deteriorate, we can ask, is this progress?"

In Wilensky's view, real wage decreases are achieved by labor crunching and union busting, mass insecurity, industrial conflict, unproductive welfare

Figure 1.2
Employment, 1970–2003

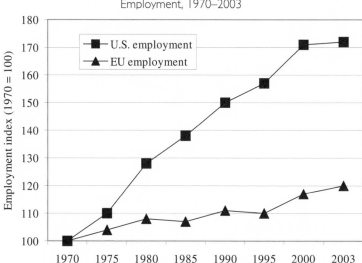

Note: Employment has grown faster in the United States than in Europe.
Source: Organization for Economic Cooperation and Development databank, 2004.

spending, high rates of divorce and abandoned children, high crime rates, and the feminization of poverty. Wilensky asks whether this brew should be labeled a "superior record of job creation." And in chapter 5, I will show that the adverse social consequences of reductions in state labor costs are not outweighed by higher rates of job creation.

But first we must explain why labor costs are so much lower in the United States. In this section, I consider six explanations that have been extensively analyzed in previous research: globalization, the weakness of the American labor movement, the role of the courts, demographic trends, the characteristics of the American welfare state, and the lack of coordinating institutions. I then consider how each of these has been exacerbated by interstate competition in the American federal system.

Globalization

Recent advances in communications and technology have made capital far more mobile than labor. The United States has become increasingly integrated into the global economy. Until the early 1970s, the United States was a net exporter of goods and services, but the balance of trade has grown increasingly negative since then. American firms and employees have thus come under growing domestic and international pressure to cut wages and benefits in order to make American industry competitive in the global marketplace.

In theory, the increasing global mobility of capital should pressure countries to reduce their tax rates, minimize regulatory burdens on business, and constrain labor costs. In practice, however, domestic politics and policies mediate the impact of the international economy on a country's labor force (Swank 2002; Drezner 2001; Wilensky 2002; Garrett 1998; Katz and Darbishire 1999). Even small countries have resisted pressures to cut labor costs. Sweden, for example, has high taxes and generous welfare policies, and pays high wages, yet it is very open to international trade and actively supports its export sector (Steinmo 1993). Sweden also provides financial and housing assistance to help displaced workers relocate to areas with a higher demand for labor.

As I will demonstrate in chapter 3, the American states most open to the international economy actually have higher labor costs than states less focused on exports or imports. Because globalization cannot fully account for these differences across countries or states, we must look elsewhere to explain the faster rate of decline in labor costs in the United States.

The Weakness of American Labor

Historically, the American labor movement has lagged far behind that of most European countries. The emerging labor movement was internally divided by conflicts over race and immigrants, as well as differences in strategy and philosophy between the craft unions of the American Federation of Labor (AFL) and the industrial-union approach favored by the Congress of Industrial Organizations (CIO). Labor leaders such as Samuel Gompers explicitly rejected the idea of a separate labor party, preferring to work within the two major parties; and the American single-district, first-past-the-post electoral system discourages third parties. Although socialist candidates have occasionally made a strong showing (Eugene V. Debs in 1918, Henry Wallace in 1948), no viable socialist or labor party has emerged at the national level (although socialists have won a few elective offices in some states and cities, e.g., New York, Wisconsin, and Milwaukee).

In comparison with other industrialized countries, the United States has a very low proportion of its workforce belonging to labor unions. Furthermore, this proportion has declined by more than 50 percent since its peak in the early 1950s—a rate of decline higher than in any other industrialized country (Scruggs and Lange 2002; Wilensky 2002).

Why is the labor movement in the United States so weak? Standard explanations include the organizational strategies of the American labor movement, the lack of a viable labor party, and the limited appeal of socialism in an individualistic country (Lipset and Marks 2000). Sexton (1991) attributes union weakness to active repression, both legal and extralegal, by businesses, their legal advisers, and Republican presidential administrations. Countries like Belgium, which utilize labor unions to finance and administer unemployment insurance (the Ghent system), thereby provide selective benefits to encourage workers to join a union. Unionization rates are indeed higher in such countries (Ebbinghaus and Visser 2000).

The structure of American industry has also changed since the 1950s, with much less emphasis on heavy manufacturing in large-scale plants. American unions have thus lost many members in declining industries like coal mining, steel, and automobile manufacturing, and they have found it far more difficult to organize white-collar workers or service employers. Yet other industrialized countries, such as Canada, have also lost manufacturing jobs, but have not experienced a commensurate decline in levels of unionization (Scruggs and Lange 2002).

The position of American labor was further weakened by actions of the Reagan and both the George H. W. Bush and George W. Bush administrations. When President Reagan fired the striking air traffic controllers in 1981, the message to labor was clear: Work stoppages were risky, and people who wanted to keep their jobs had to be prepared to accept cuts in wages or benefits (Nordlund 1998). In fact, according to Bureau of Labor Statistics data, the number of strikes in the United States has fallen sharply since 1980. Also under Reagan and both Bush administrations, appointees to the Department of Labor were mostly sympathetic to business. Responses to complaints of unfair labor practices were long delayed and were more often decided in favor of employers. The secretary of labor under the current George W. Bush administration, Elaine Chao, has placed far more emphasis on combating alleged union "corruption" than in addressing unfair labor practices by business.

As a consequence of both industrial challenge and concerted legal and political opposition by the Reagan administration, American unions by the 1980s were in no position to counter pressures for "give-backs" in wages and benefits. As Golden (1997) has shown, union leaders often gave in to such demands because seniority rules protected their own jobs. But unions themselves have also been criticized from within for not dedicating sufficient resources to organizing. Union efforts were sometimes devoted to raiding members from other unions rather than to recruiting unorganized workers. John Sweeney, of the Service Employees International Union, was elected president of the AFL-CIO in 1995 on a platform pledging to put much more effort into organizing additional workers. But as of 2004 no net increase in labor union membership had occurred, in part because the ongoing loss of union jobs in manufacturing outweighed some organizing gains in the public sector and among service workers. And in 2005 several large unions left the AFL-CIO because of disagreements over the scope and pace of Sweeney's organizing efforts.

The Role of American Courts

Historically, the U.S. state and federal courts have not been helpful to labor. As Skocpol (1992, 226) notes, "American trade unions were profoundly threatened in their very organizational existence by the aggressive use of court injunctions against strikes and boycotts." Before the 1930s, the Supreme Court consistently upheld the right of "freedom of contract" under the Fourteenth Amendment. This meant that if a worker disliked the wages, hours, or working conditions an employer demanded, he or she was free to seek employment elsewhere. By this legal logic, union organizing and collective bargaining would only interfere with individual freedom and due process. Both state and federal courts thus struck down laws to limit hours or overtime, establish minimum wages, improve worker safety, or even restrict child labor (Berry 1986). As the Supreme Court stated in its *Lochner v. New York* decision (1905), "There must be more than the mere fact of the possible existence of some small amount of unhealthiness to warrant legislative interference with liberty. Limiting the hours in which grown and intelligent men may labor to earn their living, are mere meddlesome interferences with the rights of the individual."

The Court did make an exception, but only for women, in its 1908 *Mueller* decision. The justices argued that because of women's physical weaknesses and the importance of their primary role as mothers, governmental restrictions on hours or weight lifting were permissible. American women's reform groups at first hailed this decision, the first time the Court had accepted any restrictions on the principle of freedom of contract. But many feminists soon recognized that the ensuing "protective" legislation meant that fewer women were hired, they were paid less, and they were less likely to be promoted into management positions (Baer 1978).

The burden of adverse judicial rulings also affected labor organizing strategies. In fact, after the Civil War Republicans used the courts to ensure that rulings favorable to business interests could not be countermanded by transient election results or legislative majorities sympathetic to labor (Gillman 2002). The AFL often despaired of making gains through elections or legislation in individual states, because the courts so quickly overturned them. The AFL instead tried to use strikes or negotiations with specific employers, rather than a concerted national effort to support social insurance or regulations favorable to labor (Skocpol 1992, 227).

It was not until the New Deal that efforts to extend workplace protections to men and child laborers, as well as women, received Supreme Court approval, but only after President Franklin Roosevelt threatened to "pack" the Court with additional appointees more sympathetic to his views. Roosevelt's New Deal included a number of laws designed to encourage labor unions and raise wages: Social Security, the Wagner Act, and the Fair Labor Standards Act. And these indeed passed constitutional muster by the Supreme Court after the famous "switch in time that saved nine." But as we shall see, significant aspects of the New Deal were seriously undercut by the 1947 Taft-Hartley Act, which returned crucial aspects of labor regulation to the states.

Until quite recently, U.S. courts have consistently upheld the principle of "employment at will," which gives employers broad discretion to hire and fire for any reason (Stieber 1984). Unless workers are covered by collective-bargaining contracts that mandate arbitration or grievance procedures, they may be fired for any economic or noneconomic reasons. Since the 1960s, the doctrine of "wrongful discharge" has evolved to recognize that employees' interests, dignity, and economic security merited some protection in a society increasingly dependent on wage earnings (Ballam 2000). Courts in many states have upheld public policy exemptions, so that workers cannot be dismissed for whistle blowing, jury or National Guard service, filing a workers' compensation claim, or refusing to perform an unlawful act. But as Stieber (1984, 35) notes, courts in most states "interpret the public policy exception so narrowly as to give it only very limited application."

As a result of the employment-at-will doctrine, employment protection is far weaker in the United States than in other industrialized nations. By contrast, most European countries have laws prohibiting unjust discharge (OECD 1999). However, as Wohlers and Weinert (1988, 216) state, "In the EC [European Community] countries, the high direct and indirect costs associated with dismissals make employers less willing to recruit." American employers thus have much greater latitude in personnel matters than their European counterparts enjoy. Recent American laws prohibiting racial or sex discrimination or sexual harassment, mandating family leave, or requiring accommodations for persons with disabilities have constrained these freedoms to some degree. But these laws are not always enforced, and because the burden of proof (and the cost of litigation) usually falls on the employee, most people who are fired do not pursue legal remedies. One function of labor unions has been to shield workers from unjust dismissals, but many fewer workers today have access to the protection of contract bargaining agreements or union grievance procedures. And the AFL-CIO claims that workers are routinely fired because of their efforts to organize a union. This is illegal under regulations of the National Labor Relations Board, but few employers have been subject to enforcement efforts (Bronfenbrenner 2003). Business and conservatives, however, would argue that elaborate grievance procedures, as provided by many civil service laws and by contracts with public employee and teachers' unions, make it almost impossible to fire workers even for gross incompetence, and thus greatly reduce productivity in those sectors (Maranto 1999).

Demographic Trends

The United States has higher birthrates than most European countries, especially among the Hispanic population. Thus there is a ready pool of workers competing for jobs, which tends to depress wages. Because women have entered the labor force in sizable numbers since the 1950s, the United States also has a higher labor force participation rate for women than do most European countries, although this varies considerably by state. However, the "gender gap" in wages in the United States is considerably larger than that in most European countries (Stetson 1997). Many fewer women qualify for unemployment benefits, health care coverage, and pensions, in part because more of them work part time. And unlike in Europe, family leave in the United States is unpaid and limited to firms with more than fifty employees. Thus for employers, hiring more women can be a way to cut labor costs. But stagnant wages and unemployment for men have also pushed more American women into the labor force to support their families.

Wohlers and Weinert (1988) note the success of the United States in integrating sizable numbers of new workers (women, young people, immigrants) into the labor force. And Wilensky (2002) credits much of the growth in the American labor force to such demographic factors; he cites evidence that a growing labor supply helps create its own demand for jobs providing services and housing. However, a major economic consequence of this large pool of potential workers is downward pressure on wages. And exactly for this reason, most American labor unions have historically been hostile to organizing women or minorities. Threats by employers to evict illegal immigrants have proven to be an effective means of discouraging union organizing efforts. Groups opposed to a liberal immigration policy argue that immigrants will take jobs and wages away from native-born Americans (FAIR 2000), although economists dispute these effects (Simon 1999).

U.S. Census data indicate that 85 percent of new entrants into the twenty-first-century labor force will be female and/or minority (Judy and D'Amico 1997, 113). By the late 1990s, most labor leaders in the United States were aware of these trends, and they had recognized that if unions were to survive, they must do better at organizing women and immigrants (Sweeney 1996). Efforts have been made to do so; the AFL-CIO has greatly increased its expenditures on organization drives and is targeting establishments that employ large numbers of immigrants (Greenhouse 2003). More women and minorities are emerging as officers or board members of unions. But national union leaders still encounter resistance to these organizing efforts from male members and union locals, as well as from employers determined to keep unions out. Lengthy and detailed union requirements for apprentices and journeymen also limit competition from young workers. Unions have adamantly opposed a "subminimum wage" for young and inexperienced workers because they fear older workers would thereby be displaced. And because many women and minorities work for small businesses, retail establishments, and in service industries, organizing them will not be easy.

The Welfare State and the "Social Wage"

Wohlers and Weinert (1988) stressed the importance of "wage flexibility" as a major factor encouraging high employment growth in the United States. Their analysis of employment trends in the United States, Europe, and Japan between 1973 and 1983 found that the degree of government regulation was significantly less in the United States, while interfirm or interregional labor mobility was higher. American businesses were also more mobile, and the climate for entrepreneurship was more favorable in the United States. The deregulation of industries such as trucking and aviation has increased competition in those sectors and boosted employment. In short, the United States was more "efficient" and more willing to "accept market forces" rather than trying to adjust them in favor of labor.

Wohlers and Weinert also found that the wider wage range in the United States "took better account of employment needs" by permitting greater differentials between manufacturing and service employment, and by tolerating much greater disparity in wages than was the case in Europe. Their analysis discounted differences in productivity and industrial structure as reasons for the much higher employment growth in the United States during this period. In their view, the acceleration of income inequality in the United States since 1980 may have contributed to employment growth.[12]

High labor costs (especially the social wage) and low rates of job creation, as well as high unemployment, have become major political issues in Europe as well as in the United States, especially during recessions (OECD 1995, 1999). The higher "social wage" in Europe reflects a much stronger labor movement, and labor interests are represented in parties and in government. These factors, as well as the influence of the Roman Catholic "social gospel" over Social Democratic parties in Southern Europe, formed the base of political support for the emerging welfare state. But many welfare state provisions were also rooted in the labor shortages that followed the casualties of World Wars I and II and the decline in birthrates during the Depression. Several countries adopted pronatalist policies (child care, health care, family allowances) to encourage women not only to have more children but also to remain in the labor force; these policies also add to the costs of the welfare state. The importation of "guest workers" from Eastern Europe, Turkey, and North Africa was also mandated by labor shortages (although many of these workers are not eligible for citizenship or for full welfare state benefits).

Lack of Coordinating Institutions

Wilensky's (2002) comparative analysis of nineteen rich democracies found that those with the best overall economic record (low unemployment, low inflation, high rates of economic growth) tended to be the "corporatist" states of Western Europe. In these countries, labor is a recognized partner in negotiations about policies affecting taxes, trade policy, and welfare state benefits. Rather than the ongoing business-versus-labor wrangling characteristic of the United States, labor has a "seat at the table" and the interests of workers are routinely considered. In parliamentary and multiparty systems, labor parties are also frequently part of governing coalitions.

Weiss and Hudson (1995) contrast examples of "successful" economic development in Europe and East Asia with what they term "the decline of Anglo-American capitalism." Their basic argument is that successful states such as the former West Germany and South Korea develop institutions for coordinating with the private sector to counter unbridled market forces and make long-term investment decisions (e.g., the shift from import substitution to exports, and from basic manufacturing to high technology). But in the liberal-capitalism countries of the United Kingdom and the United States, long-term investment decisions are driven by superpower status, defense priorities, and special interest pressures, rather than by a comprehensive strategy for industrial development. Savings, investment, and worker training have thus suffered in comparison with countries that have developed more effective methods for coordinating markets.

Other research has shown that more centralized structures for wage bargaining, through peak business and labor associations or a Labor Party, have also produced greater benefits for workers. Thus, "the countries least susceptible to decline have considerable institutional power over the labor market through coordinated and encompassing bargaining, centralized wage setting, and other corporatist arrangements" (Levi 2003, 48). Such countries enjoy wage moderation and low unemployment accompanied by economic growth.

In the United States, by contrast, collective bargaining is often conducted plant by plant rather than industry-wide, with a few exceptions such as the Teamsters Union and longshoremen on the East and West Coasts. Most American labor unions have a "federal" structure in which state or local councils have considerable power and independence (Levi 2003, 50). But policies set by labor's national leadership require cooperation and financial contributions by union locals, and these may not always be forthcoming. Thus few union locals responded to AFL-CIO president John Sweeney's call for greater spending on union organizing efforts (Lerner 2003).

THE IMPACT OF COMPETITIVE FEDERALISM ON LABOR COSTS

All the above factors have been analyzed extensively in previous research, and they clearly help explain the differences in labor costs and employment trends between the United States and Europe. However, none of these explanations explicitly consider federalism or the realities of interstate competition. But I argue in this book that the existence of the American states exacerbates the impact of each of these six factors on labor costs.

First of all, the American states actively compete with each other in the global marketplace, thus augmenting the national impact of globalization. The states have entered bidding wars to entice foreign investment, especially that of large automobile manufacturing plants, and they have offered major subsidies to foreign firms such as Toyota (which went to Kentucky),

Mercedes-Benz (to Alabama), and Volkswagen (to Pennsylvania) (Yanarella and Green 1990).

Second, the weakness of American labor is exacerbated by interstate competition for jobs and business investment, and by the role of state laws (especially right-to-work laws) affecting unions. Companies advising businesses on location decisions (e.g., Fantus, Grant-Thornton) routinely compare states in terms of their labor policies, taxation, and regulations.

Third, the William Rehnquist Supreme Court granted increasing discretion to state courts in many policy areas. State courts, especially in more conservative states, have tended to uphold restrictions on labor organizing efforts and to strike down most exceptions to the doctrine of "employment at will." Walsh and Schwarz (1996) report that twenty-six states have taken a very narrow view of public policy exceptions, and seven states (mostly in the South) recognize no exceptions at all. In those states, a person can lose his or her job for serving on a jury or with the National Guard in Iraq.

Fourth, demographic trends also vary among the states. In response to trends in population or economic growth, states have adopted laws to try to exclude or entice immigration, retain young people, or attract retirees. Americans are far more mobile than Europeans, and they do not face language barriers if they relocate (Long 1991). The rapid pace of internal and foreign migration has had profound political and social consequences for the United States and has shifted political and economic power from the Northeast and Midwest to the Sunbelt (Gimpel 1999). In California and Arizona, ballot propositions have attempted to deny welfare and other benefits to illegal immigrants, although state courts have struck down many of the more onerous provisions supported by the voters. California governor Pete Wilson was reelected in 1994 in part because his campaign successfully blamed high unemployment in California on illegal immigrants (Hansen 1999a). By contrast, many employers (especially in agribusiness) depend on a ready supply of low-paid migrant workers, and they have used their influence in Congress to make sure such workers can continue to enter the United States (Gimpel and Edwards 1999).

Fifth, the American welfare state is far more limited than its European counterparts, at least in part because eligibility and benefit levels for many social policies are set by the states. As Peterson (1995) has argued, the American federal system discourages high or progressive taxes and spending on social programs because businesses and the wealthy can threaten to move to lower-cost states. States are similarly concerned that their unemployment or workers' compensation benefits may be too high relative to levels in neighboring states. State legislatures regularly compare welfare benefits with those of their neighbors because they fear becoming "welfare magnets" and attracting undesirables (immigrants, welfare mothers). Despite empirical evidence that benefit differentials do not play much of a role in relocation decisions (Schram and Krueger 1995; Peterson and Rom 1990), the public, the media, and state legislators often believe otherwise.

Sixth and finally, the American federal system itself is a prime example of a "lack of coordinating institutions." Recent Supreme Court decisions—and trends toward policy devolution in areas such as health care, education, and welfare—have given states even greater discretion over policy. State and local governments have made at least some attempts to share expertise and develop better policies on regional issues. Examples include the Great Lakes Regional Commission, the Appalachian Regional Commission, the Port Authority of New York and New Jersey, the Northeast-Midwest Institute, the Southern Growth Policies Board, the National Governors' Association, the National Conference of State Legislatures, and organizations of professionals in various state government departments. But the logic of interstate (or intraregional) competition consistently overwhelms efforts by such entities. And without federal funding, coordinating institutions such as the Advisory Commission on Intergovernmental Relations have folded. By contrast, as Thomas (2000) has shown, members of the European Union (and to a lesser degree Canada) have been far more successful in restricting zero-sum competition for business and investment among states or provinces, and they have developed effective enforcement mechanisms.

I would argue, therefore, that interstate competition is a major factor keeping American labor costs low. Further evidence to support this reasoning will be presented in subsequent chapters. But to establish the importance of a state role in restricting labor costs, it must be shown that state policies have an effect independent of the federal government's policies (Hendrick and Garand 1991). Brace (1993) has demonstrated that not only are state trends in personal income independent of national economic trends, but they have become increasingly so in recent years. Accordingly, I will consider trends in federal labor costs based on minimum-wage laws, payroll taxes, and the impact of different presidential administrations on labor regulation. As I will show, these factors have less impact on state economies than do state labor costs. However, federal defense spending does contribute to state economic growth.

PLAN OF THE BOOK

The argument proceeds as follows. In chapter 2, I review the historic role of the American states in fostering economic development and regulating the cost of labor. Competition among states for jobs, people, and business investment has played a major role in state efforts to boost their economies, although some federal initiatives (the New Deal, the War on Poverty) have attempted to limit the most egregious effects of such competition. I next describe in more detail how the American states continue to influence the relative cost of labor. The states have considerable latitude in the regulation of labor relations and (unlike more centralized European countries) share with the federal government the costs and administration of worker benefits. I develop a measure of state labor costs, for the period 1970–2000, based on five elements: labor union density, right-to-work laws, unemployment benefits, workers' compensation, and manufacturing wages. Trends in this index since 1970 show a considerable overall decline, although with some variation across the individual components. Further, trends in state labor costs will be shown to be independent of national government policies, such as Social Security taxes, minimum-wage laws, defense spending, and the impact of different presidential administrations on labor policies.

Despite the overall decline, some states have reduced labor costs far more than others. However, I find little evidence for policy convergence as a consequence of globalization. In chapter 3, I consider several explanations for state differences in labor cost trends. Political factors (particularly voter turnout and the strength of public employee unions) prove to be far better predictors of trends in labor costs than demographic trends or economic factors such as the size of the manufacturing sector and openness to the international economy. I also consider how reductions in state labor costs have been packaged and marketed to the public and the media, primarily by the logic of interstate competition and a rhetorical emphasis on "jobs" as a desirable policy outcome.

In chapter 4, I analyze several economic consequences of trends in state labor costs. Neoliberal economic theory would predict higher rates of job creation and lower unemployment in states with lower labor costs. Though I do find some evidence for those effects, they must be compared with other results of declining labor costs: slower growth in personal income, productivity, and gross state product. Nor do declining labor costs appear to provide much advantage in the international economy; foreign investment is marginally higher in higher-cost states, whereas export growth is strongest in states with high levels of defense spending and higher labor costs. Unemployment is actually lower, and labor force growth stronger, in states that combine high labor costs and high levels of exports or foreign direct investment. Further, my measure of state labor costs appears to have a greater impact on state economies than do trends in federal policies affecting the cost of labor.

Chapter 5 considers some possible social and political consequences of trends in state labor costs. Despite some modest gains in employment, states experiencing declining labor costs also experience declining voter turnout, higher crime and suicide rates, family instability, and slower declines in poverty rates. And employment gains fail to counter any of these adverse effects, primarily because the new jobs created are generally low paid. These results point to the difficult choices facing state governments: to create a few more low-wage jobs or to provide a better quality of life for all their citizens.

In the concluding chapter 6, I summarize the evidence that the American federal system accounts both for the weakness of American labor and for differences in labor costs between the United States and other industrial democracies. I discuss several strategies that have been attempted to reverse the downward trend in labor costs: better union organizing efforts, minimum-wage and living-wage laws, greater investment in education and worker training. I also consider the possibility that soaring medical costs will lead both business and workers to embrace a greater public role in health coverage. All these policies face strong political opposition, especially given the logic of interstate competition. But by highlighting the state role in declining labor costs, and the adverse social consequences thereof, I hope this book contributes to the ongoing debate over the impact of globalization and strategies to minimize its adverse effects on American workers.

CHAPTER TWO

The State Role in Labor Costs

THIS CHAPTER REVIEWS THE historic and contemporary state role in regulating the cost of labor. Labor policies constitute one of the many efforts that the fifty U.S. states have pursued to foster economic development, including tax and location incentives, regulatory relief for business, development of infrastructure, and investment in human capital. A central argument of this book is that competition among states in a federal system has exerted steady downward pressure on the cost of labor in the United States.

Before the 1930s, the states exhibited considerable variation in labor policy. Some (particularly in the South) pursued a deliberate low-wage strategy and made concerted efforts to inhibit union organizing. Others, however, pioneered policies designed to protect workers' rights, health, and safety, and to increase their wages. As this chapter shows, the New Deal adopted several policies developed in the more progressive states in order to raise wages nationwide, support labor organizing efforts, and provide assistance to the unemployed. But these attempts to nationalize labor markets proved to be a hard sell politically in a country steeped in the ethos of laissez-faire, states' rights, and individualism. Efforts to gain sufficient congressional support to pass Social Security, unemployment programs, and the Fair Labor Standards Act (the minimum-wage law) made it necessary for President Franklin Roosevelt to accede to a considerable state role in policy, finance, and administration. The 1947 Taft-Hartley Act further strengthened the state role in setting labor costs, and it thus contributed to renewed interstate competition after the New Deal interregnum.

After giving a brief overview of this history, I will describe the policies that states currently employ to regulate the cost of labor: right-to-work laws, state minimum-wage and prevailing-wage policies, regulation of union organizing and political activity, exceptions to the doctrine of employment at will, unemployment benefits, and workers' compensation. On the basis of five of these policies, I develop a comprehensive measure of state labor costs and describe trends in this indicator and its components since 1970. I also develop an index of federal labor costs based on trends since 1970 in minimum-wage laws, Social Security payroll taxes, and the policies of different presidential administrations. Trends over time in this index prove to be largely independent of trends in state labor costs.

STATES AND LABOR COSTS BEFORE THE NEW DEAL

The American federal system was devised in part as a response to the economic diversity of the thirteen original colonies. No colony or state was willing to join a federation on terms that would reduce its comparative advantage, whether that was based on trade with Europe and the Caribbean, banking and finance, or agriculture dependent on a plantation economy (Bednar, Eskridge, and Ferejohn 2001). Some tough bargaining was necessary at the Constitutional Convention in Philadelphia to persuade states that they would be better off with a unified national market and currency.

The Constitution gave taxing power to Congress and put an end to the states' major source of revenue before 1789: tariffs on imports from other states (Hansen 1983). But the Constitution also included compensatory measures to guarantee states' boundaries, require that they give "full faith and credit" to other states' laws, balance the representation of larger and smaller states in Congress and the Electoral College, and provide for more adequate national defense than under the nearly bankrupt Articles of Confederation government. One infamous compromise allowed the slave trade to continue until 1808. The broader issue of slavery was debated in Philadelphia, but the southern states would probably not have ratified the Constitution if slavery had not been permitted (Collier and Collier 1987).

According to some analysts, the American federal system was established on the assumption that positive economic gains would result from political union (Wibbles 2000; Weingast 1994). The comparative advantage of different sources of wealth would be preserved, fostering trade among the states through the creation of a common market. Both American and European capital would be drawn to the states or cities where the greatest profits could be made, and the resulting competition would foster greater efficiency. Population and investment could freely migrate to states or regions offering the preferred mix of taxes, services, and economic opportunities, without the tariff barriers that had been the norm between states before 1789. Throughout the nineteenth century, vigorous and often partisan debates ensued as to whether the states or the national government should be responsible for internal improvements (roads, canals, railroads), banking, or currency (North 1983).

The South has competed for business and investment on the basis of low labor costs since the days of slavery. After Reconstruction, Jim Crow laws in the former Confederate states (enforced as necessary by the Ku Klux Klan and lynchings) helped to maintain a quiescent rural labor force, with living and working conditions only marginally better than in the slavery era. Educational opportunities for both blacks and poor whites were limited, both by segregation and by lack of public investment. Given the prevalence of tenant farming and sharecropping, agricultural workers were dependent on their employers for housing and were usually in debt to them for seeds, tools, food, and clothing (Wood 1986). Miners in company towns were similarly indebted to coal mining operators. Because few other economic options were available in mining or agricultural communities, workers were basically forced to take whatever wages were offered. Union organizers from the North received a hostile reception from southern elites.

As V. O. Key (1949) argued, low voter turnout (of both blacks and whites) and lack of party competition further limited any efforts by the "have-nots" to organize to improve their living or working conditions. The "white primary," poll taxes, and onerous voter-registration requirements reduced voter turnout by both blacks and poor whites. Not until the Voting Rights Act of 1965 (bitterly opposed by southern proponents of "states' rights") were these state restrictions effectively overturned by the presence of federal registrars.

Child labor also helped employers in certain industries (coal mining, textiles, and agriculture) to limit labor costs. Until the 1930s, federal and state courts consistently resisted any limitations on child labor as an infringement on the right of individuals to freedom of contract. Beginning in the 1880s, women's groups and other reformers initiated efforts to countermand the courts with a constitutional amendment banning child labor. This received strong support in Congress but never succeeded in passing a sufficient number of states. Businesses that supported child labor argued in favor of states' rights and depicted the reformers as promoting communism (Berry 1986, 55).

Despite such opposition, by 1920 most states had enacted laws restricting child labor. The passage of such laws was a crucial factor in gaining legislative support for mothers' pensions in several northeastern and midwestern states, so that widowed or abandoned mothers could afford to stay home to supervise young children and allow them to attend school. But in other (primarily southern) states, "entrenched economic interests" favored keeping a high proportion of child laborers in manufacturing or coal mining (Skocpol 1992, 464), because they could be paid far less than adults. As Berry (1986, 46) notes, "By 1900 one child in six between the ages of ten and fifteen worked for wages"; this amounted to close to 2 million children nationwide who were at work rather than in school.

Ultimately, however, the reformers achieved their goal through federal legislation. The Fair Labor Standards Act of 1938 included provisions that effectively ended most child labor (farm or migrant labor by children was still allowed). The Supreme Court initially struck down the act, along with many other New Deal measures, as infringements on freedom of contract and undue federal interference in the states. But after Roosevelt threatened to "pack" the Supreme Court by appointing additional justices (presumably more sympathetic to his policies), the sitting justices changed their views of the constitutionality of New Deal policies; this was the infamous "switch in time that saved nine." The Fair Labor Standards Act was ultimately upheld in *U.S. v. Darby Lumber Co.* (1941).

Certain economic interests, particularly producers of textiles and alcoholic beverages, opposed women's suffrage because they feared that the franchise would lead to both higher wages for working women and a ban on child labor (Stetson 1997). These interests provided much of the funding for organized opposition to the ratification of women's suffrage at the state level. The Supreme Court's 1908 *Mueller* decision did uphold state limits on hours and weight lifting for working women, on the grounds that women's weaker physiological structure and reproductive roles made it reasonable to provide special protection for female employees without violating the Fourteenth Amendment. Many reformers welcomed this ruling, and other states followed New York's lead and enacted such "protective" legislation.[1]

After the Civil War, private charities, settlement houses, ethnic group societies, and workingmen's associations became the innovators and administrators of programs to provide insurance for workers or social assistance to the unemployed, new immigrants, and the destitute (Skocpol 1992, 265). By 1913, with the establishment of the Federal Reserve and adoption of the income tax, a larger national role in budget and fiscal policy was established. But before World War I, state and local government spending far exceeded that of the federal government, and most government services were provided by subnational governments. As Skocpol (1992) has shown, the corruption associated with party patronage and Civil War pensions convinced most reform advocates that politicians could not be trusted with major new social spending programs. "The reform-minded middle class public was not a very receptive audience for messages about new public spending for adult male wage-earners" (Skocpol 1992, 261). Thus voters in New York and California rejected new constitutions that would have set up state-level workers' compensation programs.

Nevertheless, several eastern and midwestern states endeavored to improve conditions for labor by expanding on these private initiatives. Populists, Socialists, and Progressives advocated policies designed to enhance union strength, limit child labor, and regulate hours of work or overtime (Hofstadter 1955). The Triangle Shirtwaist Factory fire in 1911, in which nearly 200 women sweatshop employees in New York City burned to death, led to public outrage, and state and local governments began to impose building codes and minimum worker-safety requirements on businesses. However, these were not always enforced, and any workers who complained could quickly lose their jobs. Yet pioneer state policies to protect workers' health, pensions, organizing rights, and job security became the basis for the American welfare state, and many of these state innovations became national policy during the New Deal. Wisconsin, for example, pioneered workers' compensation and old-age security programs; many of its immigrants came from European countries that already employed such policies.

Also after the Civil War, many states and localities increased their investment in education. As Skocpol (1992, 89) notes, "The early democratization of the white male electorate ensured that masses of ordinary Americans could support public schooling as a right of democratic citizenship." By 1900, public primary and high schools were widespread, and American investment in education far exceeded that of Europe. Land-grant state universities established after the Morrill Act of 1862 provided their graduates with the technological skills for an increasingly industrial economy. These colleges also fostered research in agriculture, and productivity soared in that sector as county agents spread information on new farming methods to the grassroots. Thurow (1980) argues that such public support for agriculture constituted the first successful example of a sector-specific industrial policy in the United States. Even in the South, the Tuskegee Institute and the establishment of black colleges helped to raise the skills and the wages of at least some African Americans, although segregation still limited their opportunities.

However, some states (especially those in the Upper Midwest) invested far more than others in human capital. But even better-educated workers did not always benefit from higher wages; high rates of immigration from both Europe and Asia, as well as periodic recessions and business opposition to unions, helped to restrain wage growth. Several reformist movements (Populists, Progressives, the free-silver movement) emerged to try to reduce the power of business cartels and robber barons over the distribution of wealth. The Sherman Antitrust Act of 1890 was intended by many progressive reformers to restrain the predatory tactics of giant corporate trusts, and it did help limit the control of railroads over the marketing of agricultural products (and thus farmers' incomes). After 1900, groups such as the National Consumers' League began a push for state legislation of minimum-wage laws—but only for women, who were not only paid less but faced limitations on hours worked enacted as a result of the *Mueller* decision (Skocpol 1992, 410). Many labor unions actually opposed minimum-wage laws for men, fearing that they would become ceilings rather than floors and would interfere with collective bargaining (p. 412).

The states also played an active role in the suppression of labor union organizing. Before World War I, most state legislatures were controlled by business interests. Governors could summon state militias to break strikes and provide security for scab labor. Labor union organizers risked being jailed as "outside agitators" or for disturbing the peace, and any who were not U.S. citizens could be (and often were) deported. Under the "due process" clause of the Fourteenth Amendment and similar state constitutional provisions, state as well as federal courts could void union contracts and any efforts by state legislatures to enact laws concerning hours of work, working conditions, limits on child labor, or union recognition. Courts soon began to use the Sherman Antitrust Act to ban as "conspiracies" most union efforts to organize or to mount strikes. By 1920, state courts had struck down more than 300 labor laws (Skocpol 1992, 229).

As a consequence, many unionization drives in industries were dismal failures. After the Homestead strike of 1892 was brutally terminated, union activity in the steel mills all but ended, and some earlier gains in pay or reduced work weeks were rescinded (Sexton 1991, 84). Craft or guild unions (the basis for the American Federation of Labor, or AFL) had more success, because both employers and consumers needed their high levels of skill. And these unions often managed to restrict entry into their particular trade, to maintain their bargaining power. However, the 1894 Pullman strike, initiated by the railroad unions after the rail companies cut wages by 25 to 40 percent, included many craftsmen and skilled workers. The violent strike was nevertheless broken after President Grover Cleveland sent in U.S. Army troops, although in this case the governor of Illinois and the mayor of Chicago supported the strikers (Sexton 1991, 107–11).

During World War I, the need for high levels of production of war matériel led to at least some improvements in the climate for workers. President Woodrow Wilson used his war powers to give some sanction to unionization, and from 1915 to 1920 union membership increased to more than 5 million (Sexton 1991, 114). The Clayton Antitrust Act, passed by a Democratic Congress in 1914, appeared to exempt labor from the antitrust provisions of the Sherman Act. The employment and industrial-production concerns of World War I led to brief experimentation with a National Employment Service office to consolidate listings of job openings. However, as Skocpol (1992) notes, this national policy did not survive the war, and employment services reverted to the states.

After the war, a return to a Republican administration, a severe depression, and fear of communism and socialism all contributed to widespread attacks on unions. In Sexton's words, "The 1920s roared for business and whimpered for labor" (1991, 114). Republican-dominated state and federal courts ruled that the Clayton Antitrust Act did apply to unions, and they used it to stymie union organizing. A few states passed laws to curb injunctions, forbid the discharge of workers for union activity, or provide for workers' rights to organize, but all of these were struck down by court interpretation. Courts in several states also imposed a ban on even peaceful picketing, and they used injunctions to break strikes (Sexton 1991, 116). While corporate profits soared, AFL membership plummeted, real wages declined, and unemployment increased to 10 percent of the labor force even before 1929.

The 1920s also witnessed major new developments in interstate competition for business. In 1926, Mississippi, facing high levels of unemployment because of the mechanization of cotton picking, implemented an act to balance agriculture with industry. The state offered significant tax breaks and low wages to lure textile factories from New England. Many such factories did relocate, and other states began to emulate Mississippi's initiatives (Gilmore 1960; Wood 1986).

NEW DEAL EFFORTS TO NATIONALIZE LABOR MARKETS

When Franklin Delano Roosevelt took office as president in March 1933, unemployment stood at 20 percent, severe deflation had cut wages and property values, and consumer demand had plummeted. The Smoot-Hawley Tariff Act of 1930, which set up the highest tariff barriers in American history, had all but choked off international trade. Poor economic conditions were so widespread that Americans finally began to question the traditional values of rugged individualism, laissez-faire, limited government, and a balanced budget. A high-turnout election led to rejection of the Herbert Hoover administration, its business allies, and the Republican Party. State and local governments had lost most of their previous sources of revenue, and they backed the repeal of Prohibition as a quick remedy to refill their coffers. Social unrest was widespread; riots, strikes, and the Bonus March on Washington by impoverished World War I veterans convinced Hoover and many business leaders that a socialist or communist revolution might be imminent (Goldston 1985).

All these factors led to popular and political support for a larger federal role in social and economic policy, and to the creation of the American welfare state (Stein 1996; Skocpol 1992). The Roosevelt administration wanted to put purchasing power into the hands of workers by adopting a federal minimum wage and creating jobs through the Civilian Conservation Corps and public works projects. Legislation to support labor unions was also a New Deal priority. Although in his 1932 campaign Roosevelt (like Hoover) had promised to balance the budget, his administration soon moved to go off the gold standard and to adopt Keynesian deficit spending policies to boost the stagnant economy.

But these New Deal efforts to raise wages and nationalize labor markets came at a price. FDR had sizable Democratic majorities in both houses of Congress. Yet the "conservative coalition" of Republicans and southern Democrats was nevertheless strong enough to demand significant concessions, and most businesses remained hostile to the New Deal. To pass Social Security, for example, the Roosevelt administration had to agree to exempt agricultural and domestic workers, many of whom were African American and/or southern (Derthick 1979). The payroll tax for Social Security was also highly regressive, because higher incomes were not subject to it.[2] The unemployment insurance system was set up to be jointly administered by the states and the federal government, with the states given latitude to establish coverage and benefit levels to reflect local conditions. These provisions, so different from the patterns adopted by more centralized European countries, were likewise necessary to gain congressional approval (Wise 1989). As Mettler (1998) agues, social and employment policies determined by the states were much less likely to be as inclusive as national standards for eligibility and administration, and they adversely affected groups lacking political power (especially women and minorities).

Members of the Conservative Coalition in Congress were also opposed to a federal minimum wage, which they saw as an unprecedented intrusion of the federal government into the relationship between employer and employee. Southern representatives in Congress argued that a nation-wide minimum wage would undercut the South's regional low-wage advantage and thus hinder its economic development. Other observers, however, argued that southern opposition to a minimum wage also stemmed from reluctance to pay black workers the same as whites (Schulman 1991). To gain congressional passage, the Fair Labor Standards Act of 1938, which established a federal minimum wage and rules concerning overtime pay, exempted tenant farmers and domestic workers (the large majority of whom were African American) from its provisions (Paulsen 1996). Despite the southern states' strategies to retain lower labor costs, personal income in the South did rise relative to the rest of the country, partly as a result of New Deal programs such as the Tennessee Valley Authority, agricultural price supports, and rural electrification (Bernat 2001). Even before the New Deal, the Norris-LaGuardia Act of 1932 had outlawed yellow-dog contracts (which had made not joining a union a condition of employment). After 1935, the National Labor Relations Act (the Wagner Act) required employers to bargain in good faith with unions certified under that law.

In some industrial states, such as Michigan, labor was also protected by elected state officials, who refused to call up state militias as strikebreakers, and who recognized that the U.S. Army and federal injunctions would no longer be used to break strikes (Sexton 1991, 118). These new rules had the desired effect: Labor union membership rose dramatically, and for the first time large-scale industries (steel, automobiles) were unionized, although not without considerable grassroots efforts and widespread use of sit-down strikes. The National Labor Relations Board was established to oversee union authorizing elections and to investigate violations of the Wagner Act by both business and labor. Roosevelt's appointees to this board were generally sympathetic to labor, and his first secretary of labor, Frances Perkins, was a well-known labor reformer and feminist.

Businesses and most members of the Conservative Coalition remained opposed to these New Deal initiatives and to the growing membership and strength of labor unions. During World War II, however, the need for high levels of economic production and the continued Democratic hegemony in Washington precluded any legislative challenge to the Wagner Act. But the end of the war led to soaring inflation, considerable labor unrest, and takeover of Congress by Republicans. The stage was set for efforts to weaken unions, roll back the New Deal, and return the regulation of labor costs to the states.

TAFT-HARTLEY AND STATE RIGHT-TO-WORK LAWS

After Republicans gained control of Congress in 1946, they pushed through the Taft-Hartley Act over President Harry Truman's veto. A major provision of this act permitted states to adopt so-called right-to-work laws, which outlawed union shops. The law's provisions for a ninety-day "cooling-off" period and federal mediation also weakened the impact of strike threats. Taft-Hartley thus restored much of the interstate competition that the New Deal had attempted to reduce (Lee 1966). And since 1947, the states have competed actively to reduce labor costs.

Right-to-work laws originated in Florida and Arkansas during the 1940s. The ultimate strategy was to make labor union organizing considerably more difficult by banning "union shops." This meant that even if a labor union won an organizing election in a workplace, it could not compel employees to pay union dues. For workers, the temptation would therefore be to free-ride and gain any benefits of union recognition (higher wages, grievance procedures) without paying for them. For labor unions, however, the lack of dues and membership greatly weakened their stance vis-à-vis management in right-to-work states.

The tactics used by businesses and conservative groups such as the National Right to Work Committee (NRWC) downplayed the collective result of banning union shops: weaker unions, lower wages, more power to management. Instead, the emphasis was on familiar American values such as freedom of association and individual rights (Delaney 1998). The NRWC defines the absence of right-to-work laws as "forced unionization," and it also argues that the absence of labor unions would be an advantage in interstate competition for business. Labor unions and their allies were not persuaded by this rhetoric, and a majority of industrial states have rejected right-to-work laws.

However, in 2001 Oklahoma became the twenty-second right-to-work state. Table 2.1 lists the other right-to-work states, dates of adoption, and percent of the workforce unionized. As of 2000, the mean level of union density was 12.3 percent in right-to-work states, compared with 17.4 percent in states that allow union shops (a statistically significant difference). However, some right-to-work states, such as Alabama and Nevada, have relatively high levels of union density, reflecting a particular industrial profile (steel in Alabama, hotels and casinos in Nevada) that has facilitated unionization. The NRWC continues to lobby state legislatures for passage of additional laws, and it provides legal assistance to workers who want to challenge the payment of union dues or the use of those dues for political purposes. Its advertisements touting "individual rights" or "freedom of association" for workers regularly appear in national newspapers and magazines.

Not surprisingly, wages are generally lower in right-to-work states; as of 2000, $112 per week, compared with $128 in union-shop states.[3] Peter Eisinger, in a 1988 book critical of supply-side strategies for economic development such as tax incentives and low wages, posited that the wage differential between states with and without right-to-work laws would diminish over time. However, that does not appear to be the case; the ratio of manufacturing wages for states with and without these laws actually increased from 1.09 in 1970 to 1.13 in 2000, after peaking at 1.20 in 1990.[4]

Table 2.1
State Right-to-Work Laws

State	Date Adopted	Union Members, 1995 (%)
Alabama	1953	11.4
Arizona	1946	5.9
Arkansas	1944	7.1
Florida	1943	7.5
Georgia	1947	7.7
Idaho	1986	8.7
Indiana	1995[a]	14.9
Iowa	1947	13.0
Kansas	1958	9.6
Louisiana	1976	8.1
Mississippi	1954	5.8
Nebraska	1946	8.6
Nevada	1951	20.4
North Carolina	1947	4.1
North Dakota	1946	9.1
Oklahoma	2001	10.4
South Carolina	1954	3.7
South Dakota	1946	7.4
Tennessee	1947	9.6
Texas	1947	6.6
Utah	1955	8.4
Virginia	1947	6.8
Wyoming	1963	9.7

[a]Applies to school employees only.

Do right-to-work laws in fact weaken unions? Consider trends in unionization in four states that have enacted right-to-work laws since 1970: Florida, Idaho, Louisiana, and Wyoming. All have since experienced greater declines in union density (more than 50 percent) than the national average decline in union membership of 42 percent since 1980. Overall labor costs have declined more sharply than the national average in these four states as well. But none of these were industrial states, and all had relatively low levels of union density even before enacting right-to-work laws. Thus right-to-work laws are likely to be passed only in states where unions are already weak for other reasons, such as industrial composition, political culture, or strong business influence. But once enacted, they certainly make union organizing efforts more difficult.

Considerable research has found that right-to-work laws indeed have an impact on business location decisions and state economic growth (Dye 1980; Newman 1983; Hansen 1984). And as we shall see, right-to-work states tend to have other limitations on labor costs as well, stemming in part from a lack of labor union influence. Right-to-work laws may thus have a cumulative effect on state public policy.

CONTEMPORARY STATE EFFORTS TO RESTRAIN LABOR COSTS

Instead of national policies, on the New Deal model, to raise southern wages and limit low-wage competition, recent years have witnessed efforts by states to enhance their international or regional "competitiveness" by keeping the lid on labor costs. Cummings (1998) has termed these trends the "Dixification" of America" because other states have copied many antiunion and low-wage policies long prevalent in the South. Since the 1970s, many states have reduced workers' compensation, restricted eligibility for unemployment benefits, and limited strikes by public employees. States have also used measures such as hiring migrant workers, prison labor, or bans on secondary boycotts to inhibit union organizing efforts and keep wages down.

A few states have adopted laws to try to protect workers, such as right-to-know laws concerning hazardous substances, or plant-closing laws requiring advance notification of layoffs.[5] But as Portz (1990) has shown, such laws face business opposition and threats to relocate to states with lower regulatory burdens. States and localities are even reluctant to try to reclaim their investment via "clawback" provisions when subsidized companies move elsewhere, taking with them jobs and equipment provided at public expense. Thus, after a decade of tax incentives and union concessions to keep the company in a place that had been making refrigerators for more than fifty years, Maytag closed its factory in Galesburg, Illinois, in October 2004, terminating 1,600 workers. But the town decided not to bill Maytag for the value of its tax breaks, because of concern that this might discourage the potential for future business investment (Egan 2004).

Wages

The states differ considerably in average wages. As of 2000, hourly manufacturing wages ranged from $19.20 in Michigan to $10.71 in South Dakota. Obviously, manufacturing wages are largely determined by economic factors: the business cycle, demand for skilled labor, and national and international competition in particular industries. But levels of unionization, prevailing-wage provisions, and state policies affecting union organizing and minimum wages influence wages in manufacturing as well as in other sectors. Time-series data for the states are only available for wages in manufacturing. As figure 2.1 shows, manufacturing wages (in constant dollars) declined between 1970 and 1992 but increased sharply thereafter.

State policies can have a direct impact on wages via state minimum-wage laws, prevailing-wage laws for construction workers, and pay levels for public employees. State policies can also influence wages indirectly, by

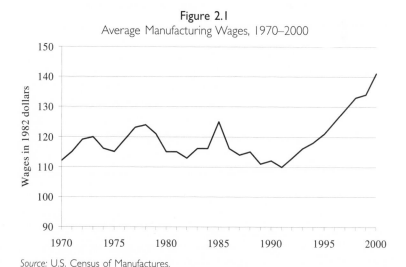

Figure 2.1
Average Manufacturing Wages, 1970–2000

Source: U.S. Census of Manufactures.

making it more or less difficult for labor unions to organize and strike, because unionized workers consistently earn more than nonunion workers. A few states have enacted comparable-worth laws for public employees, and such laws have led to increased wages for women.[6]

Minimum-Wage Laws

Minimum-wage laws have been subject to vigorous debate between liberal and conservative interests at the state as well as federal levels. Conservatives argue that a higher minimum wage leads to fewer jobs. Recent evidence (Card and Krueger 1995) has suggested that any such effect would be quite small, although the research remains highly contentious (see Levin-Waldman 2001 for a summary). Liberals and unions in the states argue for a higher minimum wage on the basis of fairness, especially because executive compensation has been rising so much faster than wages (AFL-CIO 2005). They also cite the need to maintain consumer demand and to support families. Despite dire predictions from conservatives, employment in fact grew at a healthy clip after the federal minimum wage was raised in 1993.

The federal minimum wage has lagged well behind inflation; the current rate of $5.15 per hour has not been increased since 1997, and is at its lowest value in real dollars since 1949 (Gaynor 2005b). But further increases are unlikely in a Republican-controlled Congress. As of 2005, eighteen states had adopted minimum-wage laws above the federal minimum (table 2.2), although the number and types of employees covered vary considerably. Most of these were large industrial states. Yet despite the Republican sweep in the 2004 election, two Sunbelt states that supported George W. Bush (Florida and Nevada) also voted to increase the state minimum wage. Also as of 2004, two states (Kansas and Ohio) had minimum wages below the federal minimum, although the higher (federal) minimum wage legally prevails for most workers. Seven states (New Mexico, Tennessee, Alabama, Mississippi, Louisiana, Florida, and South Carolina) have no minimum-wage law. By federal statute, wages in the District of Columbia are set one dollar above the federal minimum.

In some states where the cost of living is high, such as Alaska, Hawaii, and California, higher minimum wages are often considered a business necessity for attracting and retaining workers. But other high-wage states such as New York have resisted recent calls for a higher minimum wage, although that state has had minimum wages higher than the federal minimum in many previous years. In the fall of 2004, New York Republican governor George Pataki vetoed a minimum-wage provision passed overwhelmingly by both

Table 2.2
State Minimum Wage Laws, 2005

State	Minimum Wages above Federal Minimum of $5.15	Job Growth, 2001–4 (%)
Alaska	7.15	6.0
California	6.75	1.7
Connecticut	7.10	−2.1
Delaware	6.15	−0.4
District of Columbia	6.15	na
Florida	6.15[a,b]	9.7
Hawaii	6.25	3.2
Illinois	6.50	−1.6
Maine	6.25	0.0
Maryland	6.15	3.6
Massachusetts	6.75	−4.3
Minnesota	6.15	6.7
Nevada	6.15[b]	19.1
New Jersey	6.15	4.5
New York	6.00	4.2
Oregon	7.25[a]	−1.2
Rhode Island	6.75	−3.6
Vermont	6.75[a]	−0.2
Washington	7.35[a]	−2.3
Wisconsin	5.70	4.9

[a]Indexed to inflation.
[b]Increase approved by referendum during the 2004 presidential election.
Sources: Minimum-wage laws in Gaynor (2005b). Job growth: author's calculations from Bureau of Labor Statistics data.

houses of the state legislature, and he expressed the classic logic for doing so: concern that New York jobs would move to Pennsylvania or New Jersey. Election-year politics prevailed, however, and in a bipartisan vote the New York State Senate overturned Pataki's veto in November 2004.

Overall wages are indeed higher in states with minimum wages above the federal level, but even in those states coverage is usually limited to only part of the labor force. What about trends in job growth? As table 2.2 shows, the record is mixed; some states with higher minimum wages in fact experienced strong job growth after 2001, but others fared poorly. However, some states without higher minimum wages, such as West Virginia, Michigan, and many of the Great Plains states, have had significantly higher than average unemployment in recent years, reflecting economic difficulties in key industries such as farming and coal mining.

The impact of minimum-wage rates is especially pronounced among low-income groups, particularly women coming off welfare and workers who are younger or older than prime-age workers (McCrate 1997). Hout (1997) and Card (2001) attribute much of the recent growth in income inequality in the United States to the fact that federal and state minimum-wage levels have fallen further and further behind inflation rates and the cost of living (particularly housing costs). In constant (2003) dollars, the minimum wage in 2005 was worth only $4.65, whereas the minimum wage in 1972 was $7.12—sufficient to raise the incomes of full-time minimum-wage workers above the federal poverty level. The passage of welfare reform in 1996 pushed millions of former welfare recipients into the labor force, forcing them to compete for low-wage jobs and depressing wages even further (Bartik 1999).

Although the debate over the minimum wage tends to be highly partisan, one compensatory program has enjoyed bipartisan support. Use of the federal Earned Income Tax Credit (EITC) has expanded greatly since the Ronald Reagan administration. EITCs provide a refundable tax credit to reduce federal income tax liability and offset recent increases in Social Security taxes. Many states have also adopted EITCs to provide some benefit to the working poor and to offset the regressive impact of recent increases in state sales and excise taxes.[7] Adopting EITCs is more politically palatable than increasing the minimum wage for state governments, because the cost of the tax credits is borne by the state's taxpayers rather than by private businesses.

States also differ in the degree to which they require *prevailing wage laws* on state-financed construction projects. These laws are generally interpreted to mean that workers on those projects must receive union-scale wages. Unions and their Democratic allies of course prefer prevailing-wage laws, but states facing budget shortfalls and taxpayer resistance may accede to pressures from employers to repeal such laws. Forty-two states had prevailing-wage laws as of 1975, but ten have since repealed them, thus encouraging the hiring of nonunion (and usually lower-cost) labor for public construction projects (Council of State Governments, *The Book of the States 2002–3*, 286). President Bush suspended the federal prevailing-wage law (the Davis-Bacon Act) in the Gulf Coast in the aftermath of Hurricane Katrina (Edsall 2005). But he was forced to reinstate it after outraged state officials, labor union leaders, and congressional Democrats protested that it was unfair to pay workers low wages to rebuild their homes and communities.

Labor Union Membership

One of the most striking trends in American politics has been the dramatic decline since the 1950s in union members as a share of the workforce, from 33 to 13 percent (figure 2.2). Other industrialized countries have averaged only a 3 percent decline (Wallerstein and Western 2000). Traditional labor organizations (primarily the AFL-CIO) have declined 79 percent in membership since 1970 (Farber and Western 2001).

Labor union membership as a percentage of the labor force has declined in every state since 1970. The states still differ considerably in union membership in both the public and private sectors, from a highs of more than 30 percent in New York, Michigan, and Pennsylvania, to less than 5 percent in many southern states. Unionization levels among state public employees are now considerably higher than those in the private sector, and even increased 4 percent between 1986 and 1999. Teachers' unions and organizations, primarily the National Education Association (NEA), received the highest number of first-place mentions in Thomas and Hrebenar's (1999) ranking of the forty most influential interests in the American states. However, three states (Georgia, Texas, and South Carolina) have abolished civil service laws pertaining to new public-sector

Figure 2.2
Percent of Labor Force Unionized, 1970–2000

Sources: Bureau of Labor Statistics data before 1982, Bureau of National Affairs thereafter (see note 9 to chapter 2).

employees, who can now be hired and fired at will (*Federal Human Resources Week* 2002).

Despite the overall decline in unions' membership and power, they are still perceived as a powerful political threat by many Republicans. The NRWC's Legal Defense Foundation claims that "in-kind" contributions from labor (mailings, telephone banks, voter turnout drives) amount to millions of dollars in illegal campaign contributions (National Institute for Labor Relations Research 1997). In 2002, President Bush successfully persuaded Congress that employees of his new Department of Homeland Security would not be covered by Civil Service protections against involuntary transfers or termination (Lee and Barr 2002). And in 2004, President Bush's secretary of education, Rod Paige, aroused the ire of the NEA by referring to it as a "terrorist organization" because of its steadfast opposition to school vouchers and the Bush administration's No Child Left Behind Act.[8]

Numerous factors have been considered to explain the decline in labor union density in the United States.[9] Economic factors include increased international competition and the loss of manufacturing jobs; union organizing is far more difficult in the service, financial, and retail sectors. Political factors include the opposition to unions by Republican presidential administrations, whose secretaries of labor and National Labor Relations Board (NLRB) appointments are generally not sympathetic to unions. And labor unions themselves have spent much less money and effort on organizational drives in recent years. According to AFL-CIO organizing director Richard Bensinger, 10 percent of unions were doing 90 percent of organizing efforts, and the bulk of labor's resources went into servicing union contracts rather than organizing workers (quoted in *Business Week*, October 16, 2000, 118–20).

Nissen stresses the concerted opposition to unions by employers: "Professional anti-union consultants and strident anti-union management behavior are major determinants of union organizing success or failure" (2003, 324). He also notes the increasingly unfavorable legal climate for labor since World War II; even if workers win an NLRB union election, employer refusal to bargain a first union contract frequently kills the union. Sexton (1991) describes many historical and contemporary instances of brutal repression of labor unions by corporations and their allies in state or national government.

These analyses, however, consistently downplay the role of interstate competition in our federal system as a factor in the weakness of American labor. But in addition to right-to-work laws, the states have considerable influence on the status of labor unions. And their efforts to create a "favorable business climate" often include efforts to reduce labor costs and limit the influence of organized labor. Collective bargaining laws for public employees, and restrictions on their right to strike, also vary across states. Some state laws prohibit awarding state contracts to employers found to be in violation of the National Labor Relations Act. A few states have barred the use of strikebreakers, or the use of prisoners on work release or furlough to replace strikers. Some states are more lenient than others concerning migrant or child labor, and these workers are often paid less than the minimum wage or the prevailing union wage.

State policies also influence the political role of labor. The Supreme Court's 1988 decision in *Communication Workers of America v. Beck* ruled that union dues could only be used for collective bargaining, contract administration, and grievance procedures, not for political or charitable contributions. The Court further ruled that workers are entitled to a financial accounting of how union funds are spent. The NRWC has funded numerous legal challenges to state labor organizations under the *Beck* guidelines. Labor unions, however, view the detailed yearly financial reporting requirements as a thinly disguised effort to reduce their political and electoral influence, and they counter that businesses face no such reporting mandates.

Because of the alleged failure of the federal government to enforce the *Beck* decision, the NRWC has been backing "paycheck-protection" measures for union members in states lacking right-to-work laws. Here again, we see the use of rhetoric ("paycheck protection" sounds innocuous and beneficial to workers) to disguise a concerted effort to weaken the influence of labor. These laws require that unions must secure annual written approval from individual union members before expending any portion of their dues to support particular candidates or ballot issues, or even on voter registration drives or get-out-the-vote campaigns. As of 2004, Wyoming, Washington, Idaho, and Michigan had passed such laws, and Ohio had enacted a statute covering public employee unions. As a consequence, union fundraising for political campaigns has declined sharply in states like Michigan and Washington (Rochelle and von Spakovsky 2003, 1, 6).

In 1993, California's Republican governor Pete Wilson issued an executive order requiring notification to public employees of their rights under *Beck*. However, California voters rejected paycheck protection in hotly contested referenda in 2000 and 2005, thanks in part to active campaigns by the state's labor unions (Dively 2002). The NRWC has paycheck-protection campaigns pending in more than thirty other states. The religious right now backs them as well, because many of their leaders equate unionism with liberalism and secular humanism. The religious right would also like to constrain the political power of the teachers' unions, which tend to support Democratic candidates and have adamantly opposed the school voucher programs so important to many religious conservatives (Dreyfuss 1998).

Employment at Will

As noted in chapter 1, American state and federal courts have traditionally upheld the doctrine of "employment at will," which basically gives employers the right to hire and fire for any reason. This legal viewpoint began to shift after a 1959 decision in California, when a labor union business agent claimed that he was fired after he refused to perform an illegal act (lying under oath about his union's policies). The state's supreme court held that this constituted an unjust dismissal (Ballam 2000).

The courts in many states now realize that employees depend on their jobs for far more than wages. For many Americans, health care, pensions, insurance, and social standing are linked to employment status, and workers and their families can suffer unduly if the breadwinner loses his or her job. In addition to federal laws forbidding discrimination on the basis of race, sex, religion, or disability, courts (and occasionally legislatures) in many states have recognized a number of "public policy" exceptions to employment termination. In such states, workers cannot legally be fired because of National Guard duty, jury duty, filing a workers' compensation claim, or whistle blowing. Under the Wagner Act, employees supposedly cannot be fired for union organizing activity, although Kahlenberg (2000) cites AFL-CIO estimates that this occurs with some frequency, with one in eight union supporters fired during election campaigns.

The fifty states, however, differ considerably in the degree to which their courts or legislatures have recognized exceptions to employment at will, whether based on public policy exceptions or on the idea that a job is an "implicit contract" between employer and employee (Ballam 2000). According to Walsh and Schwarz's (1996) review of state laws and court decisions, seven states (mostly southern) recognize *no* public policy exceptions, and twenty-six other states recognize only narrowly defined exceptions. By contrast, ten states hold that jobs are based on implied contracts, and terminations require good faith and fair dealing by both parties.

Neither the courts nor advocacy groups like the American Civil Liberties Union challenge an employer's right to fire someone "for cause" (criminal activity, poor performance on the job). However, employers can claim that someone was fired "for cause" when the real issue was union organizing or jury duty. Litigation has yet to resolve many cases brought under the Americans with Disabilities Act, or whether alcoholism or drug use constitutes a remediable behavioral problem or criminal activity justifying dismissal. These legal distinctions are still evolving, and they may not be much help to individual employees who (unless they have union or Civil Service protection) may lack the legal resources to challenge their termination in court.

Perspectives on employment at will by employers and economists should also be noted. Many managers in unionized industries and the public sector claim that it is almost impossible to fire lazy or incompetent employees because of intricate union grievance procedures and Civil Service provisions (Maranto 1999). Heckman and Pagés (2004) review the literature on employment at will in the Organization for Economic Cooperation and Development's (OECD) member countries and Latin America, and they conclude that employment tends to be lower, and job growth slower, when employers face legal restrictions on their ability to fire or lay off workers. Shaughnessy (2003) estimates that on balance, wages are lower in the American states that do recognize public policy exceptions than in those where employment at will prevails; employers appear to extract a "wage premium" to compensate them for legal constraints on their ability to fire workers. As Shaughnessy's research confirms, state policies indeed influence the real cost of labor.

Unemployment Benefits

Since the New Deal, the American system of benefits to the unemployed has been jointly administered by the states and the federal government (Wise 1989). Employers are required to contribute to the state's unemployment insurance (UI) trust fund on the basis of taxable wages and their "experience" rating derived from their record of layoffs. Thus high-wage employers or firms, and those with a history of more layoffs, must contribute more to the UI trust fund. During severe economic downturns, Congress has usually provided additional funds to states with high levels of unemployment after they exhausted their trust funds.

The states vary considerably in several elements of unemployment benefits: the taxes paid by employers, the eligibility of workers for compensation, and the amount of the weekly benefits received. In some states, laid-off workers who desire part-time work are eligible for unemployment and the maximum UI benefit is indexed to state wages. Other states require laid-off workers to have worked full time for longer periods, and any changes in benefits require legislative action. Strikers, part-time workers, and the self-employed are usually ineligible. Eligibility also depends on state courts' rulings as to whether a worker quit voluntarily or was fired. In 2000, weekly benefits ranged from $136 in Mississippi to $311 in Washington and $335 in Massachusetts. Some states cover a far larger proportion of wages lost due to unemployment. In North Dakota, this was well over 45 percent in 2000; in Missouri and Indiana, it was less than 28 percent (U.S. Employment and Training Administration data cited in *Statistical Abstract of the United States 2002*, table 528).

In constant dollars, the value of state unemployment insurance benefits changed little between 1980 and 1995, but it rose slightly by 2000 (figure 2.3). However, the proportion of American workers covered by unemployment insurance has declined steadily since the 1970s, from 45 percent in 1970 to 35 percent in 2000, as has the proportion of wages received in UI benefits. In an effort to encourage business investment, many states lowered their UI tax rates during the late 1980s and 1990s, from 3.13 percent in 1985 to 1.75 percent in 2000 *(Statistical Abstract of the United States 2002*, table 529).

But many states were caught short when recessions hit and a Republican-controlled Congress after 1994 refused to bail out state trust funds. During the 1991 recession, the states, reeling from deficits, tightened eligibility standards for extended unemployment benefits until only 5 per-

Figure 2.3
State Unemployment Benefits, 1970–2000

Source: Bureau of Labor Statistics.

cent of the unemployed were eligible for such benefits, compared with virtually all the unemployed in the 1970s and 1980s (Clymer 1991). A Republican-controlled Congress failed to extend unemployment benefits beyond the usual twenty-six weeks after the 2001–2 recession.

Workers' Compensation

Workers' compensation in the United States has an interesting history, because it was largely initiated by employers rather than workers or unions. Before 1900, the prevailing legal view was that employers bore no legal or financial responsibility for workers injured on the job. Under the doctrine of freedom of contract, workers who disliked unsafe conditions were "free" to seek other employment. And under the fellow-servant rule, employees could not sue their employers for injuries caused by another employee's negligence, especially if the injured worker was even marginally responsible for the accident. Under the "assumption of risk" doctrine, workers were assumed to have bargained for higher wages to compensate for high-risk jobs (Skocpol 1992, 287).

However, rates of death or injury were high, especially in mining and heavy industries like steel manufacturing. By 1900, it was estimated that 35,000 deaths and 2 million injuries occurred every year in the United States (cited in Skocpol 1992, 289). Juries were often sympathetic to seriously injured workers or to their widows and orphans. Many businesses, therefore, backed a system of workers' compensation administered by the states, which would provide fixed benefits to injured workers and avoid the delays and potentially higher costs of litigation. Initially, labor unions were reluctant to give up workers' rights to sue. But eventually, most labor unions and reform groups backed workers' compensation, in part to aid injured workers in a timely fashion and in part to force employers to invest more money and training in worker safety.

Between 1911 and 1940, every state adopted some form of workers' compensation law (*Consumer Reports* 2000). These provided medical care and income to workers injured on the job, and death benefits to families of those who died. They also served to protect employers from costly lawsuits and unpredictable jury awards. All but the smallest businesses were required to provide workers' compensation for their employees, either from self insurance, private carriers, or state-run insurance funds. These state-mandated programs never provided generous benefits, and by the 1970s benefits were so far below the poverty level that President Richard Nixon appointed a national commission to study the problem. The commission recommended higher benefits and that totally disabled workers should receive two-thirds of their previous salaries. Most states, fearing a federal takeover of the program, raised benefits, but as of 2000, seventeen states had still not met the standards.

By the 1980s, however, workers' compensation insurers faced declining income from their investments and double-digit annual increases in medical costs. They petitioned state insurance regulators for steep increases in premiums, and they mounted a media campaign to convince legislators and the public that "fraud" was responsible for soaring rates. Malingering workers certainly existed, and state and city governments made vigorous attempts (including surreptitious videotaping of suspected malingerers) to detect fraud by employees (Young 1998). Yet even an insurance-industry group, the National Insurance Crime Bureau, found that less than 2 percent of insurance premiums paid went for fraudulent claims (cited in *Consumer Reports* 2000, 3). Protracted legal debates have also ensued over the meaning of disability and work readiness (Lemov 1997; Stone 1984).

As figure 2.4 shows, average workers' compensation payments (adjusted for inflation) soared during the 1980s. As a result, many state legislatures were persuaded that they had to cut workers' compensation costs or they would lose business to rival states. Cost-cutting policies adopted included requiring claimants to go to insurer- or employer-approved doctors, reducing the amounts and number of weeks that workers could collect, and cutting off any payments that might be covered by private pensions or Social Security. Michigan, ranked first in the country in workers' compensation coverage in 1980, reduced benefits, tightened eligibility, and limited opportunities for appeals of judgments (Jackson 1988, 122–24). Subsequent to these reforms, benefits and employer costs as a percentage of payroll dropped by more than 20 percent from 1992 to 1996. Workers' compensation insurance again became profitable and states benefited from lower rates.

However, *Consumer Reports* in 2000 documented the human cost of these "reforms:" disabled workers denied coverage by doctors in the employ of employers or insurers, lengthy delays in assessing claims, inadequate medical care, personal bankruptcy caused by soaring medical bills, and costly and protracted processes for appeals. People injured on the job often find that they must use workers' compensation for medical expenses even if the benefits are lower; their regular health care provider can refuse any medical coverage. Fraud by individuals continues to receive attention from insurers and the media, but fraud by employers, insurers, or health care providers, though far more costly, has received little regulatory attention.

Figure 2.4
State Workers' Compensation Benefits, 1970–2000

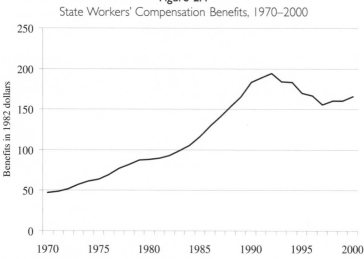

Source: Bureau of Labor Statistics.

As figure 2.4 shows, by the late 1990s workers' compensation payments again began to increase as medical costs (especially in urban areas) continued to rise far faster than overall inflation, and those costs again became a political issue. The Workers' Compensation Research Institute (WCRI), which is financed by the insurance industry, regularly publishes reports on trends in workers' compensation in the eight largest states (WCRI 2001), giving those states a strong incentive to keep their costs below those of neighboring states. Businesses in states such as California claimed that high insurance rates and overly generous payments for workers' compensation were driving them out of state. In fact, after Arnold Schwarzenegger became governor of California after the recall of Governor Gray Davis in 2003, his first priority after passing a state budget was to reform workers' compensation (National Public Radio 2004).

In relation to the cost of medical care, workers' compensation benefits are considerably lower today than in 1990 (*Consumer Reports* 2000). Interstate competition remains a major factor influencing workers' compensation coverage and benefits. But we still see considerable divergence across the states; the main reason is the higher medical costs on the East and West coasts and in urban areas.

MEASURING STATE AND FEDERAL LABOR COSTS

Thus far, I have discussed a number of policies whereby states can affect the relative cost of labor. Each policy may well have some independent impact on a state's economy, and some businesses may be more sensitive than others to particular facets of policies affecting wages, benefits, or the role of labor unions. But business investment and location decisions are likely to be based on the total impact of labor costs.

How, then, should state labor costs be measured? Commercial consultants such as Grant Thornton and Fantus prepare state rankings on tax and labor issues for their corporate clients on an annual basis, but these are often highly subjective and vary considerably over time (Fisher 2005). Two more objective measures of labor costs have been developed for other settings. First, the OECD's comparative analyses of labor costs (real wages) in industrialized countries uses a measure combining both direct wage costs and the "social wage" based on payroll taxes and regulations (OECD 1995). This facilitates comparisons across units and over time, but OECD data are for countries only and ignore federal or regional variations.[10] Second, the U.S. Bureau of Labor Statistics (BLS) calculates an employers' "Economic Costs Index" based on rates of change in several factors (wages and salaries, Social Security taxes, health insurance, retirement plans, unemployment insurance). BLS reports quarterly trends in this index by region, economic sector, and for union-versus-nonunion employees, but only since 1978 and unfortunately not for individual states.

I have therefore developed an index of state labor costs analogous to both these comprehensive measures. It combines both direct wage costs and the "social wage" (the impact on employers of state government policies and regulations) and is measured consistently over time. This index is based on five indicators available for all fifty states since 1970: labor union membership as a percent of the state labor force, presence or absence of right-to-work laws, manufacturing wages, unemployment benefits, and workers' compensation payments (the latter three in constant 1982 dollars). The combined index produces a "labor costs" score for each state for each year, 1970–2000.[11]

Table 2.3 shows labor costs by state in 1970 and 2000, and the percent change between those dates. States are ranked according to their labor costs as of 1970. The range is quite striking, with the heavily unionized Rust Belt manufacturing states at the top and the nonunion southern and western states at the bottom. There are a few surprises: Despite its poverty, West Virginia ranks relatively high in labor costs, as does Alabama; both have higher levels of union membership than most southern states. And

Vermont, despite higher levels of taxes and social services, ranks only a little above New Hampshire in the bottom quartile of state labor costs (which is otherwise dominated by right-to-work states). Table 2.3 also shows considerable variation in the percent change in labor costs between 1970 and 2000, ranging from a 43 percent decline in West Virginia to a 7 percent increase in one of the lowest-wage states, North Carolina.

The trend in state labor costs based on this consistent measure showed a decline of more than 25 percent between 1970 and 2000. Since 1970, the high-labor-cost states decreased theirs the most (averaging more than 30 percent for the top third of states as of 1970), but the low-labor-cost states also reduced their costs by more than 20 percent based on this index.

What does this index mean for a worker in a state with high or low labor costs? Compare a manufacturing worker in Michigan, the highest-scoring state in 2000, with a comparable worker in lowest-ranked South Carolina. In Michigan, the worker earns on average $19.20 per hour and is likely to be a union member; in South Carolina (a right-to-work state), manufacturing wages are only $10.96 and only 4 percent of the state's workers belong to labor unions. If the Michigan worker is injured on the job, monthly workers' compensation payments average $304, compared with $115 in South Carolina. If the Michigan worker loses his or her job, weekly benefits for the unemployed average $261, but only $206 in South Carolina.

As these examples show, state policies do have a considerable impact on labor costs. But the states are also affected by federal policies that influence the strength of unions and the cost of labor. Therefore, before we consider the relationship between labor costs and state economic and social outcomes, we must assess the impact of federal labor policies on the overall trend. As Hendrick and Garand (1991) and Brace (1993) have argued, state economic trends should not be analyzed only in terms of factors specific to the states; the national government's policies must also be taken into account.

The BLS Economic Costs Index described above is not appropriate for such an analysis, because it has only been available since 1978 and combines state and federal policies. I therefore used three yearly indicators of national trends in labor costs to construct an index of federal costs. The first is the federal minimum wage, which declined in constant (2000) dollars from $7.10 in 1970 to $5.15 in 2000. Second is the size of the payroll tax for Social Security, which increased from 4.80 percent in 1970 to 7.65 percent in 2000 for both employers and employees. Third, party and ideological differences between administrations can influence appointments to the NLRB, the Cabinet, and the enforcement of labor regulations (as

Table 2.3
State Labor Costs and Percent Change, 1970–2000

	Labor Costs (Factor Scores)		Percent Change		Labor Costs (Factor Scores)		Percent Change
	1970	2000			1970	2000	
Michigan	441	333	−24.6	Utah	267	186	−30.3
Washington	436	301	−31.2	Louisiana	254	191	−24.6
West Virginia	430	243	−43.5	Alabama	248	189	−23.9
Ohio	403	286	−29.0	Idaho	248	190	−23.6
Pennsylvania	395	272	−31.2	Tennessee	247	188	−24.2
Illinois	395	282	−28.7	Nebraska	245	184	−24.9
New York	388	332	−14.4	Arizona	243	164	−32.5
Indiana	387	265	−31.4	Wyoming	240	206	−14.3
Missouri	384	231	−39.7	Kansas	239	211	−11.9
Nevada	375	261	−30.1	Maine	234	239	2.1
Wisconsin	364	275	−24.6	North Dakota	232	170	−26.7
California	360	248	−31.0	New Hampshire	227	208	−8.6
Alaska	355	283	−20.3	Oklahoma	224	177	−20.1

Oregon	353	265	−24.7
New Jersey	345	311	−9.8
Montana	342	236	−30.9
Minnesota	336	288	−14.3
Hawaii	327	328	0.1
Kentucky	316	229	−27.3
Connecticut	308	273	−11.3
Massachusetts	303	258	−14.8
Rhode Island	297	264	−11.1
Maryland	288	251	−13.0
Delaware	286	251	−12.2
Iowa	283	243	−14.3
Colorado	279	213	−23.6
Vermont	223	212	−4.8
Arkansas	218	160	−27.1
Virginia	214	172	−19.8
Georgia	214	176	−17.3
Texas	213	166	−22.2
New Mexico	203	185	−9.3
Florida	202	171	−15.3
South Dakota	196	144	−26.6
Mississippi	181	152	−16.6
South Carolina	159	137	−13.9
North Carolina	142	152	7.4
Mean	289.8	227.0	−20.3
Standard deviation	77.8	53.2	10.3

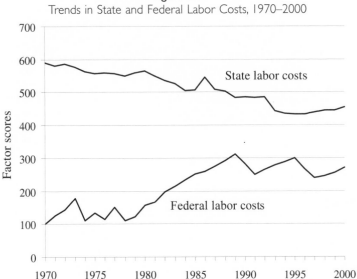

Figure 2.5
Trends in State and Federal Labor Costs, 1970–2000

Note: Since 1970, state labor costs have declined by more than 25 percent, while federal labor costs have increased.
Source: Factor scores calculated by the author.

President Reagan's breaking of the air traffic controllers' strike in 1981 demonstrated; Nordlund 1998). I therefore compare presidential administrations by using 1 for Democratic years and 2 for Republican years.

To assess the overall impact of federal changes in labor costs, I combined these three variables into a single score for each year, 1970–2000.[12] On average, overall labor costs increased by 0.25 percent a year under Democratic administrations and declined 1.0 percent a year under Republican presidents.

As figure 2.5 shows, federal and state labor costs have moved in different directions over time. Federal costs have risen somewhat since 1970; increases in Social Security payroll taxes have been partially offset by decreases in the value of the minimum wage and by the impact of different presidential administrations. But state labor costs have declined since 1970.

These results suggest that state labor costs are only marginally related to federal trends, and that changes in labor policy at the national level can-

What Matters

- The New Deal tried to reduce interstate competition over labor costs by raising the minimum wage, establishing unemployment insurance, and encouraging labor unions.
- Ever since the Taft-Hartley Act of 1947, states have returned to vigorous competition over right-to-work laws, unions, and employment protection policies.
- Labor costs can be compared across states and over time using a measure based on manufacturing wages, labor union membership, right-to-work laws, workers' compensation, and unemployment benefits.
- This combined measure shows that state labor costs have declined 25 percent since 1970 but still vary considerably across states.
- Federal labor costs (based on trends in Social Security taxes, minimum-wage levels, and the party of the president) have increased rather than decreased since 1970.

not explain the considerable variation in labor costs we observe across the fifty states.[13] In chapter 3, I turn to factors within the states to explain why state labor costs have declined since the 1970s and have fallen far more in some states than others. The index of state labor costs described above will be an essential tool for this analysis.

CHAPTER THREE

Explaining State Differences in Labor Cost Trends

STATE LABOR COSTS HAVE been heading downward since 1970, according to the comprehensive measure described in chapter 2. Yet the fifty U.S. states vary considerably in both levels and rates of change in labor costs. What accounts for these differences?

In this chapter, I find little evidence that globalization is responsible for lower state labor costs. Though state/local tax burdens and manufacturing wages have declined since 1970 and have become more similar across states, I find no such convergence in other state labor costs, personal income, or union density. State labor cost trends have been influenced less by exports or foreign direct investment (FDI) than by demographic changes in the labor force, increases in education, and the movement from mining or manufacturing to a more diversified, service-based economy. I then consider political explanations for labor cost trends: changes in state public opinion, party control of state government, labor union membership, party competition, and voter turnout. A combined analysis of all these factors reveals that domestic political trends, particularly declining voter turnout, have greater influence than the international economy on state labor costs. I conclude by considering some of the political strategies used to rationalize reductions in state labor costs, despite strong public support for labor unions and a higher minimum wage.

CONVERGENCE OR DIVERGENCE IN STATE LABOR COSTS?

At least in theory, global competition should lead to greater convergence among political units in taxes, regulatory policies, and labor costs (Barro and Sala-i-Martín 1992). The pressures of these commonly experienced international economic forces will thus challenge the autonomy of no-longer-sovereign states as they face the threat of exit by highly mobile capital. However, the influence of the global economy can also be exerted through the power of ideologies or ideas: "States alter institutions and regulations because a set of beliefs has developed sufficient normative power that leaders fear looking like laggards if they do not adopt similar policies" (Drezner 2001, 57).

The free-market logic of neoliberalism has powerful and well-financed adherents who have not been shy about making demands on individual nations or on international agencies like the World Bank or the International Monetary Fund. Neoliberals favor lower taxes, reduced government regulation, and cuts in social spending. Their claim is that greater market liberalism will be a powerful spur to economic growth, and this claim is pressed even if the evidence to support it is lacking (Collins 1998; Stiglitz 2002). As Cohen (2001, 160) asserts, "Globalization is not something that simply happens 'out there' but is manifested in the structure of social life within societies and communities. . . . The politics of globalization is primarily a struggle between political forces that is largely played out within the realm of particular states." Although Cohen was referring to nation-states, the fifty U.S. states provide an ideal opportunity to test the relative impact of the international economy and domestic political or social factors on labor costs.

Does globalization lead to greater convergence? If so, we would expect to find evidence of a "race to the bottom" as states or nations with higher levels of taxing, spending, or government regulation are forced to emulate those with low taxes and weak regulations. Previous empirical research on this question has produced conflicting results depending on the units selected, the time period covered, the specific policies analyzed, or whether alternative explanations for convergence are considered. Potoski and Prakash (2004) find a marked lack of convergence in compliance with international business standards among both European countries and the American states.[1] Though Bernat (2001) found that per capita personal income was becoming more equal across the American states, most such convergence took place *before* 1980, even though both foreign trade and investment have increased much more since that date.

Drezner (2001) found little evidence among countries belonging to the Organization for Economic Cooperation and Development (OECD) of a race to the bottom in environmental standards, and Potoski (2001) likewise found no such effect among American states in terms of clean air regulations. Donahue (1997) reports a trend toward convergence at a lower level for state spending on welfare and higher education, but no such "race to the bottom" in other policy areas. Bailey and Rom (2004) found greater reductions in spending in state-financed than in federally financed social services. But in their analysis, competition among the states appeared to be a more important factor than global economic pressures.

What about labor costs? Paradoxically, Drezner (2001, 65–69) concludes that while convergence has indeed occurred in labor standards worldwide, it has tended toward *stricter* rather than looser standards with respect to workers' health and safety conditions, rules against child or forced labor, and the right to unionize. He found that the OECD, the International Labor Organization, and the North American Free Trade Agreement (NAFTA) in the United States have all moved toward stronger enforcement of higher standards, and many developing countries have also adopted at least some international standards in their foreign enterprise zones. Conversely, Human Rights Watch (2000) has censured the United States because of its lack of worker protection or support of union organizing efforts. Questions remain as to how well labor standards are enforced in any country. The United States has long outlawed sweatshops, for example, but by all accounts they still flourish in urban ethnic enclaves (Branigan 1997). The AFL-CIO claims that NAFTA regulations concerning worker rights and safety have seldom been enforced in either Mexico or the United States. Despite international efforts, child labor continues in developing countries like India and Pakistan, and among some immigrant communities in Western Europe.

States must compete to attract business, and foreign trade and investment constitute a growing share of state economies. We might therefore expect that, over time, the states would become more alike with respect to both labor costs and taxes. One way to analyze trends in variability or similarity is to use a measure called the coefficient of concordance, W. The higher the value of W, the greater the spread of values around the mean. So if W becomes smaller over time, this indicates that the units being analyzed are becoming more similar.[2]

Table 3.1 uses W to compare the fifty states in 1970, 1985, and 2000 in terms of the index of overall labor costs, as well as the individual components of that index, per capita personal income, and state/local taxes. The results indicate only marginal evidence for convergence in labor costs; W decreased only very slightly between 1970 and 2000. Variability in the components of the overall index shows both convergence and divergence; manufacturing wages have converged to some degree, but variability in labor union

Table 3.1

Convergence in State Labor Costs and Taxes, 1970–2000

	Coefficient of Concordance (W)[a]			Convergence since 1970?
	1970	1985	2000	
Overall labor cost index	0.268	0.221	0.234	Slight
Union density	0.372	0.335	0.461	Divergence
Manufacturing wages	0.148	0.136	0.113	Slight
Unemployment benefits	0.150	0.151	0.164	No
Workers' compensation payments	0.438	0.548	0.447	No
Per capita personal income	0.155	0.152	0.152	No
State/local taxes as percent of personal income[b]	0.231	0.175	0.127	Convergence

[a]The standard deviation divided by the mean.
[b]Alaska is excluded because of extreme values; its revenues derive largely from severance taxes and fluctuate with oil prices.

membership across states has actually increased, from W of 0.37 in 1970 to 0.46 in 2000. The W values show almost no change in the distribution of per capita personal income or of unemployment benefits during this time period. Workers' compensation benefits exhibit greater variability than the other index components, reflecting much higher medical costs in urban areas of the Northeast and on the West Coast, but they have converged since 1990 following the state reform efforts discussed in chapter 2.

When we look at state/local taxes as a percent of personal income,[3] a different pattern emerges: the coefficient of concordance decreased considerably, from 0.23 in 1970 to 0.13 in 2000. But state/local taxes actually increased from 11.4 percent of personal income in 1970 to 12.5 percent as of 1985, and then declined to 10.5 percent by 2000. The business cycle accounts for at least part of this curvilinear pattern; because almost all states are required to balance their budgets, their tax burdens of necessity increase during recessions but decrease during good times such as the late 1990s. Hallerberg and Basinger (1999) argue that tax changes respond to political factors (specifically the relative strength of important interest groups in a country) rather than to uniform international trends. But table 3.1 suggests at least some evidence for tax convergence in the American states since 1970.

If policy convergence is indeed due to global economic pressures, we would expect the states most affected by the international economy to show faster declines in labor costs and taxes. Conversely, if labor costs reflect state policy choices, party and ideological differences, or the relative influence of business and labor, trends over time in labor costs and taxes should reflect these domestic factors. And when I compare these alternative explanations for state differences in labor costs, domestic factors indeed prove to be more important.

STATES IN THE INTERNATIONAL ECONOMY

The United States as a whole has become far more closely linked to the international economy since the 1970s. Exports and FDI have increased. Imports have grown even faster, and the United States has seen a huge trade deficit in recent years. Much of the current national debt is held by foreign investors; since George W. Bush became president in 2001, 92 percent of the $1 trillion increase in publicly held debt has been financed by foreign lenders (*New York Times* 2004). Immigration (both legal and illegal) has surged as well (Scott 2002). Foreign-born workers contribute billions of dollars to the American economy, and the money many of them send home to their families has a major impact on the economies of countries like Mexico, Guatemala, and the Dominican Republic.

Although the American states are affected by all these factors to some degree, they vary considerably in their direct exposure to the international economy. Table 3.2 lists the states that rank in the top quartile on three indicators as of 2000. The first is the value of manufacturing exports originating in a state; the thirteen states in the top quartile accounted for 71 percent of the total value of U.S. exports. Second is the value of FDI in property and businesses; again, the top quartile of states accounted for a large proportion (66 percent) of the total.[4] Third is the number of foreign-born immigrants, 2000–1; the top thirteen states alone attracted more than 80 percent of immigrants. Border states (Texas, Arizona, Florida, and California) have for years attracted the most immigrants, but several southern and midwestern states are now experiencing increased immigration as well.[5]

Ideally, we would also have some measure of the amount of state job losses due either to imports or to outsourcing (i.e., the growing tendency of American companies to move jobs to countries like India, where wages are much lower). The media, labor unions, and state/local governments have tried to estimate these job losses; the business reporter Lou Dobbs (2004) anticipates that outsourcing will cost the United States 10 million jobs by 2010. But reliable government statistics on job loss are missing (Uchitelle 2003). According to Tonelson (2002, 16), "Such data are locked away in the records of the world's multinational corporations. U.S.-owned multinationals have

Table 3.2

States in Top Quartile of Exports,
Foreign Direct Investment (FDI), and Immigration

Value of Exports (millions), 2000		Value of FDI (millions), 2000		Number of Foreign Immigrants, 2000–1	
California	119,640	California	120,949	California	343,693
Texas	103,866	Texas	110,853	New York	159,126
New York	42,846	New York	71,657	Texas	134,597
Michigan	33,845	Illinois	46,416	Florida	122,430
Washington	32,215	Michigan	39,090	Illinois	75,160
Illinois	31,438	Florida	38,281	New Jersey	60,361
Florida	26,543	New Jersey	36,734	Arizona	28,918
Ohio	26,322	Pennsylvania	34,170	Georgia	28,376
Massachusetts	20,514	Louisiana	31,050	Virginia	28,340
Pennsylvania	18,792	Indiana	30,095	Washington	27,301
New Jersey	18,638	North Carolina	29,777	North Carolina	26,903
North Carolina	17,946	Georgia	29,739	Massachusetts	25,710
Louisiana	16,814	Alaska	28,992	Michigan	24,215

dissuaded the U.S. government from seeking much of the data. Opening their books could reveal valuable business secrets to competitors. They also undoubtedly appreciate the public-relations disaster that releasing their job-exporting activity would create."

Tonelson further argues that many products counted as "exports" are in fact products shipped to foreign production facilities from their U.S. parents, and are therefore as responsible for job losses as the imports that compete with American-made goods. Thus the measures of the percent decline in manufacturing jobs and the value of exports that I will be using are probably picking up some of these jobs lost to imports or to outsourcing.

In theory, the states most exposed to the international economy should experience the greatest economic and political pressures to constrain labor costs. In chapter 4, I will explore in more detail the relationship between state labor costs and both domestic and international economic trends. But at this point, a simpler test will be used: Have the states that account for the bulk of American exports, FDI, and immigration experienced the greatest declines in labor costs or taxes? Table 3.3 compares trends for states in the top quartiles on these three measures with the remaining states.

The results indicate little support for the argument that the international economy is driving trends in either taxes or state labor costs. As of 2000, the absolute levels of state labor costs (based on the factor scores for 1980–2000) were highest in states in the top quartiles. Labor costs declined across all these state groupings, but the rates of decline were actually slower in states with the highest levels of exports, FDI, or immigration.[6] Though state/local taxes declined between 1980 and 2000 as a percent of personal income, they declined even faster in the states with lower levels of exports or FDI.

Is greater exposure to the international economy associated with loss of manufacturing jobs or declines in union membership? On the contrary; I found that manufacturing jobs *increased* by exactly the same amount, 6 percent, between 1982 and 1997 in states in the highest *and* lowest quartiles of exports. And not surprisingly, manufacturing jobs also increased in the states with the highest levels of FDI. Union membership showed almost exactly the same rate of decline (around 40 percent) whether a state ranked high or low in exports or FDI.

Economists disagree on the impact of exports, imports, and immigration on trends in wages and employment. Research results vary depending on the measures used, how jobs are classified, and the time period covered; some industries with little import competition have experienced high rates of job loss.[7] And Leichenko (2000) found that in some regions and industries, even increases in exports were associated with job losses, because of productivity

Table 3.3

Exports, Foreign Direct Investment (FDI), Immigration, and Trends in State Labor Costs

	Labor Costs (Factor Scores), 2000	Change in Labor Costs, 1980–2000 (%)	State/Local Taxes as % Personal Income[b]	Change in Taxes, 1980–2000 (%)
Value of exports				
Top quartile[a]	113	–18.0	11.07	–3.0
Other states	76	–19.3	10.35	–8.0
Value of FDI				
Top quartile[a]	109	–17.3	10.86	–4.1
Other states	79	–19.5	10.42	–7.2
Immigration, 2000				
Top quartile[a]	155	–16.7	10.63	–8.0
Other states	85	–20.7	10.50	–7.2

[a]States listed in table 3.2.
[b]Excluding Alaska because of high severance tax revenue.

gains derived from investment in capital rather than labor. But imports have clearly cost some American workers their jobs, even in some of the lowest-wage states like the Carolinas and Arkansas (Becker 2004). However, many other factors influence wage and employment trends, including technological change and the composition of the labor force. Minorities, older workers, and women may find it especially difficult to find comparable jobs if U.S. factories close or move overseas, but younger and highly skilled workers fare considerably better. As economist Lori Kletzer (1998, 425) concludes, "The jury is still out with respect to whether trade has a large or small impact on the domestic labor market. However, virtually all studies conclude that increasing internationalization alone cannot explain the large changes in employment and relative wages that have occurred in the U.S. labor market since the late 1970s."

What factors other than international trade or migration might explain the downward trend in state labor costs? I now consider several possible domestic explanations: first, economic or demographic developments within the states since the 1970s; second, trends in partisanship and party control of state governments; and third, changes in popular attitudes, voter turnout, and union mobilization.

ECONOMIC AND DEMOGRAPHIC TRENDS AND STATE LABOR COSTS

Since the 1970s, the American states have undergone profound economic and demographic transitions. Much of the decline in state labor costs has been attributed to increased international economic competition in sectors such as steel or automobiles, and to the loss of highly paid manufacturing jobs in those sectors. The American economy has moved away from heavy manufacturing and mining into services, which are harder to unionize and usually pay far less.

We might therefore expect that a decline in the proportion of jobs in manufacturing would be associated with declining state labor costs. But states with more diverse economies should have higher labor costs, both because of greater competition for workers and because diverse economies are less likely to be affected by downturns in manufacturing employment or exports. My indicator of labor force diversity is the difference between total state employment and the proportion accounted for by manufacturing plus services. According to this indicator, Connecticut, New York, and Minnesota have the most diverse labor forces; the least diversified include rural states such as West Virginia, Arkansas, and Idaho.[8]

The supply of labor should also influence labor costs; the larger the pool of available workers, the greater the ability of employers to keep wages and benefits low. Groups like the Federation for American Immigration Reform (FAIR 2000) and most labor unions have been concerned that high levels of foreign immigration (both legal and illegal) since the 1960s have suppressed wages for American workers. Most labor unions strongly opposed NAFTA for exactly that reason. However, highly skilled and well-educated workers should be able to command a wage premium and higher benefits.

The American labor force has changed dramatically as more women have entered full- and part-time employment (Kelly 1991). Female labor force participation rates vary considerably across the states, although they have converged somewhat since the 1970s. The highest participation rates for women are found in Wisconsin, Iowa, Alaska, and Minnesota (all over 68 percent as of 2000) and the lowest in West Virginia (47 percent). Women have traditionally been harder to organize than white males, and many labor unions have been concerned that women's entry into male-dominated fields would drive down wages (Fletcher and Hurd 2000). Although women's wages as a percent of men's increased between 1960 and 2000, women working full time year round still earn only 76 percent as much as comparably employed men.[9]

We would expect that the lower the percent of women in the labor force, the lower state labor costs will be, because women not currently employed represent a pool of potential workers that could depress wages. Women's "willingness" to work part time or at low wages has even been used as an incentive to attract business. Robert Ady, the president of the site-selection consultation agency Fantus, used the term "phantom workers" to describe women returning to work part time after their children are grown. He advised localities to advertise the availability of these "phantoms" as a "low-cost source of skilled labor" (cited in White 1987, 21). Women workers also predominate in the low-wage textile and poultry-processing plants that have boosted manufacturing jobs in the South, and in the sweatshops that have reappeared in large numbers in the U.S. garment industry (Branigan 1997). Bartik (1999) estimated that the 1996 welfare reform law has had a considerable negative effect on wages for women (especially those with less than high school degrees) after 2 to 3 million previous welfare recipients were compelled to enter the labor force because of new work requirements and time limits on welfare benefits. And indeed, women's wages as a percent of men's have declined since 2000 after years of steady increases (Hartmann 2004).

Conversely, educational levels across the United States have risen considerably since the 1970s, and the wage gap between high school dropouts and those with college degrees has been increasing (Collins 1998, 11). Workforce productivity levels have also increased during this time period, and they are strongly linked to increases in the number of college graduates and in state educational spending.[10] One would expect that a better-trained labor force would demand higher wages, and states with higher proportions of high school and/or college graduates should thus have higher labor costs.

Table 3.4 summarizes the relationship between changes in these economic or demographic indicators and trends in state labor costs.[11] As expected, states with more of the labor force employed in manufacturing as 1980 had higher labor costs. However, increases in manufacturing employment have been associated with *lower* labor costs since 1980. The explanation for this unexpected result is that jobs in manufacturing have been increasing faster in, or relocating to, low-wage right-to-work states where unions are weak. Thus the states with the most growth in manufacturing jobs since 1980 include North Dakota (64 percent), Georgia (58 percent), Arizona (55 percent), and South Dakota (55 percent). As Stull and Broadway (2004) have documented, highly paid unionized jobs in the meatpacking industry have moved from Chicago to rural Kansas and Arkansas, where recent immigrants can be hired at far lower wages, and deportation threats have been used to discourage union efforts to organize immigrants.

Table 3.4 also shows that, as expected, growth in service-sector employment is linked to declining labor costs. Also as expected, state economies that have become more diverse since 1980 have experienced rising labor costs; this is a pattern characteristic of states in the Northeast plus Wisconsin and Minnesota. In these states, expanding job opportunities in finance, real estate, insurance, transportation, and government provide options other than manufacturing or services, and are more immune to recessions.

Productivity (i.e., manufacturing value added) was positively associated with higher state labor costs as of 1980. But productivity advances since then have *not* been linked to increases in labor costs. To some degree, this may reflect management decisions to substitute capital for labor, thus increasing unemployment and exerting downward pressure on wages (Belman 1992). Also, given the sharp decline in labor union members as a percent of the labor force, American workers are now in a weak position to demand wage increases linked to productivity gains (Sexton 1991; Volgy, Schwarz, and Imwalle 1996). Perhaps for that reason, executive compensation has soared in the United States since the 1980s while wages have stagnated (Galbraith 1998; AFL-CIO 2005).

Table 3.4

Links between Economic and Labor Supply Variables and State Labor Costs

Variable	Link with Labor Costs (Factor Score), 1982	Link with % Change 1982–97[a]
Economic indicators		
% of state labor force employed in manufacturing	Positive	Negative
% of state labor force employed in services	Weak positive	Negative
Labor force diversity	None	Positive
Manufacturing productivity (value added per worker)	Strong positive	Weak negative

Variable	Link with Labor Costs (Factor Score), 1980	Link with % Change 1980–2000[b]
Labor supply		
Proportion of foreign-born immigrants in a state	Negative	Negative
Proportion of women in the labor force	Negative	Negative
Proportion of high school graduates in the state	Strong positive	Strong positive
Proportion of college graduates in the state	Positive	None

[a]Link between % change in labor costs, 1982–97, and % change in the variable to the left.

[b]Link between % change in labor costs, 1980–2000, and % change in the variable to the left.

Note: "Positive": Higher values for indicators listed on the left are associated with higher values of labor costs in 1980, or increases in labor costs since 1980. "Negative": Higher values for indicators listed on the left are associated with lower values of labor costs in 1980, or declines in labor costs since 1980. "None": No relationship between labor costs and the indicator on the left. This table is based on the Pearson correlations in appendix A.

Table 3.4 also shows the expected negative relationship between labor costs and the proportion of women in the labor force as of 1980. Also as anticipated, states where women's labor force participation rates have increased the most (thus expanding the labor supply) have indeed experienced somewhat greater labor cost declines. As of 1980, high immigration rates were strongly and negatively related to state labor costs, which have also been edging downward since 1980 in states with the largest influx of immigrants from abroad.

By contrast, the proportion of high school graduates in a state as of 1980, as well as the increase in high school graduates, are positively linked to higher state labor costs. The relationships with the proportion of college graduates are also positive, although weaker. Better-educated workers do indeed appear to command a wage premium; the financial payoff of a college education and graduate training rose to an all-time high in the late 1990s. Industries that hire large proportions of college graduates also invest heavily in technology, which has likewise boosted productivity (Hall 2000).

STATE LABOR COSTS, LABOR UNIONS, AND PARTISAN TRENDS

Since the New Deal, the Democratic and Republican parties have been at odds over labor issues. As described in chapter 2, President Franklin Roosevelt's efforts to increase the minimum wage and encourage unionization met with strong resistance in Congress from a Conservative Coalition composed of both Republicans and southern Democrats. Since that time, federal labor policy has varied considerably, depending on which party was in control of Congress and/or the presidency. My indicator of trends in federal labor costs (chapter 2) showed a clear pattern of increases under Democratic presidential administrations and even sharper decreases under Republican presidents.

We might therefore expect labor policies to vary across the states as a function of which party controls the government. But popular attitudes must be considered as well; what are the trends in public support for labor unions, the minimum wage, or government economic activism, and how do these vary across the states? And how well do trends in party control of state government reflect popular preferences? Since the 1970s, Democratic Party influence in state government has declined, and state electorates have become more conservative ideologically. But parties in the states have become more competitive in recent years, and the proportion of divided state governments has increased. As I will show, voter turnout has more impact on state labor costs than either partisan or ideological trends.

Party coalitions in the states have been transformed since the 1960s, most notably the change in the once solidly Democratic South (Black and Black 2002). The proportion of state legislative seats held by Democrats fell from a peak of 68 percent in the post-Watergate years of 1975–76 to only 52 percent in 2000. The proportion of Democratic governors declined from 74 to 34 percent during the same period.[12]

Is the decline in Democratic Party control a factor in the decline of state labor costs? This is not a straightforward question to answer, because national party positions are not necessarily supported by the state parties. These represent their own unique constituencies and reflect very different histories and institutions (Jewell and Morehouse 2001). Republicans in New England or New York are quite different from those in South Dakota or Arizona; the legacy of urban machine politics may still apply to Democrats in Massachusetts or Pennsylvania but not to those in California or Minnesota. Thus, even though the national Democratic Party has been an ally of organized labor since the New Deal, we would expect variation across the states in the relationship between trends in labor costs and the Democratic proportion of the legislature.

Conversely, the national parties have become more ideologically cohesive during the past thirty years; we now find few conservative southern Democrats or liberal northern Republicans in Congress, and party-line voting has increased. Both national parties have increased their financial and regulatory influence over state parties, and both have intervened to assist favored candidates for governor or to influence party control of the state legislature (Bibby and Holbrook 1999). We might thus expect state parties to have moved closer to the ideology of their respective national party.

Further, we must remember the distinctive history of the South. Although solidly Democratic after Reconstruction, its legacy of a plantation economy, elite dominance, and a lack of party competition (Key 1949) led to weak unions, low labor costs, regressive taxes, and (after 1947) the adoption of right-to-work laws. Southern Democrats in Congress were active opponents of much of the New Deal labor legislation. But ever since Barry Goldwater carried six southern states in 1964, the Republican Party in the South has steadily gained in state legislative seats and elections for governor and Congress. Southern Republicans have inherited the conservative Democratic legacy of support for business, low levels of taxation and government spending, and opposition to labor unions. By contrast, the few remaining Democrats in the South have been elected with sizable proportions of African American votes and have become considerably more liberal than southern Republicans (although usually less so than northern

Democrats). But the number of southern Democrats has been declining, in part because of Republican efforts to concentrate African Americans in a few districts (Toner 2004).

The components of each party's coalition have changed in other ways as well. The proportion of liberal Republicans has declined in many northern or midwestern states, reflecting the growing influence of the religious right in the Republican Party. The Democrats' religious base has also changed; Catholic voters in northern and midwestern states used to be reliable Democrats. Ever since Pope Leo issued the encyclical *Rerum Novarum* in 1891, the Roman Catholic Church has been critical of the social costs of untrammeled capitalism and has supported the right of workers to organize. As Brewer (2003) has shown, American Catholics have traditionally been much more likely than Protestants to support the "social gospel" and to favor government efforts to help the poor and to uphold the rights and dignity of workers. And sizable numbers of Catholic immigrants from Ireland, Italy, and Eastern Europe were staunch union members.

However, in recent years Brewer (2003) finds much less support among Catholics for government activism, whether on behalf of job creation, health care, or more spending on social services. As working-class Catholics from European ethnic groups moved up the socioeconomic ladder and to the suburbs, they became more similar in viewpoints to their Protestant neighbors and less likely to be union members. Polsby and Wildavsky (2004, 32) estimate that the Catholic proportion of the Democratic national coalition has declined from 47 percent in 1960 to 39 percent in 2000; the union proportion of the Democratic coalition declined from 31 to 19 percent during the same period.

At the state level, the falloff in union density is at least part of the explanation for the declining number of state legislative seats held by Democrats. One of the most striking trends in American politics is the dramatic decline since the 1950s in union members as a percent of the workforce (from 33 to 13 percent), while other industrialized countries averaged only a 3 percent decline (Wallerstein and Western 2000). Traditional labor organizations (primarily AFL-CIO affiliates) have declined 79 percent in membership since 1970 (Farber and Western 2001). However, unionization levels among state public employees are now considerably higher than those in the private sector, and even increased 5 percent between 1986 and 1999.[13] Teachers' unions and organizations, in particular the National Education Association, received the highest number of first-place mentions in Thomas and Hrebenar's (1999) ranking of the forty most influential interest groups in the American states. They also note the declining influence of organized labor; the AFL-CIO was ranked seventeenth in 1990 but only twelfth in 1999. But "white collar unions—particularly state and local employees—have risen to prominence and held on even as partisan control has changed" (1999, 133).

The states still differ considerably in union membership in both the public and private sectors. As of 2000, more than 30 percent of the labor force in New York, Michigan, Pennsylvania, Washington, and West Virginia was labor union members, while Southern states like Arkansas and the Carolinas had union membership in the single digits. In New York, more than 70 percent of public employees were union members in 2000, and Connecticut, Rhode Island, Wisconsin, and New Jersey have more than 60 percent of the public labor force unionized. The greater the clout of organized labor in a state, the more difficult it should be to reduce unemployment benefits, limit workers' compensation awards or eligibility, or counter union efforts to organize or strike. In California in 2000, labor unions successfully mobilized to defeat a paycheck-protection initiative, despite massive spending by conservative and business groups (Dively 2002). And the Washington State Teachers' Union was instrumental in defeating a 2004 initiative that would have authorized the establishment of charter schools, although that measure had been backed by Microsoft chairman Bill Gates's considerable resources (Dillon 2004).

But labor unions may not always pursue a unified strategy because of interunion or intraunion battles over leadership, strategy, or which public officials to support (Cohen 2002; Golden and Pontussen 1992; Golden 1997). And labor union members do not always vote as their union leaders would wish; 37 percent of them supported George W. Bush in 2000 and 38 percent in 2004. Issues such as gun control, same-sex marriage, abortion, and other "moral values" are often more important to many union families than jobs, and Republican candidates have made successful use of these "wedge" issues to lure union members away from the Democrats (Zernike and Broder 2004; Frank 2004).

Perceptions of relative power or influence, or of the legitimacy of unions, may be just as important as objective measures based on membership or contributions from political action committees (PACs). In the Thomas and Hrebenar state interest-group studies, legislators, academics, and media observers often rated labor unions and/or the AFL-CIO as quite influential in their state, even if labor union membership was low. Nevada is one such example: It is a right-to-work state, but labor unions are concentrated in the two most urban counties and play a major role in Democratic Party politics (Driggs 1987).

Even through business far outspends labor in donations to PACs and political campaigns, and union membership levels are already at historic lows, many Republicans in both Congress and the states still feel threatened by labor's alleged political clout. The National Right to Work Committee claims that if in-kind contributions (printing, grassroots organizing) were included, labor's campaign contributions would exceed those of business PACs (National Institute for Labor Relations Research 1997). Conservatives have been pushing for burdensome auditing requirements to further weaken the influence of union PACs, and such "paycheck-protection" laws have been introduced in thirty-five states.

How have these party trends played out in the states? The top graph in figure 3.1 shows the trend in the proportion of state legislative seats held by Democrats. We see a dramatic decline in the South (the eleven states of the former Confederacy) but a highly variable pattern in the other states: a peak after the post-Watergate 1974 elections, then a sharp decline after 1994. The bottom graph in figure 3.1 shows the trend in labor cost factor scores in the South compared with other states. Although average costs have declined in both groups of states, declines have been sharper in non-southern states. Southern labor costs had lower labor costs throughout this period, but their average rate of decline has been smaller.

Given these variable patterns, it is not surprising to find little relationship between the state labor cost measure and the Democratic percent of state legislators. In the non-southern states, the relationship is positive as expected but still modest.[14] In comparison with the strong partisan differences between presidential administrations described above, we see little relationship between the party of the governor and the trend in state labor costs. State labor cost factor scores over the period 1970–2000 averaged 258 under Republican governors and 255 under Democratic governors—hardly a significant difference.

Although the proportion of Republican governors increased dramatically between 1974 and 1994, both in the South and elsewhere, in many states Republican governors have faced Democratic legislatures. As Fiorina (1996, 25) has shown, the proportion of unified state governments decreased from 85 percent in 1946 to 45 percent in 1990, and changes in a partisan issue such as labor costs may be less likely under divided governments. However, some Republican governors have been able to counter the efforts of Democratic legislators to maintain higher levels of wages and benefits. Thus one of Governor Arnold Schwarzenegger's first actions after taking office in 2003 was to push through major cuts in California's workers' compensation benefits, despite the objections of the state's unions and the

Figure 3.1

Trends in Labor Costs and Percent Democratic Legislators,
South versus Non-South

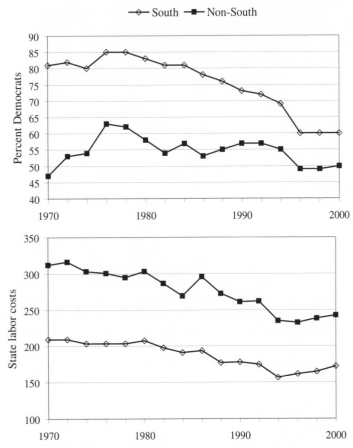

Note: Labor costs have declined more rapidly outside the South. Southern states have lower state labor costs and many fewer Democrats in state legislatures than in 1970.

Democratic-controlled legislature. And the decline in union density has deprived Democrats in many states of one of their strongest bases of support.

Has the increasing nationalization of state parties affected the fit between party control and labor costs? When we compare the links between the state labor costs measure and the Democratic percentage of state legislators (table 3.5), we see that the overall relationship is stronger in 2000 than in 1980.

Table 3.5
Links between State Party Dominance, Ideology, Partisanship,
and Declines in State Labor Costs, 1980–2000

Characteristic	All	South	Non-South
Democratic % of State Legislature			
1980	Positive	Negative	Positive
2000	Positive	Strong negative	Strong positive
Percent change	None	Strong negative	Positive
State ideology[a]			
1977–88	Strong positive	Strong positive	Strong positive
1989–99	Strong positive	Strong positive	Strong positive
Percent change	None	Strong positive	None
State partisanship[b]			
1977–88	None	Strong negative	None
1989–99	Weak negative	Strong positive	Weak negative
Percent change	None	Strong positive	Weak negative

[a]Higher values = more conservative public opinion.
[b]Higher values = more Republican Party identification.
Note: "Positive": Higher values for indicators listed on the left are associated with slower declines in state labor costs since 1980. "Negative": Higher values for indicators listed on the left are associated with larger declines in labor costs since 1980. "None": No relationship between labor costs and the indicator on the left. This table is based on the Pearson correlations in appendix A.

In the South, the relationship is actually negative, because the growing Republican ascendancy has combined with economic conservatism and declining labor costs. Outside the South, the relationship between the percent change, 1980–2000, in the Democratic percent of state legislators and state labor costs is modestly positive. This evidence suggests that state parties, like their national counterparts, are becoming more polarized and ideological. And legislative partisanship is indeed related to trends in state labor costs.

PUBLIC PREFERENCES AND IDEOLOGY

Let us now consider trends in the preferences of the general public. Does the decline in state labor costs reflect increasing antipathy toward labor unions? On the contrary, Gallup Polls show that Americans remain broadly supportive of unionization. Responses to the question "Do you approve or disapprove of labor unions?" show little evidence of change over time; there was 60 percent approval in both 1972 and 2001.[15] Other national survey data confirm consistent positive perceptions of labor unions. Since 1972, the American National Election Studies (ANES) surveys at the University of Michigan have asked respondents to place various political and social groups on a "feeling thermometer," where 100 equals a strongly positive assessment, 50 indicates a neutral response, and 0 shows a negative reaction. These "feeling thermometer" ratings for labor unions have also shown little change over time, averaging 56 in 1972 and 55 in 2000.

However, during this same period, the thermometer scores for labor unions showed increasing divergence between Democratic and Republican identifiers. Thermometer scores for "big business" likewise changed little during the period (also averaging around 55), but these too had become more partisan by the 1990s (Hansen and McLean 2003). And as Lipset and Schneider (1987) have argued, Americans have become more distrustful of most American institutions, including business and labor as well as government.

Other Gallup Poll data indicate broad popular support for raising the minimum wage. In 2001, for example, the public agreed that "Congress should raise the minimum wage" by a strong margin of 80 to 18 percent, and similar percentages approved raising it in 1985. And despite Republican gains in the 2004 election, voters in two states that supported Bush for president (Florida and Nevada) nevertheless approved ballot measures to raise their state's minimum wage. The Florida measure was an amendment to the state's constitution and mandated regular future increases in the state minimum wage to reflect cost-of-living increases, thus bypassing opposition by the Republican majority in the state legislature. Oregon, Vermont, and Washington have likewise indexed state minimum wages to the cost of living (Gaynor 2005b).

By contrast, a question on government-guaranteed jobs, posed repeatedly on the ANES surveys since 1972, suggests a more conservative trend in public attitudes. Respondents are asked to place themselves on a 7-point scale ranging from 1, "The government should see to it that each person has a job and a good standard of living," to 7, "Each person should get ahead on his own." Unlike the labor union thermometer scores, support for government job guarantees has trended downward since 1972; the highest mean score was recorded in 2000, when the lowest-ever proportion of respondents (7.7 percent) selecting the position that the government should guarantee jobs and living standards. As with the thermometer scores for unions and business, views of job/income guarantees have become much more partisan over time. Public skepticism may also have grown because of the perceived failure of previous government job-creation policies (Mucciaroni 1992; Lafer 2002).

Responses to this 7-point job-guarantee scale vary across the states as well. Respondents from western states such as Arizona, Nebraska, and Utah were most likely to favor individual responsibility, while greater support for government job guarantees was found in both northern liberal states (Delaware, Maine) and poor southern ones (Arkansas, Kentucky) (Hansen 1996). Higher state mean scores, 1972–96, suggest more conservative attitudes and are indeed associated with greater declines in state labor costs between 1980 and 2000.[16]

However, the ANES surveys are not designed to provide good state-level estimates of public attitudes, both because of small samples and because in any given election year a number of smaller states are not included in the national survey at all. A better estimate of state public opinion has been developed by Erikson, Wright, and McIver (1993) (hereafter EWM). They used responses to questions on party identification and ideology based on telephone polls conducted by CBS News and the *New York Times*, and they then aggregated these by state and year. Using this methodology, they created measures of partisanship and ideology for forty-eight states (Alaska and Hawaii excluded), 1977–88, and for all fifty states, 1989–99. Although state partisanship has fluctuated considerably, the scores for state ideology have shown a strong trend over time in the more conservative direction.[17]

We would therefore expect to see the most decline in labor costs in states where public opinion has moved closer to the conservative ideological position. But the more liberal and/or Democratic states should have higher labor costs. To test these hypotheses, I analyzed the linkages between state labor costs and levels of both partisanship and ideology (the EWM measures) as of 1980 and 2000 (table 3.5). Lower scores on the EWM ideology and partisanship scales indicate support for more liberal and Democratic views. I also examined the relationship between the change in state labor costs, 1980–2000, and changes in both partisanship and ideology. The results are shown separately for southern and non-southern states, given the partisan changes in that region noted above.

As table 3.5 shows, more liberal ideological views were indeed associated with higher levels of state labor costs. These relationships became somewhat stronger between 1980 and 2000, especially in the South, where we see strong links between trends in ideology and in state labor costs. In the South, the relationship between Democratic partisanship and labor costs is strongly negative, because Republican ascendancy there accords with more conservative ideological preferences. However, in the non-southern states, the public's ideological preferences are more closely linked than partisanship to levels and trends in state labor costs; relationships with partisanship are weak and negative in both 1989–99 and 1977–88.

EWM (p. 75) also developed a measure of state policy liberalism, based on indicators of education, welfare, criminal justice, and tax policies (but not labor policies) in the states for the 1980s. They report strong positive relationships between state policy liberalism and their measures of both state partisanship and ideology, even when they took into account socioeconomic factors such as wealth, urbanization, or education. I found a strong relationship between the EWM index of state policy liberalism and my labor costs factor scores for the states as of 1980. States scoring higher on EWM policy liberalism also had slower rates of decline in labor costs between 1980 and 2000.

EWM (p. 134) report a weaker relationship between state partisanship and policy (their index of state policy liberalism) than with ideology. Their explanation is that party elites must balance appeals to the ideologies of party activists with the need for electoral support from independents and moderates. Also, in more liberal states both Republicans and Democrats tend to be more liberal (while both parties are more conservative in more conservative states), so partisanship again fails to predict either policy or positions on issues. Table 3.5 shows the same patterns with my indicator of state labor costs; there are much stronger links with ideology than with partisanship. Only in the South do we see evidence that the decline in state labor costs is associated with both partisan and ideological change.

This analysis of trends in popular preferences provides somewhat paradoxical results. National survey data show that popular support for labor unions and for increases in the minimum wage have remained fairly strong since the 1970s. Both partisanship and the proportion of Democrats elected to state legislatures have fluctuated during the past thirty years. But the EWM data and the ANES question on government job/income guarantees suggest a conservative trend in citizen ideology. In both southern and non-southern states, ideological preferences are linked to both levels and trends in state labor costs. However, state labor costs tend to be higher, and to decline more slowly, if more Democrats are elected to state legislatures.

VOTER TURNOUT AND TRENDS IN STATE LABOR COSTS

The last political factor to be considered in relation to trends in state labor costs is voter turnout. V. O. Key's classic *Southern Politics* (1949) described how the lack of party competition and the operation of Jim Crow laws led to very low voter turnout by poor whites as well as African Americans. There was thus little popular challenge to an elite-dominated political system based on segregation, low wages, and regressive taxes. Key theorized that in more competitive states, both political parties would have an incentive to mobilize voters by promising higher levels of government services and by appealing to working-class and low-income individuals.

Considerable research in state politics has demonstrated at least some linkages among party competition, voter turnout, and more progressive social policies in the states (Hill, Leighley, and Hinton-Anderson 1995). However, since the 1960s voter turnout in the United States has declined, despite a higher turnout by African Americans in the South after enforcement of the Voting Rights Act of 1965. Although state voter registration restrictions have eased considerably, especially since the National Voter Registration Act of 1993 (Highton 2004), turnout has not increased. One reason for this trend is the expansion of the electorate due to the enfranchisement of young voters after 1968; they tend to vote at very low rates. A second reason is the switch to gubernatorial elections in nonpresidential years; only fourteen states still vote for governors and president at the same time.[18] Voter turnout is generally 15 to 20 percent lower in off-year or midterm elections.

A third reason for declining turnout is the drop in labor union membership. In earlier years, organized labor was an effective force for mobilizing and educating lower-income voters (Asher et al. 2001). Leighley and Nagler (2003) estimate that the turnout by voters in the bottom third of the income distribution would be 10 percent higher today if union membership had remained at 1964 levels, and the class bias in participation would be much weaker. The American Political Science Association's (APSA) report on political inequality (Task Force on Inequality 2004) linked reductions in voter turnout since the 1960s to reduced civic engagement (including membership in labor unions as well as other organizations) and growing distrust of government. The APSA authors further argued that the major political parties are increasingly responsive to the contributors and activists in their base and have neglected public policies with genuine popular appeal, such as education, health care, or a higher minimum wage. This lack of government responsiveness has fostered popular cynicism and even less incentive for political involvement.

Have state trends in voter turnout since the 1980s affected trends in state labor costs? Elections for governor provide a better test of state-level voting turnout than would presidential elections. Aggregating state turnout data across several elections is necessary because of fluctuations in turnout between gubernatorial elections held in presidential versus nonpresidential years, and because voter interest increases in more highly competitive elections for open seats when no incumbent governor is present (Carsey 2000). Comparing average state turnout levels in gubernatorial elections between 1981–88 and more recent years (1996–2002) permits us to estimate the overall trend in voter participation.[19]

According to these aggregated measures, the states vary considerably in turnout rates in gubernatorial elections. For the period 1996–2002, the lowest turnout rates (below 30 percent) were found in Arizona, Texas, Kentucky, and Nevada; the highest rates (above 60 percent) prevailed in Minnesota and Montana. Mean state voter turnout declined 4 percent between 1981–88 and 1996–2002, with the greatest drops in Kentucky and Michigan (–20 percent) and California and Idaho (–19 percent). Fast-growing states with younger populations and sizable proportions of immigrants, such as Nevada and Texas, tend to have a lower turnout. But turnout has increased in several states (Florida, New Hampshire, South Carolina) with an influx of retirees, who tend to vote in sizable numbers. Turnout rates have also risen in states with increasing proportions of college graduates. States where the electorate has become more Democratic likewise show an increased voter turnout; this relationship is especially strong in the South, where the African American turnout has grown considerably since the Voting Rights Act of 1965.

Figure 3.2 suggests that declining voter turnout in state elections could indeed be part of the explanation for declining labor costs. In the ten states where turnout actually increased between 1981–88 and 1996–2002, state labor costs declined only 10 percent between 1980 and 2000. But in the ten states where voter turnout has declined the most, labor costs fell an average of 23 percent. There is thus a strong relationship between state voter turnout and labor costs. And as the next section shows, voter turnout indeed shows a strong link to trends in state labor costs—even when other political and economic factors are taken into account.

COMPARING ECONOMIC, INTERNATIONAL, AND POLITICAL FACTORS

It is now time to compare these diverse explanations for changes in state labor costs since the 1970s. If the neorealist economic paradigm is correct, the states most closely linked to the international economy will have ex-

Figure 3.2
Declines in Voter Turnout and State Labor Costs

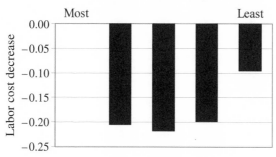

Decline in voter turnout (quintiles)

Note: State labor costs decreased more from 1980 to 2000 in states where voter turnout has declined the most. Voter turnout decline is the difference between the average turnout for 1996 to 2002 and the average for 1981 to 1988.

perienced the greatest decline in labor costs. But I have also described the impact of several other economic, demographic, and political factors; are these more or less important than the global economy? A statistical technique, regression analysis, can help show us how much each of these factors contributes to explaining trends in state labor costs when the impact of other factors is also considered.

In this multivariate analysis, the impact of globalization will be assessed using the measures of state exports and FDI described above. Several economic and demographic indicators that could influence state labor costs will also be included. First is the percent change since 1980 in manufacturing employment; the prediction is that movement out of this sector into services will lead to lower wages, lower levels of unionization, and thus lower labor costs. Second is the proportion of the state population with a college degree; better-educated people should be more productive and should command higher wages.

Three political factors will also be included in the analysis. First is the percent of public-sector union members in a state as of 1986. The expectation is that states with high levels of public employee union members will be able to mobilize against any efforts by business groups or Republicans to reduce labor costs. Second is the change in state ideology between 1977–88 and 1989–99 (the EWM measures); as we have already seen, this estimate of public opinion is more closely linked to trends in labor costs than either state partisanship or the percent of Democrats in the state legislature. Third is the trend in voter turnout; the greater the proportion of the electorate that is mobilized, the more incentive politicians have to appeal to minority and working-class citizens. The measure to be used here is the change in average turnout for gubernatorial elections between 1981–88 and 1996–2002, as described above.

The results of this analysis are shown by the graphs in figures 3.3 and 3.4 (the statistical analysis on which these graphs are based is described in appendix A). The length and direction of the bars in these graphs indicate whether each factor considered is associated with higher or lower labor costs. The longer the bar, the more important that variable is after taking into account the influence of all the other variables. Two separate indicators of international influence are used in these statistical models. Figure 3.3 includes the *percent change* in exports and state FDI since 1981; figure 3.4 uses the *level* of both exports and FDI as of 1985 to predict changes in state labor costs since then.

The most striking finding is the *lack* of impact of globalization. In figure 3.3, neither of the bar lines for the percent change in FDI or state exports since 1981 is long enough to suggest any substantial effect on state labor costs. In figure 3.4, based on the levels of exposure to the global economy as of 1985, the bar lines for both exports and FDI are negligible as well. In fact, the direction of the bar line for FDI is positive; this means

Figure 3.3
Change in State Labor Costs, 1980–2000, and Trends in Exports and FDI

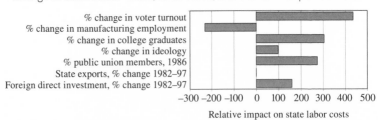

Note: Values are standardized regression coefficients. Those above +200 or below −200 suggest a substantial and statistically significant relationship. Trends in state labor costs since 1980 are better explained by changes in voter turnout, education, and public union membership than by trends in exports or foreign direct investment.

Figure 3.4
Change in State Labor Costs, 1980–2000, and Levels of Exports and FDI, 1981

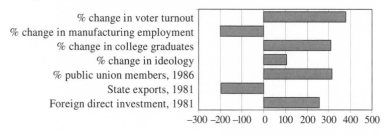

Impact on state labor costs

Note: Values are standardized regression coefficients. Those above +200 or below −200 suggest a substantial and statistically significant relationship. This model is similar to figure 3.3, but it now includes the absolute levels of state exports and foreign direct investment (FDI) as of 1981. FDI levels are linked to increases in labor costs since 1980, while export levels and increases in manufacturing employment are linked to declining labor costs.

that the *greater* the value of direct foreign investment in a state, the *greater* the increase in labor costs since the 1980s.

In both graphs, bar lines for the economic and demographic factors support the predictions suggested earlier in the chapter: somewhat faster decline in labor costs in states where manufacturing employment has grown, but a significant upward trend in labor costs in states where the proportion of college graduates has increased. The proportion of public employee union members as of 1986 is also associated with higher state labor costs.

Turning now to the results for the political variables, we see that increasing levels of voter turnout between 1981–88 and 1996–2002 are linked to higher state labor costs (or, as depicted in figure 3.2, slower rates of decline in those costs). This confirms the link between popular mobilization and greater benefits for the working class. But results for ideology are unexpected; once other factors are considered, the conservative shift in state public opinion has had no significant impact on trends in labor costs. State labor costs are evidently influenced more by *mobilized* preferences (indicated by longer bar lines for voter turnout and the proportion of public employees unionized) than by trends in public opinion.

Inspired by Key's (1949) research on one-party Southern politics, political scientists have anticipated that party competition would influence both voter turnout and public policy. Holbrook and Van Dunk (1993) examined a broad range of policies and found that electoral competition had a strong influence on policy outcomes, even when controlling for other important influences such as state wealth and partisanship. However, I found no relationship between party competition and the decline in state labor costs since 1980.[20]

What can we conclude from this analysis? Clearly, economic and labor supply factors influence trends in state labor costs, which rise with the level of education of a state's citizens and decline in states that have gained manufacturing jobs (as noted above, primarily the low-wage, nonunion states). But it is *domestic* economic factors that matter; neither the level nor rates of change in exposure to the international economy had the expected impact on state labor costs. And additional statistical analysis found that immigration likewise had no independent or significant impact on state labor cost trends.

Politics matters as well, supporting the arguments of those who emphasize social and cultural factors that mediate the impact of global economic trends. States with increasing voter turnout have experienced much slower rates of decline in labor costs. And the effect of voter turnout is more important than either ideology or the mobilizing impact of public employee unions. States with higher levels of voter turnout have evidently been able to resist both political and economic pressures to reduce the cost of labor.

However, most states have experienced declining voter turnout since the 1980s. Decreasing involvement in voting as well as other forms of civic engagement has led to much less government emphasis on policies benefiting middle- and working-class voters (Hacker et al. 2004; Task Force on Inequality 2004). The overall downward trend in state labor costs may thus reflect growing civic disengagement, only partially offset by the mobilizing efforts of public employee unions. In fact, state labor union density showed a considerably stronger relationship with voter turnout in the 1980s than after 1996.[21]

Labor unions may have helped boost turnout in years past, but the most effective grassroots mobilizing today involves people who worship regularly in theologically conservative churches (both evangelical Protestants and charismatic Roman Catholics). The values of these ardent churchgoers stress individual salvation rather than the Catholic social gospel or any public responsibility to create jobs or raise living standards (Brewer 2003; Barker and Carman 2003). Such religious groups have also mobilized against unions and in support of "paycheck-protection" initiatives, in part to weaken opposition by teachers' unions to school vouchers (Dreyfuss 1998). Morality concerns (abortion, stem cell research, gay marriage) are far more important to most voters on the religious right than are issues of job loss, deindustrialization, and stagnant wages. Frank (2004) argues that such issues have been deliberately fomented by economic conservatives to further stimulate distrust of government and opposition to taxes, and to distract working-class voters from their own economic interests.

It remains to be seen whether the higher levels of voter turnout experienced in the hotly contested 2004 presidential election will carry over into state contests, especially because most gubernatorial elections are held in off years and have lower turnout. However, the record turnout in 2004 produced a Republican sweep, stimulated in part by gay marriage bans on the ballot in several states (Zernike and Broder 2004). Higher turnout may therefore not have the political and social effects the APSA Inequality Task Force expects if it is motivated by moral and religious concerns rather than by economic issues.

Further evidence of the importance of ordinary voters is the decision by France and the Netherlands in June 2005 to reject the proposed constitution for the European Union. Though better-off citizens accepted arguments by political and business leaders that a united Europe would benefit from increased trade, younger, working-class, and unemployed voters feared increased competition from the low-wage countries of Eastern and Southern Europe, expanded immigration, and loss of generous welfare state benefits. These voters, motivated by "lost jobs, lost growth and lost confidence" (Cohen 2005) used national referenda on the proposed constitution to force their leaders to rethink the costs of a closer European union.

CONCLUSION

The model of a liberal market economy predicts that international economic forces will cause labor costs to decline and to become more similar across regions and sectors. While state labor costs in the fifty American states have indeed declined since 1970, the results presented in this chapter cast considerable doubt on the convergence model. Instead, I have found continued divergence in labor costs across the states, although state/local taxes have converged to some degree. Further, when we compare states with the highest and lowest levels of immigration, exports, or FDI, the results challenge neoliberal expectations: We see *slower* rates of decrease in labor costs and taxes in the states with the closest links to the global economy.

This chapter has considered several reasons why the American states differ in labor costs, and why they have experienced different rates of decline in those costs since 1970. As many political scientists have concluded (summarized in Drezner 2001), domestic political structures and historical institutions influence and condition economic change and mediate the impact of globalization on the welfare state and social equity. A statistical analysis comparing indicators of globalization with other state political and economic trends showed that domestic rather than international factors account for trends in state labor costs. The growing weakness of labor unions and the trend toward a more conservative ideology in most states are part of the reason for the decline in labor costs since 1970, although declining voter turnout is even more important. The impact of the declining numbers of Democrats in state legislatures may be a factor as well (at least outside the South), although the increasing proportion of divided governments in the states may dampen any impact of partisan swings. Thus the impact of the governor's party on trends in state labor costs was considerably weaker than that observed for differences in national labor cost trends across presidential administrations.

Public opinion surveys suggest at least some degree of popular support for labor unions and for higher wages. It is difficult to imagine that campaigning on the basis of low wages and reduced benefits would be a winning strategy for state elected officials. How, then, have most states been able to implement policies to reduce the cost of labor?

First, we have seen widespread evidence of business concern with labor costs and opposition to unions. Business interests wield considerable political influence in almost all states, backed by high-priced lobbying efforts and campaign contributions (Thomas and Hrebenar 1999). Governors would strongly prefer cutting ribbons to open new plants than having to explain why yet another company is closing its doors. They have been quick to claim credit for any indications of business expansion, whether or not state policies were responsible (Grady 1987).

Second, organized labor has lost much of its clout in many states and in Washington. It can thus offer little in the way of countervailing power to prevent the increasing dominance of business interests. Third, state Democratic parties are not all as liberal as their congressional counterparts; and as we have seen, the proportion of Democratic governors and state legislators has declined since the 1970s. Barrilleaux, Holbrook, and Langer (2002) find little evidence of higher welfare spending in the states until the Democratic proportion of the state legislature reaches 63 percent; and as of 2004, only Massachusetts and California came close to that level. Liberal Republicans in northern and midwestern states may have been at least somewhat supportive of labor in past years, but they are also declining in number.

Fourth, interstate competition is intense. Businesses can credibly threaten to move out or to invest elsewhere if they do not receive policy concessions, such as tax incentives, regulatory relief, or limitations on labor unions. State residents are also loath to see jobs or retail sales move to other states, and they may thus be persuaded that the logic of interstate competition requires cuts in business taxes, labor costs, or workers' compensation benefits. Peterson (1995) argued that states should invest more in education and infrastructure to encourage economic development, but interstate competition over taxes appears to have diminished state support for these investment policies as well (Brace 2001).

Fifth and finally, the public's major concern in most gubernatorial elections is with jobs and unemployment (Herzik and Brown 1991; Hansen 1999b; Cohen and King 2004). Most are willing to accept policies that are marketed as likely to create jobs, and tax incentives for business are usually sold to legislators and the media on that basis. The frames used to define policies, and the symbols attached to them, can be even more persuasive than their actual impact (Schram and Krueger 1995). Evidence that tax subsidies or weaker regulations are responsible for creating any new jobs usually comes much later, if at all (Thompson 1983; LeRoy and Slocum 1999). As we will see in chapter 4, job creation is actually stronger in states with higher rather than lower tax burdens. But the inflated statistics and anecdotes generated by state commerce or economic development interests, and touted by the business media, usually overwhelm objective attempts at econometric analysis.

Despite their concern with the state's employment picture, voters do not necessarily go along with every business demand. When the details of the "deal" that brought Mercedes-Benz to Alabama in 1994 were made public, voters were outraged by the promised giveaways to the German automaker, including guaranteed purchases of Mercedes cars for the state fleet, tax abatements stretching years into the future, and the state's agreeing to pay the salaries (described as "training wages") of all newly hired plant workers for the first year (Watson, Gardner, and Montjoy 2001). The governor who had brought in this "prize," Jim Folsom, was defeated in the next election. Likewise, sports stadium projects are usually advertised as engines of local job creation, despite a lack of convincing evidence, but voters in several metropolitan areas have voted down stadium financing deals that would have enriched the sports franchise owners at public expense (Cagan and DeMause 1998; Euchner 1998).

Voters may tolerate reductions in state labor costs if job creation rates are strong (as they were in the 1980s in the Sunbelt and in the 1990s in almost all states). As chapter 4 will show, at least between 1970 and 2000, lower state labor costs were indeed associated with lower unemployment and higher rates of job creation. But what if job creation rates slow down? In 2004, the United States experienced an economic recovery (eleven straight quarters of growth) but still had a million fewer jobs than at the beginning of the 2001 recession. Although George W. Bush narrowly carried Ohio (the state with the largest loss of manufacturing jobs) in 2004, elected officials may still experience voters' wrath if the promised jobs do not result from ongoing efforts to reduce labor costs.

What Matters

- The global economy does not explain the decline in state labor costs. In fact, states with the highest levels of exports, foreign direct investment, or immigration have reduced their labor costs less than have other states.

- Manufacturing jobs are increasing in a few low-wage states, but labor costs are higher in states with higher levels of education and more diversified economies.

- Domestic rather than international politics accounts for trends in state labor costs. We see more reductions in labor costs in southern states and in states with weaker public employee unions, more Republicans in state legislatures, and low or declining voter turnout.

- Although Americans have become somewhat more conservative in ideology, and are skeptical of government job creation efforts, they remain supportive of labor unions and strongly favor a higher minimum wage.

- Reductions in state labor costs have been justified by the rhetoric of globalization and interstate competition, and by promises that more jobs will be created.

- Business strength and labor union weakness have made it easier to reduce wages and benefits overall, but not as much in states with higher voter turnout and more Democrats elected to state legislatures.

CHAPTER FOUR

The Economic Effects of Cutting Labor Costs

AS THE PREVIOUS CHAPTER has shown, state-level factors have accounted for much of the variation in labor costs in the United States since the 1970s. The fifty U.S. states also vary greatly in their exposure to the international economy, and thus they provide an ideal laboratory for examining the economic and social effects of labor costs. This chapter analyzes the economic impact of state labor costs in an increasingly interdependent global economy. In addition to employment trends, I consider a range of other state economic outcomes: the growth since the 1970s in gross state product (GSP), personal income, productivity, exports, and foreign investment. And I also describe how links to the international economy affect the impact of labor costs on state economic outcomes.

I first review what previous research has told us about economic trends in the states. On that basis, I develop several hypotheses to predict the impact of labor costs on state economic growth and employment trends. The next two sections of this chapter describe other state and federal policies that could also influence state economic trends: state/local taxes, federal labor costs, and defense spending. We must consider these as well to better understand the impact of state labor costs. The fourth section discusses the data and measures used to test the hypotheses, and the final section summarizes the results.

These results (summarized in tables 4.2 and 4.3 below) challenge the theory that cutting the cost of labor will enhance competitiveness. States with high labor costs are in fact doing better with respect to economic growth, exports, and foreign direct investment (FDI). The strong links among high labor costs, productivity growth, and defense spending provide some states with a competitive advantage in the increasingly specialized global economy. And state labor costs have independent effects on economic growth even when we consider trends in federal labor costs, taxes, and defense spending. Nevertheless, higher state labor costs do tend to increase unemployment and lead to slower rates of job creation. As the next chapter will show, whatever the economic advantages, reductions in labor costs have adverse social consequences for the states: slower declines in poverty rates, lower personal income, family disruption, declining voter turnout, and higher crime rates. State policymakers must therefore confront some difficult policy choices.

PREVIOUS RESEARCH ON STATE LABOR COSTS AND ECONOMIC DEVELOPMENT

Much of the recent research on interstate competition for jobs and investment has stressed the role of taxes and business incentives (Peterson 1995; Brace 1993; Bartik 1991; Crain 2003). Eisinger (1988) claimed that factors such as taxes and right-to-work laws would diminish in importance as states moved to newer entrepreneurial strategies to boost investment and innovation. But state experiments with industrial and entrepreneurial policies in the 1980s were never adequately implemented or fully funded, and most fell victim to the state fiscal crises of the early 1990s. Brace (2001) argued that the states were moving "back to an inglorious future," emulating the tax incentives and antiunion, low-wage strategies long characteristic of the southern states—what Cummings (1998) calls the "Dixification of America."

Research on business investment and location decisions has usually found the cost of labor to be far more salient to employers than either state taxes or state/local business incentives. Studies of plant location decisions in the American states reveal that while access to markets was the most important factor cited by business leaders, labor issues (wages, nonunion labor, skilled workers) were a close second, well ahead of state/local taxes [Calzonetti and Walker (1991)]. Manufacturing wages and right-to-work laws also figure prominently in commercial rankings of state business climates by Grant Thornton, Fantus, and the editors of *Site Selection Handbook*.[1] Goodman (1979) claimed that "while government incentives like tax breaks and job training help to influence where a business decides to locate, labor conditions, especially wages and the level of union power, play an even more prominent role." Thompson (1983, 365) concluded that "the effects of wage rates and other economic costs of production far outweigh any advantages [tax] incentives might offer."

Most economists and owners of businesses argue that high unemployment and slow economic growth are the likely consequences of any efforts by governments or labor unions to raise wages and benefits above market rates. Vedder and Gallaway (1993) insist that unemployment would disappear if labor unions, minimum-wage laws, and welfare policies were abolished. Many employers oppose unions because they interfere with managerial prerogatives to hire and fire, slow productivity, and reduce profits. In economic models emphasizing the efficiency of markets, labor unions are usually depicted as "rent-seeking" organizations receiving higher wages and better benefits than would be warranted by a free market for labor. In Lindbeck and Snower's (1988) terms, labor union members and others who are currently employed are the "insiders," who try to limit competition from "outsiders" (the unemployed, immigrants, nonunion labor) who could bid down wages and benefits. Unions use strikes, picket lines, boycotts, and go-slow or work-to-rule strategies to raise the cost to employers of trying to keep wages and benefits low.

At the national level, Freeman and Medoff (1984) estimated that higher union wages cost the economy approximately 0.3 percent of gross national product. At the state level, Bartik (1985) found that branch-plant location decisions were strongly affected by labor union density, while state taxes played a much smaller role. Several earlier studies of the American states found evidence that higher growth rates in some states (particularly in the Sunbelt) were based in part on right-to-work laws and weak unions (Dye 1980; Hansen 1984; Newman 1983). The National Right to Work Committee makes a similar argument when it tries to persuade more states to adopt right-to-work laws. Minimum-wage laws at both state and federal levels have likewise come under attack for increasing unemployment.[2]

However, other research has found high labor costs and unionization to have positive as well as negative economic effects. Freeman and Medoff (1984) counterbalanced their analysis of unions' negative impact on efficiency with the economic benefits unions could offer to employers: reduced turnover costs, upgrading of workers' skills, and productivity gains. Unionization forces management to invest more in capital and technology to offset the higher cost of labor. This may affect nonunion workplaces as well: "To survive, nonunion competitors often increase their use of technology and train workers in new skills, making them eligible for higher wages. The ultimate beneficiary is the overall economy" (Center for Policy Alternatives 2004a). Belman (1992) and Wilson (1995) argue that unionized labor is more stable and productive, in part because management is motivated to enhance efficiency by investing more in capital and technology, and in part because of lower turnover rates in unionized industries.

Research on state economies has produced divergent results concerning the impact of labor costs on productivity. Doucouliagos and Laroche (2003) found that the productivity effects of unions varied considerably across industries and over time. Pantuosco, Parker, and Stone's (2001) analysis of state data from 1978 to 1994 found that although unions increase the rate of wage inflation, "wage inflation has a significant positive link to productivity growth" (p. 5). In a similar vein, V. O. Key argued in *Southern Politics* (1949) that agricultural productivity in the South lagged because of a surplus of cheap labor, and that early southern "smokestack chasing" economic development efforts were designed to quell the outward migration of surplus or seasonal agricultural labor.

The impact of unions on state employment and population trends has also led to conflicting results. Pantuosco, Parker, and Stone (2001) found that unions adversely affected unemployment, growth in GSP, and population growth. Though higher union wages might attract workers, the higher unemployment rates associated with greater union density could increase labor migration out of a state. By contrast, Partridge and Rickman (1995) found that unionization was not significantly related to state unemployment rates once they considered industrial composition and nondemographic labor market variables. Simon (1999) found that high wages and high levels of union density, in addition to boosting productivity, also encouraged in-migration. Innovative high-technology industries demand a well-educated labor force, and they may have to pay a wage premium to attract skilled workers. High labor costs in the states may thus be associated with faster rates of growth in personal income, GSP, and population, and with a higher proportion of well-educated workers in professional and managerial positions. State revenues are likely to benefit as well from skilled workers' higher earnings.

What about the impact of the global economy? Neoliberal economists would expect greater reductions in labor costs in states most closely linked to international trade and thus facing greater competitive pressures. Still, the empirical evidence to date is mixed. Fox and Lee (1996) found that FDI, 1985–90, was indeed higher where wages and unemployment were lower, but they noted no consistent effects of right-to-work laws on FDI. However, they also found that foreign firms preferred to locate in proximity to other foreign firms and in states with well-developed infrastructure. Thus New York, New Jersey, and California attract sizable foreign investment despite their high wages and taxes. Friedman and others (1992) found a significant positive relationship between labor force productivity and state FDI, 1977–88. Yet weak unions and lower wages helped attract Japanese and German automobile manufacturers to states like Kentucky, South Carolina, and Alabama (Yanarella and Green 1990; Watson, Gardner, and Montjoy 2001). Previous research on the impact of labor costs on exports is likewise mixed. Kletzer (2002) found that some manufacturing industries (particularly apparel) experienced a loss of jobs and declining wages due to imports. Leichenko's regional analysis (2000) found that while the West gained jobs in relation to exports, the Northeast lost some. But the consensus among economists is that for the U.S. economy as a whole, exports (of both goods and services) contribute to a growth in jobs as well as to economic growth (Stiglitz 2002; Karoly and Panis 2004). The U.S. comparative advantage in exports lies in high-technology and high-value-added goods like aircraft and computers (Helpmann 1999; Porter 2002). Low-wage states in the United States have been losing jobs to even lower-wage developing countries. Thus even substantial cuts in state wages, workers' compensation, or unemployment benefits would not make American factories competitive with those in Honduras or Sri Lanka. The United States has very little trade with the developing countries that have the lowest labor costs (DiTella and Vogel 2003). However, as of 2004 the United States was experiencing a sizable trade deficit with Western Europe; despite their higher levels of taxes and a higher social wage, European countries were exporting far more to the United States than they were importing from it.[3] And by 2005 the United States' enormous trade deficit with China had become a major political issue.

Why has previous research on state labor costs produced such divergent results? One reason is that the proclivities of researchers and their funders can affect the design and interpretation of research on the politically charged issues of unions and wages. Conclusions reached by the conservative Cato Institute or Heritage Foundation concerning labor costs differ considerably from those of the prolabor Center for Policy Alternatives or the Upjohn Institute. Second, the choice of methods can influence results. Though sophisticated statistical analyses by economists have found both positive and negative effects of labor unions, surveys of business managers concerning their location decisions usually find strong antipathy toward organized labor. Business interests lobby vigorously for reductions in state labor costs, but their prime motivation may be to limit union power rather than to lower the costs of production (Sexton 1991). Wilson (1995) suggests that business opposition to unions is often based on the limitations they impose on managerial prerogatives, rather than on cost factors. According to Baumol, Blackman, and Wolff (1989, 262), "Downsizing firms end up spending less money on wages relative to output. . . . That is just another way of saying that downsizing is profitable at least partly because it is an effective way to hold down wages. We may be led to say that this is the dirty little secret of downsizing."

Third, previous research on state labor costs has led to conflicting conclusions because analysts considered different states and time periods. It is thus difficult to determine whether the relationship between state labor costs and economic outcomes has changed over time or relative to national or international trends. Crouch (1998) is critical of previous studies of taxes and employment trends by the Organization for Economic Cooperation and Development (OECD) because the analyses frequently excluded countries or time periods that did not support its neoliberal conclusions. The dependent variables used in different studies (branch plant locations, trends in personal income or GSP, employment rates, productivity) vary so much that it has seldom been possible to compare effects. It is certainly plausible that labor costs might have divergent effects on different economic outcomes, but few have considered these alternatives. Pantuosco, Parker, and Stone's (2001) recent work, tracking reciprocal relationships among state economic outcomes, is a notable exception.

Fourth, since 1970 the American economy has become much more closely integrated with the world economy. The value of FDI has soared, as have manufacturing exports and the number of jobs linked to exports. In theory, the increasing global mobility of capital should pressure countries (and states) to lower their tax rates, minimize regulatory burdens on business, and reduce labor costs. But previous studies of the American states have not established whether global trends have put even greater pressure on labor costs over time, or whether the states most open to the international economy have been the most constrained to reduce labor costs. Chapter 2 showed little empirical evidence for convergence across the states in either labor costs or personal income.

Fifth and finally, labor costs have been measured in several different ways in previous studies. No single indicator is ideal, particularly because different economic sectors may be sensitive to different cost factors. Time-series data on wages for states are available only for manufacturing, although this sector has been shrinking as state economies have become more diverse.[4] As I have shown, union density and other aspects of labor regulation vary within as well as between right-to-work and union-shop states. And the usual indicator of union density (the percent of workers who are union members) may not reflect the actual influence of organized labor in state politics. Comprehensive indicators of national labor costs have been calculated, such as the Economic Costs Index developed by the U.S. Bureau of Labor Statistics (BLS), or the OECD's measures of the social wage or employment protection. But no such index has been used in previous studies of state labor costs.

We must also ask whether business investment or location decisions respond to labor costs, or whether they reflect broader dimensions of state economies, such as taxes, markets, or the supply of skilled labor. State policymakers need to know whether a policy change (adopting a right-to-work law, raising the minimum wage, cutting taxes) will produce identifiable short- or long-term changes (for better or worse) in economic indicators. And they need to know whether reductions in labor costs are more or less effective in stimulating growth than tax breaks or other economic development policies.

This chapter's analysis attempts to address these problems. First, a comprehensive index of state labor costs has been developed, analogous to the BLS Economic Costs Index, to assess the combined impact of wages and benefits over a considerable period (1970–2000) for all fifty states. Both levels and changes in state labor costs can be considered on the basis of this comprehensive index. Second, to highlight some of the trade-offs involving labor costs, different economic outcomes (trends in GSP, productivity, personal income, unemployment, and job creation) are compared, as are several social and political trends. Third, measures are included (specifically the value of state exports and FDI) to assess how a state's success in the global economy is affected by trends in labor costs. Fourth, any exclusion of anomalous states because of missing data or extreme values is noted.

Finally, any assessment of the impact of labor costs should consider how other state and federal policies affect state economic trends. I now discuss how state taxes, federal labor costs, and defense spending could heighten or counterbalance the impact of state labor costs.

STATE/LOCAL TAXES AND STATE ECONOMIES

For decades, state officials have used a variety of tax strategies to try to lure businesses. State tax laws provide for a variety of deductions, exemptions, and subsidies for certain businesses, individuals, or areas; states with higher tax rates are more likely to make use of such subsidies. The proportion of state revenue derived from corporate income taxes has fallen considerably since the 1970s, while the number of tax subsidies has grown.[5]

Economists have long disputed the impact of state taxes on economic growth. The preponderance of earlier research reported negligible effects, especially on employment trends, because state taxes constitute only a relatively small part of the expenses of most businesses. Eisinger (1988) argued that states were moving away from strategies as tax breaks because of their lack of impact. States began to experiment with more active entrepreneurial strategies during the 1980s to boost investment and create new jobs, rather than trying to entice them away from other states. But many of these innovative strategies were short-lived, and the 1990s saw a return to interstate tax competition.

More recent research gives taxes a somewhat larger role in state economies. Helms (1985) found that state taxes may indeed have an impact if one considers how the revenue is used; spending on education and infrastructure has more positive economic effects than spending on welfare. According to Crain (2003), although state income taxes had no impact on the growth of state personal income, sales taxes did have a significant negative effect. Hansen's (2001b) analysis using 1980–95 data found that job growth, productivity, and FDI were actually higher in states with higher tax burdens, while unemployment was significantly lower.

Tax policies vary considerably across the states. Most use a combination of sales and income taxes, but six states have no broad-based income tax and five have no sales tax; New Hampshire has neither. Some have a unique revenue source (gaming in Nevada, severance taxes on oil and natural gas in Alaska and Wyoming, tourism in Hawaii or Florida) that enables them to shift much of the tax burden to nonresidents. Most state tax systems are regressive, taxing lower-income groups far more heavily than the wealthy. But a few states like California or Vermont, because of progressive income taxes, have a more proportional revenue system (CTJ 2003). Excise taxes on gasoline, alcohol, or cigarettes are also sources of state revenue, and in recent years many more states have made use of lotteries and casino gambling (Pierce and Miller 2004). These revenue sources all tend to fall more heavily on lower-income earners.

The states also vary in the mix of funding between state and local governments, and in recent years many states have shifted spending to cities and counties through unfunded mandates (Conlan 1998; Posner 1998). Any comparison of the economic impact of taxes should therefore consider local as well as state revenues. The standard measure of the economic impact of taxes is the combined state/local tax burden (taxes as a percent of personal income), and this varies considerably across the states. As of 2000, the highest tax burdens were in Washington (14.5 percent), Pennsylvania (14.4 percent), New York (13.3 percent), and Wisconsin (12.2 percent); the lowest tax burdens were in Texas, Alabama, New Hampshire, and West Virginia (all less than 9 percent of personal income).

Because of both interstate competition and the influence of the global economy, we might expect tax burdens in the American states to have converged over time at a lower level. But chapter 2 revealed a more complex pattern; tax burdens (state/local taxes as a percent of personal income) increased between 1970 and 1985 and have since declined. Since the 1980s, the top marginal rates for most states' income taxes have fallen as well; New York's dropped from 14 percent in 1980 to less than 8 percent in 2004. The corporate share of state/local taxes has also fallen.

Regardless of the economists' ongoing debates over measures and methodology, taxes remain politically salient in the states. Business groups such as state chambers of commerce focus on reducing them, and tax breaks for business represent one of the major tools policymakers have used to try to influence economic growth. So any assessment of state labor costs should be compared with state and local taxes as policies that could influence state economies.

STATE ECONOMIES AND FEDERAL POLICIES

As shown in chapter 3, trends in state labor costs are determined more by endogenous factors (those internal to the states) than by exogenous factors such as ties to the international economy or trends in federal labor costs. But while states can indeed affect labor costs, the American states are not fully autonomous units in either political or economic terms. Thus any analysis of state economic trends must also consider federal policies. First is the federal role in determining labor costs, as described in chapter 2. I found that national labor costs (payroll taxes, minimum-wage rates, policies under different presidential administrations) have been only marginally related to trends in state labor costs since 1970. However, such policies may still have independent effects on the overall economy and on employment trends in the states.

Second is the national business cycle. Federal policies cannot fully control the huge and complex American economy, which is vulnerable to external shocks such as oil prices in the 1970s or the Asian monetary crisis of the late 1980s. But both monetary and fiscal policies have been used to try to control inflation, spur economic growth, and speed up recovery from economic downturns. Considerable research in both economics and political science has found that partisan and electoral factors indeed influence unemployment, inflation, and the trade-off between them.[6] To control for effects of the national business cycle on unemployment (higher during recessions, lower during recoveries), my subsequent analysis uses the *difference* between the state and national unemployment rates for each year. This measure makes political as well as economic sense; according to Wolfers (2002), voting for state governors since the 1940s has been related more to state unemployment deviations from national trends than to absolute levels.

Third, federal policies can influence state economies through defense spending. Federal aid to state and local governments (other than direct payments to individuals or third-party providers, such as Medicaid) has been declining since the 1970s, and most of the federal policies initiated in the 1960s to boost regional economies have since disappeared.[7] As domestic spending has been cut after years of federal deficits and devolution, prime defense contracts now constitute the primary form of federal spending in states (Gottlieb 1997). Although defense spending's share of the federal budget declined between the peak of the Ronald Reagan buildup in 1985 and the end of the cold war, it has been rising since 1995 and surged after the terrorist attacks on September 11, 2001.

Federal defense spending could be expected to boost a state's GSP and exports. The Defense Department annually awards billions of dollars in prime contracts, and elected officials compete fiercely for these awards. Critics have claimed that the allocation of these contracts represents political pork rather than the military's defense needs. Congress has even voted to continue the production of expensive, unreliable, or outdated equipment that the Pentagon says it no longer needs (e.g., the Osprey helicopter, the B1 bomber, and the Crusader artillery system) to keep factories open in the districts of influential members (Dao 2001; Shanker and Dao 2002).

Table 4.1 shows that whereas all states receive at least some defense spending, the major beneficiaries of prime defense contracts are California, Virginia, Texas, and Florida.[8] Only a dozen states account for 69 percent of all prime defense contracts. In six states (Alaska, Hawaii, California, Maryland, Virginia, and Washington), more than 7 percent of total employment is defense related. Military production has been a great boon to states such as Washington (home of Boeing Aircraft), Missouri (home of McDonnell Douglas) and Connecticut (home of Sikorsky Helicopters and Electric Boat). One in three manufacturing jobs in Connecticut were defense related as of 1992 (McGee 1993).

The United States leads the world in arms sales ($13.3 billion in 2003, 45 percent of the world's total); it sells more than the next twenty nations combined (Federation of Concerned Scientists 2003). Without arms exports, the American balance of trade would be even more negative. Aircraft and other armaments constitute a major portion of total U.S. exports; more than 80 percent of U.S. fighter jets are now produced for export (Sennott 1996). Most armaments are high-technology, high-value-added

Table 4.1
Prime Defense Contracts by State, 2000 (billions of dollars)

California	$9,380	Hawaii	$599
Virginia	7,046	Tennessee	558
Texas	6,276	South Carolina	542
Florida	3,342	Utah	491
Maryland	2,572	Kentucky	470
Massachusetts	2,448	Kansas	460
Arizona	2,350	Alaska	428
Missouri	2,329	Wisconsin	398
Pennsylvania	2,050	Maine	398
New York	1,983	New Mexico	336
Georgia	1,896	Iowa	320
Alabama	1,708	Rhode Island	217
Ohio	1,591	New Hampshire	206
New Jersey	1,518	Arkansas	176
Colorado	1,141	Oregon	145
Washington	1,131	Nevada	144
Connecticut	1,126	Nebraska	123
Louisiana	1,002	Vermont	123
Illinois	831	Idaho	108
Indiana	831	North Dakota	67
Mississippi	805	Wyoming	52
Minnesota	754	Montana	47
Michigan	749	South Dakota	46
Oklahoma	723	Delaware	46
North Carolina	619	West Virginia	23

goods produced by skilled and well-paid workers, and contracts for their development and production are avidly sought by defense contractors and politicians in the states where these firms are located. Defense spending could also be related to productivity gains in particular states. Much of U.S. research and development spending has been under military auspices, particularly the Defense Advanced Research Projects Agency, where the Internet originated. Highly skilled workers are needed in factories producing the most advanced aircraft, weapons, and computer technology (Saal 2001).

Does defense spending boost state employment? Markusen and others (1991) argued that economic recovery after the 1981–82 recession was fueled largely by the surge in defense spending under the Reagan administration, and that Sunbelt states were the major beneficiaries. Congress has resisted military base closings and the cancellation of defense production because of its concern with losing jobs.[9] And in response to state and local concerns about the economic impact of base closings, Congress has appropriated millions to affected districts to retool military bases as sites for factories, prisons, or community colleges, although the presence of toxic or radioactive wastes at many sites limits their use.

Conversely, recent trends may have reduced any impact of defense spending on job creation. Since the 1970s, "defense employment has become more the preserve of the middle class, including many scientists, engineers, and technicians, and less the domain of mass-production operatives and unskilled laborers" (Higgs 1990, xix). Thus fewer jobs are generated per dollar spent. And Kinsella (1990) argues that military spending absorbs more output from the capital-intensive manufacturing sector and less from the labor-intensive service sector. Further, many labor unions have objected to the outsourcing of defense contracting jobs to lower-cost producers overseas. The Defense Department has often used such "production offsets" to boost its sales of armaments to particular countries (Sennott 1996; Tonelson 2002). The Pentagon has also shown some preference for locating major production facilities in nonunion states to save money on labor costs (Markusen et al. 1991).

Research on the economic effects of defense spending has yet to produce definitive results. Kinsella (1990) found no significant relationship between defense spending and U.S. interest rates, prices, or unemployment, although defense spending did boost national output (gross domestic product, or GDP) at least in the short term. Critics on the left claim that production for the domestic market would benefit the economy far more than does arms production (Gottlieb 1997; Melman 1974). Gold (2002) cites a study by the Congressional Budget Office, which found that every $10 billion spent on weapons generated 404,000 fewer jobs than $10 billion spent on civilian programs. But there is far more political support in Congress (especially among Republicans) for expanded military spending than for investment in domestic policies.

Power politics—including intensive lobbying by defense industries, the role of congressional appropriations committees, and interservice rivalry—may have far more to do with the awarding of prime contracts than either military or economic considerations (Rundquist, Lee, and Rhee 1996; Carsey and Rundquist 1999; Gold 2002). And Mayer (1991) found evidence that presidents have used prime contracts selectively to enhance their reelection chances. Therefore, given the billions of dollars involved, the impact of federal defense spending should not be ignored in any analysis of state economic trends.

HYPOTHESES, DATA, AND MEASURES

Much previous research on labor costs has concentrated on their adverse employment effects. But as indicated by the literature cited above, labor costs can have an impact on several different aspects of economic growth—some positively, others negatively. Therefore this analysis will compare several distinct dimensions of state economies: unemployment, rates of job creation, GSP, per capita personal income, FDI, and exports.

One would expect to find higher *unemployment* and slower *rates of job growth* in states with higher labor costs; this is certainly the consensus of previous research in economics. Here, I analyze trends in the mean annual unemployment rate, as calculated by the BLS for each state based on the proportion of people in the labor force who are out of work but actively seeking work. This rate thus excludes people not in the labor market (housewives, students, retirees, discouraged workers). As explained above, the state rate will be subtracted from the national rate to control for trends in the national economy. To analyze job growth, I use the annual rate of change in the number of persons employed in a state, based on payroll data supplied to the BLS.[10] State data for both unemployment and labor force trends are taken from BLS data given in annual editions of the *Statistical Abstract of the United States*.

As already noted, previous research has produced mixed results concerning the impact of the international economy on the states: long-term advantages for the U.S. economy as a whole, but adverse short-term effects on particular industries or regions. I use the same two measures described in chapter 3 to assess a state's exposure to global economic trends. First is the dollar value of state *manufacturing exports*, based on data from the *Census of Manufactures*, 1970–2000. Second is the total amount of *FDI* in a state; this has been available on a state-by-state basis only since 1978.[11] Both measures use constant dollars so that the results are not affected by inflation.

On the basis of previous research, state labor costs are expected to show a positive relationship with three additional aspects of state economies. The first is *GSP*; analogous to GDP for the U.S. economy as a whole, it represents the gross market value of goods and services produced by labor and property located within a state. GSP is also measured in constant dollars (using the GDP price deflator) to control for inflation, and it is adjusted for the size of a state's labor force.[12] The second aspect is *personal income per capita*, which also is measured in constant dollars to control for inflation.

The third aspect of state economies considered is *productivity*. A state with a productive labor force may have a comparative advantage in growth rates, personal income, and international trade even if its labor costs are high. Conversely, gains in productivity could lead to fewer jobs (at least in the short term) if capital and technology were substituted for labor. Productivity is measured by the annual rate of change in the value of manufactured goods in a state, relative to the size of the state's labor force.[13] Though other measures of productivity have been developed for national economic data, this is the only one for which state data are available for the 1970–2000 period. Larger industrial states tend to be highly productive, although a few rural states in the West top the list; the poorer southern states tend to rank lowest. Both productivity and labor costs are used to predict trends in unemployment, job creation, exports, FDI, GSP, and growth in personal income.

Any assessment of the economic impact of state labor costs must account for the role of federal policies such as minimum-wage laws, Social Security payroll tax rates, and labor policy differences across presidential administrations. State and federal labor costs are indexed by the factor scores for 1970–2000 described above. Including these two measures can help determine whether state or national labor cost factors have more of an impact on state economic outcomes, and whether trends in state labor costs are indeed independent of national trends (as the analysis described in chapter 2 suggested).

To assess the effects of federal defense spending on state economic trends, I use the value (in constant dollars) of defense prime contracts in a state in a given year.[14] Defense spending is expected to show a positive relationship with state exports and GSP. Its effects on employment and productivity may be positive as well, although previous research has not always supported those conclusions. Finally, an indicator of the overall tax burden (total state/local taxes as a percent of state personal income) is used to assess the economic influence of taxes and to compare their impact with that of labor costs.

THE ECONOMIC EFFECTS OF STATE LABOR COSTS

I have just described measures of six different aspects of state economies: unemployment, rates of job growth, GSP, per capita personal income, exports, and FDI. I now use these measures to assess the effects of labor costs on state economies. But state labor costs are not the only factor influencing these economic outcomes; so federal labor costs, defense spending, productivity, and state/local tax burdens must also be included in the analysis.

The period to be analyzed is 1970 to 2000 (1978 to 2000 for FDI) for all fifty states. Because the methods required to analyze such time-series data are somewhat technical, statistical methods and detailed tables are included in appendix B. The results of the analysis are summarized in tables 4.2 and 4.3. In these tables, the economic outcomes (called the dependent variables) are listed down the side of each table. State labor costs and the other predictors (the independent variables) are listed across the top of each table. Within the table, an asterisk indicates that the predictor variable was positively related to an economic outcome (e.g., GSP or unemployment), even when the other predictor variables were taken into account. A double asterisk indicates an especially strong positive relationship. A minus sign with an asterisk indicates a strong but negative relationship. And NS stands for "not significant," indicating that any relationship between two variables was so weak that it could easily be due to chance alone.

The results shown in table 4.2 support most mainstream economists' predictions concerning the adverse employment effects of increasing wages and benefits; unemployment is considerably higher in states with higher labor costs, and labor force growth is considerably slower. By contrast, state labor costs are strongly and positively associated with *higher* levels of GSP, personal income—and exports. But FDI seems to be unaffected by state labor costs, which calls into question Fox and Lee's (1996) findings that foreign firms are more attracted to low-wage states.

Table 4.2 also shows that state labor costs have a sizable impact on state economies, even when we take into account the influence of federal labor costs. Federal labor costs show no relationship with GSP, but they are linked to higher rates of growth in personal income, exports, and FDI. Surprisingly, federal labor costs are associated with faster rather than slower growth in the state labor force. However, as expected, they are also linked to higher state unemployment rates. And because our indicator of state unemployment is the *difference* between state and federal unemployment rates, the impact of federal labor costs is not due to recessions or other fluctuations in the business cycle.

Another federal policy, defense spending, also shows strong effects on state economic trends. GSP, personal income, labor force growth, exports, and FDI all rise as defense spending increases. Defense spending is also associated with faster growth in the labor force; the strong political support from state and local officials (and members of Congress) for expanding military spending and keeping military bases open apparently has at least some empirical economic basis. In light of these strong effects, it is surprising to see that defense spending has little if any impact on state

Table 4.2

Predictions of State Economic Outcomes, 1970–2000

State Economic Outcomes	Predictor Variables					
	State Labor Costs	Federal Labor Costs	Defense Spending	State/Local Taxes	Manufacturing Productivity	R^2
Gross state product	**	NS	**	NS	NS	0.49
Personal income	**	**	**	**	(*)	0.42
Unemployment	*	*	NS	NS	NS (−)	0.13
Job growth	−*	**	**	**	NS (+)	0.46
Exports	**	*	**	−*	NS	0.33
Foreign direct investment	NS	*	**	NS	NS	0.37

Note: Table entries show how each of the predictor variables (listed across the top) affect state economic outcomes (listed down the side). R^2 tells us how well these predictor variables combine to explain each economic outcome. Values range from 0.0 for no explanation up to 1.0 for full explanation.

Key:

(*) Modest impact on economic outcome. Marginal statistical significance ($p < .10$).

*   Sizeable impact on economic outcome. Statistically significant ($p < .05$).

** Very strong impact on economic outcome. Statistically significant ($p < .01$).

−* Negative and statistically significant relationship ($p < .05$) to economic outcome.

NS Very weak relationship with economic outcome; not statistically significant.

Table 4.3

Combined Impact of Exports, Foreign Direct Investment (FDI), and State Labor Costs (SLC) on Gross State Product, Personal Income, Unemployment, and Job Growth

State Economic Outcomes	Predictor Variables[a]				
	SLC	Federal Labor Costs	Exports * SLC[b]	FDI * SLC[b]	R^2
Gross state product					
Exports interaction	−*	−*	**		0.82
FDI interaction	NS	−*		**	0.89
Personal income					
Exports interaction	**	**	−*		0.44
FDI interaction	*	*		(*)	0.43
Unemployment					
Exports interaction	**	**	NS		0.14
FDI interaction	**	**		−*	0.16
Job growth					
Exports interaction	−*	**	**		0.48
FDI interaction	−*	**		**	0.55

Note: Table entries show how each of the predictor variables (listed across the top) affect state economic outcomes (listed down the side). R^2 tells us how well these predictor variables combine to explain each economic outcome. Values range from 0.0 for no explanation up to 1.0 for full explanation.

Key:

(*) Modest impact on economic outcome. Marginal statistical significance ($p < .10$).

* Sizable impact on economic outcome. Statistically significant ($p < .05$).

** Very strong impact on economic outcome. Statistically significant ($p < .01$).

−* Negative and statistically significant relationship ($p < .05$) to economic outcome.

NS Very weak relationship with economic outcome; not statistically significant.

[a]Other variables in the equations (defense spending, state/local taxes, productivity, exports, and FDI) are not shown here. See appendix B for full tables.

[b]Interaction term: exports or FDI multiplied by SLC.

unemployment rates, although this result has been confirmed by previous research. One reason may be that defense industries hesitate to locate in central cities, where unemployment tends to be highest. Another reason is that defense production has a much lower multiplier effect on employment than other types of industry (Kinsella 1990; Markusen et al. 1991).

Also confirming previous research, the state/local tax burden has no impact on state unemployment trends; it also shows little relationship with GSP.[15] But personal income and the labor force both appear to be growing more rapidly in states with *higher rather than lower* tax burdens. Higher tax burdens do have a significant negative impact on exports, although apparently no effect in either direction on FDI.

The impact of productivity on state economies is surprisingly weak, at least according to these indicators. However, the relationship between productivity and personal income growth is positive and close to statistical significance. Higher productivity growth also showed a modest *positive* relationship with growth in the labor force and with personal income, and it is linked to *lower* unemployment (see appendix B for the actual coefficients). Although neither relationship is statistically significant (and thus could be due to chance), both are indicative of the positive long-term effects economists such as Thurow (1999) predict would result from productivity gains—but somewhat surprising given these annual data. As noted in chapter 3, productivity (value added in manufacturing) was positively related to state labor costs prior to 1980, but not since then. These results thus support Volgy, Schwarz, and Imwalle's (1996) finding of a weaker association between wages and productivity gains in weak-labor countries (including the United States) than in those with stronger unions and labor parties.

EXPORTS, FDI, AND STATE ECONOMIC TRENDS

These same measures will now be used to test how state labor costs affect the economies of states most exposed to the international economy. The economic outcomes (the dependent variables shown in table 4.3) are GSP, personal income growth, labor force growth, and unemployment. The predictor variables are the same as in table 4.2, but with the addition of two interaction terms. The first is the product of state labor costs multiplied by the value of exports in a given year; the second is the product of state labor costs and FDI. If either of these interaction terms shows significant effects, it means that labor costs have greater influence on state economic trends in states with higher levels of exports or FDI, respectively. To simplify the presentation, the effects of defense spending, tax burdens, and productivity are not shown in table 4.3; their effects are mostly similar to those shown in table 4.2. The exact coefficients for both tables are given in appendix B, tables B.2 and B.3.

The results seriously challenge the notion that cutting labor costs enhances international competitiveness. As shown by the double asterisk for the interaction term listed in the third columns of the tables, GSP is considerably higher in states with both high labor costs and high levels of exports or FDI. The rate of personal income growth is slower in states with high levels of both exports and state labor costs, but it tends to be higher in states with high levels of both FDI and state labor costs. The combination of high labor costs and high levels of exports has no effect on state unemployment rates, but these are *significantly lower* in states with high labor costs and high FDI. Finally, the rate of growth in the state labor force is *significantly faster* in high-labor-cost states with close links to the international economy. Further, the addition of these interaction terms improves our ability to predict the values of the dependent variables. The last columns in tables 4.2 and 4.3 (the R^2 statistic, which can range from 0 to 100) tells us what proportion of an economic indicator is explained by the independent variables used in the analysis. Most dramatically, the predictions for GSP increase from an R^2 of 49 percent in table 4.2 to more than 80 percent in table 4.3; the other economic outcomes show smaller increases in R^2 values. One additional difference between tables 4.2 and 4.3 should be noted: Once the interaction term for FDI is included, defense spending is associated with significantly lower state unemployment rates.[16] However, none of the prediction equations explain unemployment very well, because the R^2 values are low.

CONCLUSION

On the basis of the analysis summarized in this chapter, the conclusion is clear: The combination of strong links to the international economy and high labor costs has generally beneficial effects on state economies. Even unemployment is lower in states (e.g., California, New York, and Illinois) that combine high labor costs and high levels of FDI. Overall, both unemployment and labor force growth are adversely affected by state labor costs, whether or not exports and FDI are included. However, state labor costs are associated with significantly higher levels of GSP, personal income, and exports. These economic advantages must be weighed against any employment disadvantages.

Tables 4.2 and 4.3 enable us to compare the effects of state and federal labor costs on state economies. The state labor costs measure proves to have a significant independent impact on several aspects of state economies; in fact, in several instances the effect is the opposite of that for federal labor costs. State labor costs also have an economic impact independent of (and in several cases larger than) that of state/local tax burdens. Clearly, they should be included in any analysis of state economic development policies.

This analysis confirms that it is important to incorporate *both* state and national factors in any analysis of state policy outcomes, as Brace (1993) and Hendrick and Garand (1991) have urged. The striking impact of federal defense spending on these state economic trends should also be emphasized. However, its lack of impact on state unemployment is even more puzzling in light of the otherwise positive economic effects of defense spending described by these equations.

As we have already seen, labor costs in different states continue to vary greatly, even though exports and FDI have soared. And as the analysis in this chapter has shown, states with higher levels of FDI or exports combined with high labor costs have experienced faster growth in GSP, personal income, and the labor force. Unemployment, usually the most politically sensitive issue in the states, is indeed lower when state or federal labor costs are higher. But the combination of high state labor costs and exports has little apparent impact on unemployment, and state unemployment is also significantly lower in states with high labor costs and high levels of FDI. We must look to domestic rather than international factors to account for the decline in state labor costs.

This chapter confirms what the analysis in chapter 3 showed: The international economy is not the major factor increasing state unemployment. And state/local taxes likewise have little impact on the unemployment rate. Brierly and Feiock (1998) describe unemployment as the "missing multiplier" that fails to decline even when other indicators of state economic growth show improvement. Also, Bartik (1991) argues that economic development policies are seldom targeted on regions with the highest unemployment. Prime defense contracts are allocated on the basis of intensive lobbying by defense industries and their congressional allies; local or regional employment trends are seldom if ever a salient factor.

Additional social factors (education levels, percent minority, percent urban, declines in mining and agricultural employment) must be taken into account to explain why high unemployment persists in particular states or regions (Pryor and Schaffer 1999). Benabou (2002) suggests that

What Matters

- Mainstream economists may be right; higher labor costs in the states mean higher unemployment and slower job growth.
- But state labor costs have substantial positive effects on other aspects of state economies: per capita personal income, gross state product, and exports.
- State labor costs influence state economic trends, even when federal policies (labor costs and defense spending) are considered.
- Federal defense spending has a strong influence on state economic growth, but it apparently has little effect on state unemployment rates.
- State and local taxes are associated with lower exports, but higher rates of growth in jobs and personal income.
- The combination of high labor costs and close ties to the international economy is advantageous for growth in gross state product, personal income, and jobs.
- Unemployment is significantly lower in states with both high labor costs and high levels of foreign investment.

high levels of incarceration have been used in some states to limit the number of unemployed people. And my data analysis showed that states with high levels of incarceration did have significantly lower unemployment rates.[17]

Because unemployment is such a politically charged issue, international influences may be a convenient scapegoat for it. In 1994, Governor Pete Wilson of California gained reelection by attributing the state's persistent high unemployment to illegal immigration from abroad (Hansen 1999a). However, the real culprit was the post–cold war decline in defense spending, which had hit California's aerospace industries particularly hard. As a campaign strategy in 2004, "blaming foreigners" was preferred to addressing the growing trade deficit (Norris 2004). In certain regions and sectors, as Kletzer (2002) has shown, jobs lost overseas exceeded jobs gained from exports and foreign investment, even if the overall economy benefited from expanded trade. But a political and media focus on selective aspects of the international economy can also deflect attention from domestic policy choices concerning organized labor, tax cuts, lack of investment in education or worker training, and the corporate excesses of such firms as Enron or WorldCom, whose bankruptcies caused the loss of thousands of American jobs. "Globalization" can be an excuse for reducing labor costs, even if (as demonstrated here and elsewhere) higher labor costs can in fact be advantageous for productivity, economic growth, and international trade.

CHAPTER FIVE

The Social and Political Consequences of Declining Labor Costs

THE ANALYSIS IN CHAPTER 4 confirmed what most economists have claimed: Rising labor costs lead to higher unemployment and slower rates of job creation. For elected officials focused on "jobs" and a general public concerned with unemployment, cutting labor costs in the hopes of creating more jobs governed the mindset of the 1980s and 1990s. But what kinds of jobs are created by lowering labor costs? What is the social impact of stagnant wages, weaker unions, and declining benefits? The "low road" to economic development, based on low wages and high levels of job insecurity, has been criticized by many for its adverse social consequences (Levin-Waldman 2001; National Center on Education and the Economy 1990). Blank (1994) predicts the "low road" will lead to rising inequality, less investment in human capital, longer work hours, and consequential stress on family life.

As this chapter shows, reductions in labor costs are indeed associated with a number of negative social outcomes in the fifty U.S. states: higher rates of poverty, crime, suicide, and family instability. And these negative outcomes are *not* counterbalanced by more positive gains resulting from higher rates of job creation.

POSSIBLE CONSEQUENCES OF REDUCING LABOR COSTS

Possible *economic consequences* of declining state labor costs include a reduction in living standards, greater poverty, slower growth in personal income, and rising levels of income inequality. As of 2004, even working full time, year round at the minimum wage failed to lift individuals or families above the federal poverty line—and Congress has not raised the minimum wage since 1997.[1] But since 1970, per capita personal income growth has risen in tandem with increases in state or federal labor costs, as shown by the analysis in chapter 4.

Growth in poverty and income inequality could have adverse consequences for the whole economy, since consumer confidence and consumer spending are major factors driving economic growth. If low-paid workers have less to spend, the reduced demand for goods and services could lead to layoffs, price deflation, bankruptcies, housing foreclosures, and ultimately recession. In 2004, after a period of wage stagnation and slow job growth, high-end merchants like Neiman Marcus reported strong sales, while sales for mass-market merchandisers like Wal-Mart and Sears declined (Rozhon 2005). The level of personal bankruptcies has also increased since the 1990s. These are exactly the reasons why the economist John Maynard Keynes advocated greater government spending during recessions: to boost consumer demand and expand the market for both goods and services. But because of interstate competition and state constitutional limits on running deficits, Keynesian economic policies are not an option for the states.[2]

Further, reductions in labor costs tend to fall most heavily on those with the least political clout: minorities, women, and people coming off welfare. These groups are less likely to have health insurance coverage and are most vulnerable to hazards in the workplace. People receiving the minimum wage are disproportionately female, and thus most severely affected if the minimum wage does not keep up with inflation. Fewer women are eligible for unemployment insurance benefits, because they are more likely to work part time and because "domestic quits" to take care of family responsibilities do not qualify for benefits.[3] Thus state cutbacks in benefits, or tighter eligibility restrictions for workers' compensation or unemployment insurance, are likely to fall most heavily on poor women and minorities.

Possible *social consequences* of declining state labor costs include higher rates of crime and domestic violence, increased drug and alcohol abuse, and higher suicide rates. The loss of well-paid jobs in the steel industry in the Pittsburgh region in the 1980s was indeed associated with a number of these adverse social outcomes (Cunningham and Martz 1986). Poverty and high levels of unemployment can put severe stress on existing families, so we would expect to see an increase in the divorce rate. When finances deteriorate, couples tend to fight more, increasing the chances that they will split up (Horin 2004).

Other indicators of social stress include more children living in poverty and in single-parent families. Wilson (1997) argues that poverty and high rates of unemployment among young black males impede the formation of new family units, producing many more single mothers. Thus more children may be born out of wedlock in states experiencing declining labor costs and living standards. And reduced health benefits could have adverse consequences for public health.

Population migration is another consequence of trends in labor costs. Higher-wage regions are likely to attract more immigrants from other states as well as from abroad. Considerable research in economics suggests that jobs follow people, rather than the reverse.[4] A steady influx of new residents into a state increases demand for goods and services and thus creates more jobs. Labor cost trends may also have an impact on the age structure of a state's population. Though retirees may prefer states with lower taxes and living costs, prime-age workers are the group most likely to relocate to higher-wage regions. This exodus may be especially pronounced among younger and more highly skilled workers, and during the 1990s many older industrial states became concerned about the "brain drain" of well-educated young professionals.[5] Several Great Plains states experienced sharp declines in population in the 1980s and 1990s as agricultural employment declined and their young people left for more promising locations (Mitchell 2004). States and cities with stable, declining, or aging populations are likely to face a serious shortfall in tax revenue as well.

Declining state labor costs may also have *political consequences*, in part as a function of the weakened influence of organized labor. According to B. Kaufman (2004, 377), "The most compelling rationale for unions among citizens and policy-makers is the traditional one of protecting the underdog and leveling the playing field." Labor unions have historically encouraged greater political activism among lower socioeconomic groups, and such mobilization can offset the political and economic power of employers and the wealthy. Recent research on voting behavior found that personal contacts—whether from precinct workers, churches, or union stewards on the shop floor—encourage political awareness and involvement (Huckfeldt and Sprague 1995; Krueger 2004). But union membership has declined precipitously since the 1970s, and this is one explanation for the overall decline in voter turnout in the United States (Asher et al. 2001; Leighley and Nagler 2004). If union density in a state decreases, unions will have fewer resources for voter registration efforts, voter education, and get-out-the-vote drives.

In addition to a falloff in voter turnout, political scientists have documented an overall decline in "social capital" (social and community involvement, organizational membership) in the United States since World War

II (Putnam 2000; Skocpol and Fiorina 1999). Much of this decline is due to a switch from mass-membership organizations (including labor unions) to advocacy groups. But social capital is also related to levels of income and education. If people must work overtime or hold two jobs to make ends meet, they will have less time for political activism or volunteer activities. Poor people are less likely to vote and to join organizations, in part because they lack the personal and social resources that encourage political involvement (Verba, Schlozman, and Brady 1995; Verba 2003). In addition, the chronic housing problems of low-income workers result in frequent moves and thus difficulties with maintaining community involvement or voter registration (Ehrenreich 2001).

Higher voting turnout has been linked to more progressive social policies in the states (Hill, Leighley, and Hinton-Anderson 1995). Avery and Peffley (2005) found less restrictive welfare eligibility in states with the highest lower-class voting rates. Union density in the states is also associated with policy liberalism, defined by Radcliff and Saiz (1998) to include more generous welfare benefits, higher education spending, higher total per capita spending, and progressive taxes that fall more heavily on the rich than on the poor. If labor unions (and their allies in the Democratic Party) have less political clout, such liberal policies are less likely. The Center for Policy Alternatives (2004a), a liberal-left organization/think tank with strong ties to organized labor, addressed these policy outcomes directly as a reason to oppose right-to-work laws and antiunion policies: "Because state law holds down wages, Right-to-Work states consistently have higher poverty and infant mortality rates, less access to health care, and poorer schools." States with low or declining voter turnout and declining labor costs should thus have more regressive tax systems and lower levels of spending on social services.

TESTING FOR THE CONSEQUENCES OF TRENDS IN STATE LABOR COSTS

The social and political trends discussed above have been subject to considerable research and much partisan debate. It is not my purpose here to review all the possible reasons for trends in poverty, social capital, voter turnout, immigration, crime rates, out-of-wedlock birthrates, and the like. This chapter poses much more basic questions: Do economic, social, or political trends vary across states as a function of trends in state labor costs? And are any negative outcomes counterbalanced by positive social effects of higher levels of employment?

To help answer these questions, I have computed the percent change in several economic, social, and political indicators between 1980 and 2000 (or a year or so in either direction, depending on data availability). I then compare changes in each of these indicators across states that have experienced three different levels of reduction in labor costs since 1980. As noted earlier, almost all states have experienced declining labor costs according to the measure I developed in chapter 2. But as table 5.1 shows, the mean rate of decline ranges from 28 percent in the top third of states to 8 percent in the bottom third.

I then calculated changes in the same economic, social, and political trends for states with three different levels of growth in the labor force since

Table 5.1
States Grouped by Changes in Labor Costs
and Size of Labor Force, 1980–2000

Decline in state labor costs:

High (group mean = –28%, N = 16)
Alabama, Alaska, Arizona, Idaho, Indiana, Mississippi, Missouri, Montana, Nebraska, North Dakota, Ohio, Pennsylvania, South Dakota, Utah, Washington, West Virginia

Medium (group mean = –21%, N = 17)
Arkansas, California, Colorado, Delaware, Illinois, Iowa, Kentucky, Louisiana, Michigan, New Mexico, New York, Oklahoma, Oregon, Tennessee, Virginia, Wisconsin, Wyoming

Low (group mean = –8%, N = 17)
Connecticut, Florida, Georgia, Hawaii, Kansas, Maine, Maryland, Massachusetts, Minnesota, Nevada, New Hampshire, New Jersey, North Carolina, Rhode Island, South Carolina, Texas, Vermont

Growth in state labor force:

High (group mean = 89%, N = 17)
Arizona, Arkansas, California, Colorado, Florida, Georgia, Idaho, Montana, Nevada, New Hampshire, New Mexico, Oregon, South Carolina, South Dakota, Utah, Washington, Wisconsin

Medium (group mean = 63%, N = 17)
Alabama, Alaska, Delaware, Indiana, Kansas, Kentucky, Maine, Maryland, Michigan, Minnesota, Mississippi, Nebraska, North Carolina, Tennessee, Texas, Vermont, Virginia

Low (group mean = 34%, N = 16)
Connecticut, Hawaii, Illinois, Iowa, Louisiana, Massachusetts, Missouri, New Jersey, New York, North Dakota, Ohio, Oklahoma, Pennsylvania, Rhode Island, West Virginia, Wyoming

---

1980. Table 5.1 also lists these states; job creation rates were nearly three times as high in the top group as in the bottom group. A comparison of economic, social, and political trends across these groupings of states will help to highlight the trade-offs between job creation and labor costs. Finally, for three of the indicators that showed the closest association with declining labor costs (violent crime rates, the proportion of children living in poverty, and voter turnout), I compared the impact of trends in state labor costs with other state trends that could influence each of these indicators. This analysis will show that declines in state labor costs have a significant independent effect on social well-being in the states. But these negative trends are not counterbalanced by high levels of job creation.[6]

ECONOMIC CONSEQUENCES OF DECLINING LABOR COSTS

The rate of growth in per capita personal income is the first economic consequence of trends in labor costs to be considered. As chapter 4 suggested, it is likely to be slower in states where wages and benefits have declined the most. The second and third economic consequences are the percent changes of families and of children living in poverty. The measures used here are the percent changes, 1980–2000, in the proportion of a state's total population or of children under eighteen years of age who fall below the federal government's official poverty line. At least according to this official indicator, the incidence of poverty fell across the United States from 10.3 percent of families in 1980 to 8.7 percent in 2000.[7] We would expect poverty rates overall and for children under eighteen to have declined the most in states that reduced labor costs the least.

A fourth economic indicator is the trend in income inequality across the states. Langer (1999) used a combination of survey and U.S. Census data to compute an index of income inequality for each state for 1959, 1969, 1979, 1989, and 1995. The higher a state's score on this index (called a Gini index), the more inequitable the distribution of wealth in a state. Thus southern states tend to have the highest levels of inequality, and northwestern and New England states the lowest.[8] According to Langer's index, as well as other measures (DiTella and Vogel 2003; Scott and Leonhardt 2005), income inequality has increased across the states as well as in the United States as a whole since the 1960s. While personal income has been rising (fueled in part by growth at the high end of the income distribution), family or household income has risen more slowly and has become more inequitably distributed since the 1980s (Ryscavage 1999). We should expect states with declining labor costs to have experienced growing inequality over time, as measured by the change in Langer's index of inequality between 1979 and 1995.

Table 5.2 shows economic trends in these four indicators for states with three different levels of change in job creation and labor costs. As expected, per capita personal income increased significantly more rapidly between 1980 and 2000 in the states where labor costs declined the least. Official poverty rates for families declined in all three groups of states, but the decline was smallest in states that experienced the greatest decrease in labor costs. Child poverty rates actually increased more than 12 percent in states where labor costs declined the most. But the lower half of table 5.2 shows no consistent relationship between the growth of a state's labor force and either increases in per capita income or declines in poverty rates. Because so many new jobs have been part time and low paid with few benefits, it is not surprising that they have not raised family living standards. However, both family and child poverty rates increased in states with the lowest levels of job creation.

According to Langer's Gini index, income inequality in the United States as a whole increased 20 percent between 1969 and 1995. Growth in the very top of the income distribution has been fueled by tax cuts, stock market gains, and high levels of compensation for corporate chief executives.

Table 5.2
Percent Change in State Labor Costs, Job Creation Rates, and Economic Trends

Type of Change	Personal Income Per Capita, 1980–2000[a]	Poverty Rate, 1979–99[b]	Child Poverty, 1979–99[b]	Income Inequality, 1979–95[c]
Decline in state labor costs				
High	256.8	−2.3	12.1	5.6
Medium	287.3	−4.1	0.0	4.0
Low	333.6	−3.4	−3.0	3.6
Growth in state labor force				
High	295.7	−2.3	4.8	4.8
Medium	314.7	−12.5	−6.6	4.1
Low	295.7	5.1	10.9	4.2

Source: Unless otherwise indicated, data are from the *Statistical Abstract of the United States.*
[a]In constant 1990 dollars.
[b]Percent of a state's population or of children under 18 living below the official federal poverty level for a family of four.
[c]Gini index for states calculated by Langer (1999).

But in the United States, unlike other advanced capitalist countries, neither taxes nor social welfare policies have provided much help to those at the bottom (Kollmeyer 2003). However, as indicated by table 5.2, states with higher labor costs have experienced *declining* income inequality since 1979, while states where jobs growth has been strong have had significantly *higher* levels of inequality. The correlations in table C.1 in the appendix provide additional statistical evidence for this conclusion.

SOCIAL CONSEQUENCES OF DECLINING LABOR COSTS

Social stress should increase as declining wages and benefits augment pressures on both mental health and family life. My first indicator of social stress is the change in the violent crime rate between 1980 and 2000. Smith (1997) found that state homicide rates reflected levels of resource deprivation in the states fifteen years earlier; his measure of resource deprivation was based on rates of poverty, per capita income, and the African American percent of the population. Conversely, lower levels of unemployment, or higher levels of job creation, in low-wage states could contribute to greater social and economic stability and thus lower crime rates, although Smith's analysis found no relationship between unemployment and state homicide rates.

Two other indicators of social stress reflect changes in family structure: the divorce rate and the number of children born to single mothers as a proportion of all births in a state. The poorest states, and low-income women overall, tend to have the highest rates of out-of-wedlock births (Luker 1996). A fourth indicator of social stress is the trend since 1980 in the suicide rate.

The results presented in table 5.3, though not unexpected, are certainly troubling. Although overall rates of violent crime in the United States have fallen since 1980, they *increased* 9 percent in states with the greatest declines in labor costs, but *fell* by 14 percent in states where labor costs declined the least. Job growth, however, had little effect on crime rates. Suicide rates were 7 percent higher in states experiencing the greatest declines in labor costs, but they were lower in states with slower rates of labor cost declines and lower rather than higher rates of job growth. The proportion of births to unmarried women has increased across the United States since 1980, but it was sharply higher in states with the greatest declines in labor costs as well as in states with the highest levels of job creation. By contrast, births to single mothers have declined sharply in one of the states with the

Table 5.3
Percent Change in State Labor Costs, Job Creation Rates,
and Social Trends, 1980–2000

Type of Change	Violent Crime Rate[a]	Divorce Rate[b]	Suicide Rate	Births to Single Mothers
Decline in state labor costs				
High	9.3	−21.3	7.2	124.2
Medium	2.1	−16.3	−5.9	104.9
Low	−13.8	−25.5	−6.9	94.3
Growth in state labor force				
High	−5.5	−26.4	−1.6	116.2
Medium	7.2	−17.3	1.3	95.6
Low	−4.9	−19.3	−6.1	110.9

Source: Unless otherwise noted, data are from the *Statistical Abstract of the United States.*
[a]*FBI Uniform Crime Reports* data.
[b]Excludes California, Colorado, Indiana, and Louisiana because of missing data.

highest labor costs, New York (L. Kaufman 2004). Thus all three of these adverse social trends are strongly associated with trends in state labor costs.

Divorce presents a somewhat different picture. The overall risk of divorce for individuals (50 percent of all marriages) has changed little since 1980, although this "divorce plateau" in the United States also reflects higher rates of cohabitation. Though divorce rates for women with college degrees have declined, rates of marriage dissolution are considerably higher among minorities and those with less education. Further, these trends have increased considerably since 1980; "those having the least resources to overcome the costs of family dissolution are experiencing the highest levels and the most increase in the risk" (Raley and Bumpass 2003, 256–57).

Confirming these conclusions, table 5.3 shows that while official divorce rates have declined since 1980 in all groups of states,[9] they have declined the most (more than 25 percent) in the states where state labor costs have declined the least. These results support Wilson's (1997) argument that stable family life is more likely when breadwinners can earn a living wage. And they call into question claims by many conservatives and members of the religious right that marriage is the solution to poverty. Instead, higher levels of education and income seem to encourage not only marriage but stable marriages (Jones-DeWeever 2002). As of 2004, the state with the lowest divorce rate was that hotbed of liberalism and gay rights, Massachu-setts—a state with very high labor costs. The southern and western Bible Belt states that voted for George Bush have far higher divorce rates (Holt 2004; Coontz 2005), as do the states creating the most new jobs.

Are these negative social outcomes counterbalanced by higher rates of job growth? Table 5.3 shows little relationship between these social indi-cators and job creation rates, although divorce rates have fallen a bit more in states with higher rather than lower job growth. Again, the likely expla-nation is that most job growth has been in low-wage jobs, and these have not been sufficient to ease the social stresses attributable to declining labor costs and living standards.

LABOR COSTS AND POPULATION TRENDS

Higher labor costs are expected to encourage population growth and in-migration, especially of working-age adults from other states or from abroad. As table 5.4 shows, based on data from the U.S. Census of Popu-lation, overall population grew faster in the states where labor costs declined the least. But the highest rates of population growth are found in states creating the most new jobs. The fastest-growing states in the country (Ne-vada, Florida, Georgia, and Texas) are among the states with the slowest rate of decline in labor costs, whereas several states with stagnant or de-clining populations (North Dakota, West Virginia, and Pennsylvania) fall in the top third of states in reductions in wages and benefits.

Table 5.4 also shows that the proportion of the population over age sixty-five years increased somewhat more rapidly in states where labor costs de-clined the most. States such as Florida, Arizona, and Arkansas welcome retirees, who may bring sizable pension incomes and who often prefer lower-cost regions with milder climates. But relatively few people over sixty-five are in the labor force earning taxable income, and many states exempt pen-sions and residential property owned by senior citizens from taxes.[10] Many people over sixty-five also require expensive social services, particularly pre-scription drug benefits and Medicaid coverage for nursing homes, and the costs of these are shared by the states and the federal government. So an increase in retirees and a decline in the proportion of prime-working-age, taxpaying adults can put serious stress on state budgets, as is the case with Japan and most Western European countries experiencing low birthrates and a rapidly graying population (Hewitt 2002).

Younger workers, particularly the well educated, constitute the most geographically mobile group in American society. So it is hardly surpris-

Table 5.4

Percent Change in State Labor Costs, Job Creation Rates,
and Population Trends, 1980–2000

Type of Change	Population	Persons over Age 65	Immigration (% Foreign Born)
Decline in state labor costs			
High	22.4	17.2	.96
Medium	19.4	14.1	2.46
Low	33.2	13.2	6.16
Growth in state labor force			
High	44.2	11.3	.85
Medium	22.4	15.5	4.79
Low	7.7	17.5	4.13

Source: Data are from the *Statistical Abstract of the United States.*

ing that prime-age workers (age twenty-six to forty-four) are moving to states with higher wages and benefits. These census trends are confirmed by survey research: Recent college graduates most concerned with salaries and employer benefits are the ones most likely to leave the region where they attended college (Hansen, Huggins, and Ban 2003). These trends also pose a dilemma for state budgets: Why invest state taxpayers' money in higher education if the best-educated graduates are likely to leave the state? The decline in state support for higher education in recent years threatens a "race to the bottom" (Donahue 1997), and indeed the United States is starting to fall behind several other industrialized countries in its rate of investment in higher education.[11]

Table 5.4 also indicates that rates of immigration increased more in those states where job growth is strongest. A few high-wage states (California, New York, New Jersey, and Illinois) for many years had high levels of foreign immigration, in part because new immigrants favor communities where they will find compatriots who speak their language and share their customs. But several other states concerned with population decline, such as Maine, Kansas, and Iowa, have made concerted efforts in recent years to attract more immigrants (Hansen 2000). As we saw in chapter 1, Arkansas is one of the states experiencing the highest rates of increase in immigration today. Because immigrants and younger workers have higher birthrates, the overall state population grows faster as well in states with the highest rates of job creation.

TRENDS IN VOTER TURNOUT
AND STATE LABOR COSTS

How do declining labor costs affect political involvement? As discussed above, state voter turnout is expected to decline along with labor costs. I computed the change in voter turnout in gubernatorial elections between 1981–88 and 1996–2002, as described in chapter 3. Average state voter turnout declined from 45 to 42 percent during this period. As figure 5.1 shows, voter turnout declined more than 8 percent in the states with the greatest decline in labor costs after 1980. But in the states with the smallest decline in labor costs, voter turnout actually averaged 4 percent higher in the 1990s than in the 1980s.[12]

Chapter 3 considered the opposite pattern of causation: low voter turnout as an explanation for declines in state labor costs. This relationship held up even when other factors influencing labor costs were considered. So which of these causal links is stronger?[13] The relationship between voter turnout and labor costs may well be reciprocal and mutually reinforcing over time. The political and policy consequences of rising political inequal-

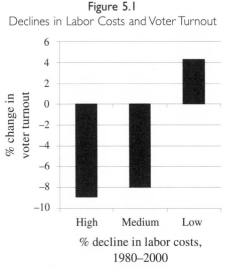

Figure 5.1
Declines in Labor Costs and Voter Turnout

% change in voter turnout

% decline in labor costs,
1980–2000

Note: Voter turnout has increased in states with the lowest declines in labor costs. The percent change in voter turnout is the difference between the average turnout for the years 1996–2002 and 1981–88.

ity include less political support for policies (health care, minimum-wage laws, spending on welfare or education) that would benefit middle- and working-class Americans. The growing perception that government is not responding to people's needs further discourages political activism and voter turnout, especially by the poor and minority groups (Hacker et al. 2004). Thus elected officials have even less incentive to support policies to benefit the less advantaged in our society, and more incentive to cater to the wealthy.

POLICY CONSEQUENCES AND DECLINING STATE LABOR COSTS

How have trends in labor costs or job creation influenced state policies? Previous research on the American states found low voter turnout and weak labor unions to be associated with more regressive tax policies and lower levels of spending on social services. As Korpi and Palme (2003) have shown, neoliberal economic policies have been linked to a worldwide shrinking of the welfare state. Let us therefore consider the relationship between trends in state labor costs and four indicators of public policy: the regressivity of a state's tax system and state per capita spending (both overall and on education and social services).

We might therefore expect those states with declining labor costs to have regressive tax systems (taxes falling more heavily on the poor). The measures of tax regressivity I will use here are the ratio of the tax burden of the highest-income group in a state to that of the lowest 20 percent of wage earners, as well as the percent change, 1991–2003, in this ratio, based on data from Citizens for Tax Justice (CTJ).[14]

Most states have highly regressive systems. Tax burdens average more than 12 percent of income for the lowest 20 percent of family incomes but less than 8 percent for the top earners (CTJ 2003, 1). Only Oregon, Maine, Minnesota, Montana, Idaho, and South Carolina have proportional or mildly progressive state tax systems. States with the highest rates of job growth also have the most regressive tax systems; the poorest families in those states pay more than 2.5 times as much of their income in state/local taxes than the richest income earners do. The ratio is only 1.9 to 1 (still highly regressive) in states with slower job growth (although with considerable variation about the mean in all three categories).

However, the results for trends in tax regressivity are unexpected. Between 1991 and 2003, most states reduced their overall level of regressivity of the major state and local taxes (those on sales, income, and property),

Table 5.5
Percent Change in State Labor Costs,
Job Creation Rates, and Political Trends

Type of Change	Tax Regressivity, 1991–2003[a]	Spending on Education, 1980–2000[b]	Spending on Welfare, 1980–2000[b]	Total Spending 1980–2000[b]
Decline in state labor costs				
High	−20.3	198	419	218
Medium	−9.2	201	341	221
Low	−2.8	229	385	241
Growth in state labor force				
High	−12.2	206	421	234
Medium	−13.3	214	381	226
Low	−5.6	209	339	220

Source: Unless otherwise indicated, data are from the Statistical Abstract of the United States.
[a]Ratio of state tax rates on the top 1 percent of income earners to tax rates on the bottom 20 percent (Citizens for Tax Justice 1991, 2003).
[b]State/local spending per capita.

so that the ratio of taxes on high-versus-low-income families declined. But as table 5.5 shows, the states with the highest rates of decline in labor costs reduced their rates of taxation of low incomes the most relative to rates of taxation on the highest incomes.[15] States with higher rates of job growth also had less regressive taxes in 2003 than in 1991.

We would expect states with declining labor costs to have slower growth in overall state/local spending, and table 5.5 show that they do, even though total spending has increased considerably since 1980. Spending on social services (education and welfare) per capita also suggests the policy impact of state economic trends.[16] It is troubling to see that the states where labor costs declined the most also experienced the slowest rate of increase in spending on education. Future productivity gains are likely to be slower in such states, making it even more difficult for them to compete internationally. But because less-educated citizens are less likely to vote, these low-wage states are unlikely to generate much popular support for increasing investment in human capital.

In contrast, spending on welfare grew much faster in the states where labor costs have declined the most—and welfare spending increased even more sharply in the states with the fastest-growing labor force. Again, the most likely explanation is that while low labor costs may produce more jobs, these jobs are likely to pay very little and provide few benefits. So poor families and their children will need higher levels of social services and income support from both state and federal governments. Because the fastest-growing states also spend relatively less on education, in future years they may face an even higher demand for welfare.

TESTING FOR THE INDEPENDENT EFFECTS OF DECLINING LABOR COSTS

The results presented thus far suggest that declining state labor costs are associated with serious economic and social problems, as well as slower population growth, declining voter turnout, and less spending on education. However, complex social problems such as crime rates, poverty, and births out of wedlock have multiple causes. Even if the trend in state labor costs is an important contributing factor, it is unlikely to be the only one.

Let us therefore take a closer look at three of the most striking trends discussed above: violent crime rates, voter turnout, and the proportion of children living in poverty. I first describe several other social or economic factors that could account for trends in each of these indicators since 1980. I then compare trends in state labor costs to these other explanatory factors. Finally, I consider whether any adverse social or economic effects of lower labor costs are outweighed by higher rates of job creation in the states.

Crime Rates

Violent crime rates in the states have been linked to the proportion of males age eighteen to twenty-five years in the population, because this is the demographic group responsible for the most criminal activity. Crime rates also tend to increase when unemployment is high, and they are higher in urban states and those with a higher proportion of minority residents or people living in poverty (Smith 1997). Recent analyses by economists suggest that access to abortion leads to lower crime rates fifteen or twenty years later. Thus an unintended impact of the 1973 *Roe v. Wade* decision was a drop in crime rates in the 1990s. As Donohue and Levitt (2001) explain, unwanted children, especially those born to young, poor, single, or minority women, are more likely to commit crimes when they grow up. In states where abortion is legal and widely available, the number of unwanted children, and thus crime rates, should be lower in later years.

To test whether declining labor costs have influenced the increase in state crime rates, 1980–2000, I compared them with trends since 1980 in the proportion of the population under age twenty-five, percent minority (Hispanic or African American), and percent of children below the poverty line. And to test for the long-term impact of legalized abortion on crime, I also included the state abortion rate as of 1980.[17] The results displayed in figure 5.2 use the same format as figures 3.3 and 3.4 in chapter 3; the length and direction of the bars in these graphs show whether a given indicator is associated with higher or lower crime rates. The longer the bar, the more important that variable is after taking into account the influence of all the other variables. The statistical analysis on which these graphs are based is described in appendix C.

Figure 5.2 confirms what Donohue and Levitt found: States with high rates of abortion as of 1980 experienced significantly lower crime rates in subsequent years, as indicated by the long bar line running in a negative direction. But even when abortion rates and other explanatory factors are taken into account, slower rates of decline in state labor costs were associated with *significantly lower* rates of violent crime.

Further, figure 5.2 shows that the impact of declining labor costs on crime rates was *not* counterbalanced by high rates of job creation; that bar line is very short. Trends in the African American population had only marginal

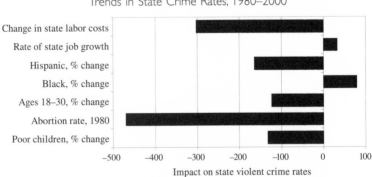

Figure 5.2
Trends in State Crime Rates, 1980–2000

Note: The interval is 1980–2000 for all but the abortion rate. Values are standardized regression coefficients. Those above +200 or below −200 suggest a substantial and statistically significant relationship. Crime rates have fallen in states with increasing labor costs and high rates of abortion in 1980. Job growth has no effect on crime rates.

effects. But an increase in Hispanics was associated with lower crime rates; as Stull and Broadway (2004) suggest, the reason may be the reluctance of non–English speakers to report crimes because of language and cultural barriers, as well as fear of immigration officials. Surprisingly, between 1980 and 2000 child poverty rates were associated with lower rather than higher crime rates, although Smith (1997) reported a strong link between income deprivation and crime rates over a longer time period.

Voter Turnout

Higher turnout rates in the states have been linked to older and more stable populations and to a "moralistic" political environment, where citizen involvement and activist government are valued (Elazar 1984). Historically, southern states and those with more arduous voter registration requirements have had lower turnout. But federal enforcement of the Voting Rights Act of 1965 and motor voter laws facilitating voter registration have mitigated those effects (Highton 2004). In the statistical analysis of voter turnout used for figure 5.3, the mean level of voter turnout 1981–88 was included to test whether any lingering effects of these historic patterns persisted. Party competition is another element expected to influence voter turnout; the

Figure 5.3
Trends in Voter Turnout, 1981–88 to 1996–2002

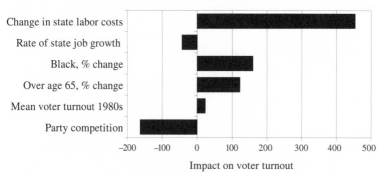

Note: The interval is 1980–2000, except voter turnout is 1981–2002 and party competition is 1980–96. Values are standardized regression coefficients. Those above +200 or below −200 suggest a substantial and statistically significant relationship. Increases in labor costs are the best predictor of increases in voter turnout. Job growth has no effect on voter turnout.

two parties have greater incentives to mobilize their supporters when elections are likely to be close.[18] Because grassroots activism by labor unions has been linked to increased voter turnout, the proportion of the state's public employees unionized as of 1986 was also included; overall union membership could not be used because it is one of the components of the labor costs index.

The graph in figure 5.3 shows that, even with these other factors controlled, states where labor costs declined the least had considerably higher levels of voter turnout after 1996 than in the 1980s. And as with crime rates, higher rates of job creation showed no countervailing impact on voter turnout. The negative bar direction shows that job growth was actually associated with *lower* turnout, because newcomers in fast-growing states tend to be younger and less likely to register or vote than older residents. The fastest-growing state in the United States, Nevada, thus had the lowest rate of voter turnout in 2000: only 31 percent of eligible voters. None of the other variables had much effect; contrary to predictions, voter turnout actually declined more in states with higher levels of interparty competition in the 1980s. Public employee unionization had a positive effect, as expected,[19] but overall labor costs had more of an impact on turnout trends.

Children Living in Poverty

What factors best predict the change since 1980 in the proportion of a state's children living in poverty? States with higher proportions of immigrants and African American residents could be expected to have higher levels of child poverty, as could states where more children have been born to single mothers (Lyter, Sills, and Oh 2003). We should also consider state abortion rates; if abortion is not readily available, more children are likely to be born to families financially unable to care for them. These factors will be compared with trends in state labor costs and job growth.

The longest bar line in figure 5.4 shows that an increased rate of births to single mothers was the best predictor of an increase in child poverty rates between 1979 and 1999. Trends in the Hispanic or African American population had only marginal effects. Yet even after taking these factors into account, child poverty rates were significantly lower in states where labor costs declined the least. And as with crime rates and voter turnout, the bar line for labor cost trends was considerably longer than that for the rate of job creation in the states. However, state abortion rates as of 1980 are associated with more rather than fewer poor children; the reason may be that

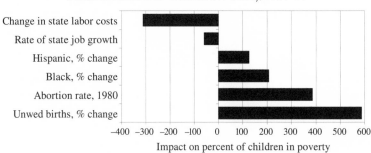

Figure 5.4
Trends in Percent of Children in Poverty, 1979–99

Impact on percent of children in poverty

Note: The interval is 1980–2000 for all but the abortion rate. Values are standardized regression coefficients. Those above +200 or below −200 suggest a substantial and statistically significant relationship. States with higher state labor costs have fewer poor children; states with high rates of births to single mothers have more poor children. Job growth has no effect on child poverty rates.

states with many families living in poverty are likely to have higher abortion rates.[20]

These results illustrated in figures 5.2, 5.3, and 5.4 strongly point to two conclusions. First, trends in state labor costs indeed have a sizable impact on social and political outcomes in the states, even when we consider other factors that might influence crime rates, voter turnout, or child poverty. And second, the deleterious impact of declining labor costs on crime rates, voter turnout, or child poverty is *not* counterbalanced by higher rates of job growth in the states.

Why do high rates of job creation fail to reduce crime rates, increase voter turnout, or decrease child poverty? Table 5.1 suggests one answer: Rapid job growth in the states does *not* produce much overall gain in per capita personal income. Department of Labor statistics demonstrate that most of the fastest-growing occupations in the United States (personal health care aides, waiters, janitors, retail clerks) pay very low wages. Most of these jobs are not unionized, and they seldom offer benefits such as health care (Appelbaum, Bernhardt, and Murname 2003). Further, the job-growth measure is based on payroll data employers submit to the Bureau of Labor Statistics, and people working more than one job may thus be counted twice. But many people are working more than one job because their pay is so low (Warren and Tyagi 2003). An increase in the number of "jobs" reported by a state's employers may therefore represent not economic growth but people's efforts to maintain family incomes and living standards in an era of rising housing and transportation prices, soaring college tuition, and declining pay and benefits.

CONCLUSION

This chapter has shown that reductions in labor costs can have serious economic and social as well as political consequences in the states: higher rates of poverty, violent crime, suicide, and births to single mothers. In states where labor costs have declined the most, state/local spending on education has grown more slowly and voter turnout has declined considerably since the 1980s.

At least by one measure (that of CTJ), state and local taxes have become slightly less regressive than in the early 1990s in states where labor costs have declined the most. However, in those same states, the poor still pay a far higher proportion of their income in taxes than do the wealthy. These results from the American states thus support the conclusions of the APSA's Task Force on Inequality (2004) about rising inequality, less government spending on social services, and declining levels of civic involvement.

The promise of the "great American job machine" is that the economy and society will benefit when more people are able to find work. But high rates of job growth in the states do not appear to be linked to improvements in most of the indicators considered here. Nor does rapid job growth counter the downside of declining labor costs; in fact, the link between job growth and overall population growth may add to social stress. And because so many new jobs are low paying and offer few benefits, they do not help families or individuals cope with the pressures of inadequate housing, lack of health care, or family instability.

Weber and Brace (1999, 13) criticize the states' emphasis on the quantity rather than the quality of jobs:

> Many jobs secured by predatory economic competition between the states and their localities are of the low-wage and low-skill variety. While this approach may provide short-term fixes to a state or local economy, in the long run it creates a potentially vulnerable workforce, subject to the vicissitudes of a rapidly changing economic landscape. Too often, low-skill jobs gained by lavish tax concessions or financial inducements do not end up producing commensurate revenues.

American voters (and politicians) remain deeply concerned about unemployment, and strongly committed to the virtues of hard work and

What Matters

- States where labor costs have declined the most have lower personal income and more poverty.
- States where labor costs have declined the most have significantly higher rates of violent crime, suicide, divorce, and births to single mothers.
- States where labor costs have declined the most spend less on education and more on welfare, but their taxes have become somewhat less regressive since 1991.
- Inequality has increased in states where labor costs have declined.
- Population and immigration are increasing faster in states with higher rates of job creation.
- Voter turnout has increased since the 1980s in states where labor costs have fallen the least, but it has decreased where labor costs have fallen the most.
- Most new jobs pay little and offer few benefits, thus increasing stress on families.
- High rates of state job creation do *not* counter the effects of declining labor costs on crime, voter turnout, or the proportion of children living in poverty.

individual effort. But can we find ways to maintain high rates of job creation without the adverse social and political consequences of declining labor costs? The final chapter of this book considers possible remedies for this dilemma.

CHAPTER SIX

· Conclusion: Lessons Learned and Policy Options for the States

THIS BOOK HAS FOCUSED on trends in labor costs in the fifty U.S. states between 1970 and 2000. By developing a measure combining wages, union density, right-to-work laws, and state-provided benefits (unemployment benefits and workers' compensation), I have been able to analyze labor costs across time and across the fifty states. I have explored why states differ, sometimes markedly, in labor costs, and what economic and social consequences have ensued.

What can a study of state labor costs tell us? First of all, the impact of globalization on the states is surprisingly modest; the states with the highest levels of exports or foreign direct investment have actually reduced labor costs less than have more insular states. I also found little evidence that ties to the international economy have led to policy convergence across the states. Further, higher rather than lower labor costs provide a comparative advantage in international trade because of the links between productivity and labor costs. Clearly, many states and economic sectors have lost jobs to lower-cost producers overseas (although no government agency collects reliable data on this politically sensitive indicator). But often low-wage states and regions prove to be the most vulnerable to such competition. The Carolinas, with the lowest labor costs in the United States, have lost thousands of jobs in the textile industries (Becker 2004). But these losses are offset by export and investment gains in other states and industries.

Second, the downward movement in state labor costs since 1970 reflects domestic political factors rather than levels of exposure to the international economy. As chapter 3 showed, increasing Republican and conservative influence in the states has been associated with declines in labor costs. States with higher voter turnout, more Democratic state legislatures, strong unions, and higher levels of education have experienced much less decline in wages and benefits. But levels of state exports or foreign direct invest-ment had little effect on trends in labor costs.

Third, interstate competition in the American federal system is a major factor driving down labor costs in the United States. Most analysts of the weakness of American labor have paid little attention to the American states or to interstate competition for business, but I have documented the myriad ways in which states have tried to compete by reducing labor costs and con-straining union influence. Encouraging such interstate competition was a deliberate policy fostered by opponents of New Deal efforts to support la-bor and raise living standards, as Mettler (1998) has argued. The rhetoric of global competition has provided a new rationale for long-standing conser-vative and business efforts to weaken labor unions and keep wages low.

Fourth, this analysis points to the need to add labor costs to any analy-sis of state economic or social policies. Political scientists who study the American states have considered interstate competition in other areas (taxa-tion, innovation, welfare spending, environmental regulation), yet they have largely ignored labor costs. But as the time-series analysis in chapter 4 dem-onstrates, state labor costs do have economic consequences, both positive (higher rates of growth in gross state product, personal income, and exports) and negative (higher unemployment, slower rates of job creation). Further, these effects are significant even when we take into account the influence of state/local taxes or federal labor costs. The strong impact of federal de-fense spending on state economic growth reinforces arguments by Brace (2001) and others that the analysis of state policies cannot ignore the fed-eral context.

Fifth and finally, a comparative perspective suggests that American fed-eralism is a major reason why labor costs tend to be lower, and labor unions weaker, in the United States than in other industrialized countries. As the European Union (EU) continues to debate the economic ramifications of the "social wage" and employment protection, it might consider the nega-tive social consequences I have documented in the American states that have reduced labor costs the most. The World Economic Forum's 2004–5 *Global Competitiveness Report* (World Economic Forum 2004) shows that many high-wage European countries are flourishing in the international economy, and the EU exports far more to the United States than America exports to the EU. Conversely, the American states might consider some of the les-sons Europe has to offer about human capital investment and restraint of competition for business subsidies.

At least before 2000, states with higher labor costs did tend to have higher rates of unemployment and slower rates of job creation. And the

United States, with lower labor costs relative to Europe, has been creating jobs at a much faster pace. But as described in chapter 5, declining state labor costs have social consequences as well: higher rates of crime, divorce, suicide, poverty, and births to single mothers, as well as lower voter turnout and lower levels of state spending on education. Nor did higher job creation rates ameliorate the adverse social consequences of declining labor costs for violent crime rates, voter turnout, or the proportion of children living in poverty.

The analysis of the economic and social effects of state labor costs in chapters 4 and 5 laid bare the central dilemma facing state governments (and all Americans): Is it possible to provide better worker protection and decent wages without costing jobs or cutting benefits? A number of possible resolutions for this central dilemma have been advocated by economists, labor, the business community, educators, and politicians. These include human capital investment, strengthening labor unions, reforming health care, and measures to raise workers' incomes and create better jobs. The European experience with globalization also suggests some policy options for restraining interstate competition, maintaining quality of life, and mitigating the burdens of job losses due to imports.

The rest of this chapter considers the pros and cons of these alternatives—and their political feasibility for the American states. But most states (and the United States as a whole) have been pursuing low-wage strategies for many years now. I argue that this represents a political choice, not an inevitable consequence of globalization, and can therefore be changed.

THE ECONOMISTS' PREFERRED ALTERNATIVE: INVESTMENT IN HUMAN CAPITAL

Most mainstream economists argue that the best way to raise wages and improve living standards is to increase productivity by investing in human capital (Brown, Green, and Lauder 2001; Baumol, Blackman, and Wolff 1989; Reich 1991). Massey (2004) anticipates that the soaring productivity gains of the past few years will soon translate into more and better jobs: "Businesses have wrested about all the additional output they can from existing workers and must start adding workers if they want to keep growing. With more people getting jobs and receiving paychecks, consumer spending can remain robust, creating the sort of internal growth fuel that keeps an economy humming during good times."

As the business cycle finally recovers from the 2000–1 recession, some employment gains are indeed likely, and the pace of job creation picked up in mid-2005. But gains in wages or incomes are far less probable.

Workers in the United States and in other weak-union countries have simply been unable to acquire for themselves much of the benefits of recent productivity gains (Volgy, Schwarz, and Imwalle 1996). The Economic Policy Institute (2004, fig. 13) has tracked the relative shares of labor compensation and corporate profits in income growth during economic recoveries since 1950. Its data show that the corporate-profits share of income growth reached an all-time high in 2003 (41 percent), relative to labor compensation's share (38 percent). In 1950, the comparable shares were 10 and 69 percent, respectively.

Despite the record long hours that Americans work, wages and family incomes have been stagnant since the 1970s, except for modest increases during the economic boom of the late 1990s. Consumer debt and bankruptcies have risen, but wealth has not, and the proportion of Americans mired in poverty remains high. As I have shown in chapters 4 and 5, high rates of job creation in the states have *not* led to increases in personal income, and they have not countered most of the adverse social effects of declines in labor costs.

Investment in education and worker training (or retraining) are proven strategies for boosting both wealth and productivity. Countries such as China and India are experiencing the benefits in economic growth from years of investment in human capital, both from their own resources and from investments by foreign corporations (Tonelson 2002). Friedman (2005) attributes much of Ireland's recent spectacular growth to public investment in education. That country plans to double the number of Ph.D. holders it produces in science and engineering by 2010. However, public investment in higher education in the United States has been decreasing rather than increasing as a share of state budgets, and most states have shifted the burden of tuition at state colleges and universities to students and their families (Hansen 2001a). Tuition at both public and private institutions of higher education has been rising much faster than inflation, and many students today graduate owing thousands in student loans. The National Education Association (NEA 2004) estimates that the cost of higher education (tuition minus grant aid) has actually increased more for students attending public rather than private institutions.

In his summer 2000 address to the National Governors' Association meeting in State College, Pennsylvania, Federal Reserve Board chairman Alan Greenspan urged the governors to invest more in human capital in their respective states. He argued that such investment was essential to enhanced productivity and economic growth in the global economy. But a RAND Corporation report (1997) described exactly the opposite trend: "What we found was a time bomb ticking under the nation's social and economic foundations. At a time when the level of education needed for productive employment is increasing, the opportunity to go to college will be denied to millions of Americans unless sweeping changes are made to control costs, halt sharp increases in tuition, and increase other sources of revenue."

Donahue (1997) foresees a "race to the bottom" in higher education, for two reasons. First, almost all states are facing severe budget constraints because of popular resistance to tax increases, reduced federal aid, unfunded mandates, and the rising cost of health care. Higher education spending can more easily be curtailed than can programs such as Medicaid or corrections. And second, highly educated young people are the most mobile group in American society and can easily move to locations offering more jobs and higher wages. The top five states in educational attainment are all in the West and have fast-growing, younger populations. But many states with a less educated workforce, such as Pennsylvania, West Virginia, and Missouri, have aging populations and high rates of out-migration by college graduates (Progressive Policy Institute 2000). Legislators in these states are increasingly reluctant to invest in higher education if graduates are likely to leave.

The Business Roundtable warns that the decline in American science and engineering degrees "could represent a profound threat to the country's global competitiveness" (cited in Gaynor 2005a). As interest in technological fields by American students has diminished, science and engineering programs at state universities have come to rely on foreign student enrollments in recent years. But because of rising tuition and problems obtaining visas due to terrorism concerns, these enrollments are now declining (Institute of International Education 2004). Fewer foreign students will reduce university enrollments and revenue, and could also hamper ongoing research efforts. Concerns have been expressed about a "reverse brain drain," with the best and the brightest students from abroad going to European rather than American universities (Webber 2004).

Political restrictions on American scientific research on topics such as stem cells and global warming could also drive away scientists, along with the patents or products they might develop (Florida 2004). California is trying to buck the trend; state voters in 2004 approved a $3 billion bond issue to provide funding for stem cell research for ten years. California hopes to attract top researchers, philanthropists, and investors to the state and boost its already considerable biotechnology industry by giving scientists a path around President George W. Bush's August 2001 ban on federal funding of new embryonic stem cell research. Several other states—including New Jersey, Connecticut, Massachusetts, Wisconsin, Minnesota, and Maryland—have also appropriated funds to encourage stem cell research and attract biotechnology investment (Jones 2005). All such states rank in the highest quartile of my indicator of state labor costs.

In contrast to higher education, public investment in elementary and secondary education has increased, with some states and localities reporting gains in student achievement (Grissmer and Flanagan 1998). As noted in chapter 5, total state per capita spending on education has risen over 200 percent since 1980 (in current dollars). Sadly, the rate of increase has been slowest in states with the greatest declines in labor costs. The United States still lags far behind most other industrial democracies in mathematics and reading scores, and high school dropout rates (especially among African Americans and Hispanics) remain high. The federal No Child Left Behind Act has mandated higher standards and extensive testing, but it has never been fully funded, and states are using easier tests of student achievement to avoid cut-offs of federal funds (Dillon 2005). Many states and localities have been forced to lay off teachers, increase class sizes, and close schools; fast-growing states like Florida and Nevada face severely crowded classrooms. New York City faces a court-ordered increase of $5.6 *billion* to provide adequate funding for its overcrowded and dilapidated schools, after years of legislative inaction (Baker 2004).

"Worker training" (or retraining) has been a politically popular mantra for both Democratic and Republican elected officials, and it is often advocated as the preferred policy option for people who lose their jobs because of deindustrialization, closure of military bases, or foreign competition. Clearly, postsecondary education and lifelong learning are needed to keep pace with a changing economy. But the rhetoric of support for worker training has seldom been matched by actual funding. Thus most of the savings from the post–cold war decline in defense spending were "used to reduce the fiscal deficit of the federal government rather than to expand civilian public investment in physical and human capital" (Bischak 1999, 16), and even the Bill Clinton administration's 1994 "public investment package" for education, training, and physical capital showed no new net investment. Moreover, it is hard to envision what "retraining" could be recommended for people with advanced degrees in computing or engineering who have lost their jobs to India, China, and Ireland because of outsourcing. Congress imposes H1-B visa fees on employers to pay for job-training programs for high-technology workers, but so far most of the money is going to basic programs for disadvantaged youth, single parents, and entry-level computer jobs (Yeomans 2001, Uchitelle 2006).

Community colleges and worker-training programs are increasingly characterized by soaring demand, high and rising tuition, and limited public funding. Howard (1997) describes how administrative problems and confusion over state/local/federal responsibility have reduced political support for job training. He concludes: "For a nation supposedly devoted to the values of work and self-sufficiency, the United States has done remarkably little with employment and training programs. The national government spends less on job training than on AFDC [Aid to Families with Dependent Children], which benefits many people who do not work for wages" (p. 161). States and local governments are also reducing public investment in this training and requiring higher tuition from community college students (NEA 2004).

The Trade Adjustment Assistance Act, initially adopted in 1974, was designed to help people who lose their jobs due to import competition. Eligible workers receive job search assistance, a relocation allowance, and extended unemployment compensation benefits as long as they are enrolled in approved classroom and/or on-the-job training. However, this act has never been adequately funded, and most of the jobs for which training is offered pay far less than those lost in manufacturing.[1] Many displaced workers have been denied eligibility or access to training programs (however, in 2005 the act was to be extended to some farmers and fishermen). Also, workers over the age of forty-five or fifty years are unlikely to be rehired regardless of their training, in part because of employer concern with the cost of their health care. But as Kletzer (2002) has shown, these are precisely the workers most adversely affected by import competition.

Lafer (2002) concludes that much of the federal and state/local funding for job training has been wasted. Some of it has gone to politically well-connected but educationally dubious diploma mills, which collect federal or state grants for student tuition and then close their doors. Training programs have been set up for jobs that no longer exist, and training for those that do often lacks appropriate instructors or equipment. Jobs programs designed for disadvantaged workers or welfare recipients often show little evidence of effectiveness (in part because of limited funding), and thus lose political support (Mucciaroni 1992). Students pay high tuition and may go into debt to do so, but many fail to graduate. Although only 10 percent of community college graduates go on to attain B.A. or B.S. degrees, people who do receive A.A. degrees or complete other postsecondary training tend to earn considerably more than those with only high school degrees or general equivalency diplomas, according to U.S. Census data on employment and earnings. So greater public investment in postsecondary job training could generate positive results, but only if funds are targeted to accredited institutions rather than diploma mills.

For many low-wage earners working long hours or holding down two jobs to make ends meet, finding the time or the money to invest in additional training or education is a difficult challenge. Workers' motivations have become a key element of human capital theory (Brown, Green, and Lauder 2001). However, if workers' increased skills are unlikely to be rewarded with higher wages, benefits, and job security, they have less incentive to invest in acquiring new skills. Because many working-class youth in the United Kingdom and African American males conclude that their future employment prospects are dismal, they drop out of secondary school and avoid vocational training programs that might indeed improve their job prospects (Royster 2003). Howell (1994) reports that even though educational test scores for young black males improved dramatically between 1971 and 1988, their real wages actually declined. It is thus not surprising that college enrollment by African American males has been falling since the 1990s (Dyer 2005).

Education remains high on the list of voters' concerns. Citizen ballot initiatives have mandated increased state spending on education and smaller class sizes in states such as Florida and California. But given the soaring budget deficits and the policy priorities of the George W. Bush administration, greater public investment in education does not appear to be a likely solution to a low-wage economy.

What about the private sector? Some larger firms like IBM do provide considerable on-the-job training, and workplace education has proven to be highly beneficial for low-wage workers (Ahlstrand, Bassi, and McMurrier 2003). Firms can also negotiate with state and local governments to have local community colleges train their workers in specific skills at public expense; such arrangements may be part of the incentive packages used to attract business. Although most businesses favor a more highly skilled labor force, they are reluctant to invest much in training workers for fear that free-riding competitors will hire them away. Some business groups like the Computer Systems Policy Project have advocated greater public investment in education or support for university research and development, to spur innovation and long-term job growth (Lohr 2004). But as Martin (1995) has shown, small businesses are better organized, and their preferences for lower taxes and less government spending usually predominate in Washington and state capitals.

Instead of worker training, Howard (1997, 82) argues that employers have been "taking a 'low-road' human resources strategy, one aimed above

all at reducing labor costs." They have contracted out to low-wage suppliers, relocated to lower-wage sites, and pushed for union wage concessions.
In response to widespread business reports of shortages of information technology workers, the Department of Labor has approved over 2 million H-
1B visas since 2000 to permit well-educated foreign workers to take jobs
in engineering and computer science, usually at wages well below those of
similarly trained Americans (Bjorhus 2002). Outsourcing even highly
skilled work to low-wage countries like India has also expanded. Forger
(2004) claims that forty-two of the fifty states now use offshore call centers
to handle inquiries about their food stamp programs.

A NEW ROLE FOR ORGANIZED LABOR?

As this analysis has shown, labor costs are indeed higher in states with higher
levels of union density. Other research in political science has linked unionization to a number of progressive policies in the American states (Radcliff
and Saiz 1998), as well as to higher voter turnout. Countries with greater
worker power have been more successful in protecting their citizens from
the negative consequences of globalization. However, union membership
(particularly in the private sector) has been declining for a generation.
Would revitalizing the American labor movement be a remedy for the ongoing decline in wages and benefits?

Organized labor is widely regarded in the business community as an
obstacle to productivity and a major factor discouraging investment. As
discussed in chapter 2, the empirical evidence is mixed as to the actual
impact of unions on employment and productivity trends in the states.
Chapter 4 showed that higher labor costs have positive links to growth in
gross state product, exports, and personal income. But any strategy to
strengthen unions has been met with implacable opposition by neoliberal
economists and business leaders, as well as by most Republicans.

Given this opposition, organized labor faces an uphill fight. The National Labor Relations Board (NLRB) has often failed to respond to claims
of unfair labor practices; union organizers have been fired for efforts to
promote union recognition; and "paycheck-protection" laws threaten to
reduce labor's role in elections. Businesses have demanded give-backs in
wages and benefits and higher copayments for health coverage. Courts have
upheld abrogation of prior commitments for employee pensions and health
care. Threats to close factories and relocate to lower-wage states or countries have been used to discourage union organizing. The country's largest
employer, Wal-Mart, is an implacable foe of unionization, and in 2005

closed its only unionized store in Quebec after its workers voted to support a union (MacKenzie 2005).

Organized labor also faces serious internal debates about its future strategies. Many white male workers are reluctant to admit female, immigrant, or minority members, fearing they will undercut wages, and are adamantly opposed to affirmative action (one reason for their considerable support for George W. Bush in 2000 and 2004). AFL-CIO president John Sweeney has urged union locals to invest more resources in organizing, but many have failed to do so. Unions often compete with each other in certification elections rather than reaching out to unorganized workers. One recent proposal would consolidate the current sixty unions into fewer than twenty to increase their bargaining power (Greenhouse 2004b). Another strategy is to focus organizing efforts on a particular geographic area or a few employers; Wal-Mart is a top priority, and union efforts have thus far kept it out of New York and Chicago. A third strategy is to penalize employers with particularly onerous labor practices, via negative publicity or consumer boycotts (Lerner 2003). Robert Greenwald's critical documentary, *Wal-Mart: The High Cost of Low Prices*, received widespread publicity in late 2005.

Another proposal backed by labor is enactment of the Employee Free Choice Act, supported by most Democrats in Congress and by Senator John Kerry during the 2004 presidential election. Before the Taft-Hartley Act, workers could gain union certification at a workplace if a majority of them simply signed union cards in private. But Taft-Hartley permitted companies to call for NLRB-supervised elections, which unions are increasingly likely to lose. NLRB elections

> gave the company time and a mechanism to use intimidation and scare tactics to discourage union votes. Instead of workers self-organizing and taking the democratic decision to form a union, now the company was allowed to be a part of that decision making process. Now the employer could effectively use the NLRB process of supervised elections to help determine when the vote is taken and under circumstances favorable to the company. And it started a whole industry of anti-labor lawyer consultants and organizations ready to intervene for the employer. (Marshall 2004)

The Employee Free Choice Act would also mandate binding arbitration to reach a first contract if one is not negotiated in a timely way; currently employers can stall for months or years before negotiating a first union contract. And last, the legislation would increase the penalties for companies and employers that use illegal tactics to stop workers from organizing. However, such legislation has little chance in a Republican-dominated Congress, even with international support from Human Rights Watch.

Another potential strategy for rejuvenating labor is advocated by Freeman and Rogers (2002): open source unionism. Prounion workers in firms where most employees prefer to remain nonunion could still affiliate with national or international unions; this strategy was used in the early years of AFL organizing. Open source unionism could expand union membership rolls and revenue from dues, as well as providing a base for future organizing efforts within firms. It could also benefit workers who change jobs often in an increasingly dynamic economy.

Despite serious obstacles, there are a few bright spots for union efforts to increase worker power. One is the persistence of the public employee unions described in chapter 3, and their success in mobilizing voters to defeat antiunion legislation. Another is that public support for labor unions is as strong today as it was in the 1970s; many workers not now represented by unions claim that they would like to be (Gallup Poll 2001). A 1997 Teamsters strike against United Parcel Service succeeded at least in part because public opinion strongly favored extending employee benefits to part-time workers (Geoghegan 1997). And third, organizing efforts have succeeded in places such as Los Angeles (janitors) and Las Vegas (casino workers and hotel employees), because employers need such service workers in these popular destination cities and cannot credibly threaten to close or relocate.

Nevertheless, worker power in the United States (and in most American states) is likely to remain far weaker than that in most other industrial democracies. It may take a major economic crisis, or a serious threat of widespread loss of benefits such as health care or Social Security, to convince American workers to vote on the basis of pocketbook issues rather than the foreign policy and "values" concerns that have dominated political discourse during recent elections (Frank 2004). Since its losses in 2004, the Democratic Party has been debating ways to combat the perceived Republican advantage on values and combating terrorism and to shift the political agenda back to health, education, and economic issues, but Democratic partisans remain deeply divided about future strategies.

CHANGING HEALTH CARE

If organized labor is likely to remain weak, support for job creation and good benefits may come from another source: the American business community. This somewhat surprising conclusion is based on the delete-rious economic impact of soaring health care costs. Unlike in Canada, Japan, and most European countries, where publicly financed health care is a basic right of citizenship, in the United States health care has largely been provided through one's employer. Unless they are over age sixty-five and eligible for Medicare, or qualify for Medicaid for reasons of poverty or disability, millions of Americans who work part time or for smaller companies lack health care benefits.

Providing health care benefits increasingly puts large companies at a comparative disadvantage. Major U.S. corporations like General Motors must compete with automakers in Japan or Italy, which do not have to pay health care costs for their employees. In 2004 GM paid $60 billion in health care benefits, which added about $1,500 to the price of every car and truck it built. With nearly half of all United Automobile Workers members eli-gible to retire within five years, GM also faces costly obligations to pro-vide future medical benefits to retirees (Garsten 2004). The double-digit annual increase in health care costs is a major reason why job creation has been so slow ever since the 2000–1 recession. And companies facing finan-cial difficulties (United Airlines and US Airways, coal mining companies) have been turning to the bankruptcy courts to get out from under con-tractual obligations to provide health care or pensions to retirees.[2]

As Rivlin (1992) argued, the cost of health care is hurting the whole U.S. economy. America spends far more per capita on health care as a per-cent of its gross national product than do competing nations, even though it ranks far worse in infant mortality and life expectancy. Rivlin estimated that 30 percent of health care spending goes to administrative costs and insurers rather than to the direct provision of medical services. President Clinton's proposal for national health care argued that the control of health care costs would free up private resources for other, more productive in-vestments. Advocates of single-payer government health insurance coun-tered that their preferred option would leave the health insurance industry out of the picture altogether and thus save even more; but for a variety of political reasons, the single-payer option was never seriously considered by Clinton's health care task force (Jacobs and Shapiro 2000; Skocpol 1997).

Yet health care benefits are a necessity for companies seeking to attract and retain skilled workers and highly educated professionals. Many larger companies would actually prefer greater public investment in health and in worker training, because both their workers and their own bottom lines would ultimately benefit (Martin 1995). Mares (2000) likewise found strong employer support for European welfare state programs such as unemployment insurance. However, in the United States opposition from small businesses and insurers effectively killed Clinton's health care proposals, because these groups had more to lose and were far better organized than the larger employers (Martin 1995; Skocpol 1997).

Another strategy to reduce health care costs received attention during the 2004 election campaign: catastrophic health care benefits. Kerry's proposal was that the government would pay 75 percent of the bills for prolonged or serious illnesses after a certain dollar amount in health care costs (e.g., $30,000 in 2006) had been reached. To qualify for the subsidy, companies would have to agree to cover their employees and to share the savings with workers. Kerry said the plan would save workers with family coverage an average of about $1,000 per year. This was touted as a major benefit to small business in particular, where the medical expenses of a single employee or family member with cancer or multiple sclerosis could drive up the company's health care premiums.

A precedent exists for such coverage: Since the 1980s, Congress has authorized payment under Medicare for kidney dialysis for persons of any age, who usually require this expensive treatment for the rest of their lives and would in most cases quickly exceed the limits on any employer health benefits or private insurance. Shifting the burden of other catastrophic illnesses to the public sector would reduce employers' health care costs and thereby permit them to hire additional employees. Ford Motor Company chairman Bill Ford and other business leaders are now advocating catastrophic health care reform. Because of this business support, catastrophic health care benefits may receive a sympathetic hearing even in a Republican-controlled Congress. But the costs may be high; the Emory University economist Kenneth Thorpe estimated the program would cost $653 billion over ten years. Kerry would have financed the plan by rolling back tax cuts for people who earn $200,000 or more a year (Wallack 2004). A Republican Congress is more likely to make such tax cuts permanent, but it may find other ways to respond to business concerns with soaring health care costs, such as imposing limits on medical liability.

INCREASING WORKERS' WAGES

Several proposals have been made to increase workers' wages directly through government action: raising the minimum wage, pay equity for women, living-wage laws, and tax breaks for the working poor. Some states have taken action on each of these.

During the 2004 presidential campaign, Kerry advocated raising the minimum wage to $7 an hour; the current minimum of $5.15 has not been raised since 1997. The public strongly favors increasing the minimum wage (77 percent, according to a 2003 Pew Research Center poll), but further action by the current Republican Congress is unlikely. However, the states listed in table 2.1 already have minimum wages set above the federal level, and others may follow. Although this remains a highly contentions and partisan issue, most economists now estimate that the unemployment impact of a higher minimum wage would be small (Levin-Waldman 2001). Higher wages would give workers more to spend and boost consumer demand, thus having a multiplier effect on the economy that could create even more jobs. And many states with higher minimum wages are generating new jobs at a healthy rate.

Other proposals to increase workers' wages have focused on more equitable wages for women, whose wages for full-time, year-round work are only about 75 percent of what men earn. Two-thirds of minimum-wage workers are women, and female-headed households are far more likely to be poor than households headed by single men or with two wage-earners. According to data from the Bureau of Labor Statistics, women earn less than men in almost every profession and job category. Some of the wage discrepancies are due to women's lack of education or training in higher-paying fields and to the obstacles many women face in balancing career and family; the United States is the only industrialized country with no paid family leave (Stetson 1997). Women have also failed to benefit from most job-training and economic development programs (Harlan 1989); they are usually steered into low-paying jobs in the "pink-collar ghetto" rather than better-paying jobs in construction or high technology.

Women may also lack some of the negotiating skills that men have used more effectively to achieve financial recompense for their training and accomplishments on the job (Babcock and Laschever 2003). But economists have concluded that sex discrimination, in recruitment, hiring, and promotion, also accounts for much of the gender gap in wages (Goldin 1990; Kelly 1991; Boraas and Rodgers 2003). Women have won several major sex-discrimination lawsuits, and they have received large class-action settlements from firms such as Mitsubishi and Morgan Stanley. However, most individual women lack the resources to pursue pay equity through the legal system or the large backlog of cases at the Equal Employment Opportunity Commission. But a class-action lawsuit is pending against Wal-Mart, alleging that the company's pay and promotion policies discriminate against women.

Paying women comparable wages would certainly boost family and individual incomes. It would move many women and their families out of poverty and off welfare (Lyter, Sills, and Oh 2003). Pay equity has been a major goal of the feminist movement and was one of the selling points for passage of the Equal Rights Amendment; Kerry advocated pay equity during the 2004 campaign as part of his appeal to women voters (Halbfinger 2004). Pay equity may be easier to achieve in the public sector; because of Civil Service laws and merit-based pay scales, Washington, DC, is the best location for women workers in the country, and women's wages there are 90 percent of men's. Women in the armed services also receive equitable pay and benefits.

A few states, such as Minnesota, have enacted comparable-worth legislation for public-sector employees. But most states have found it politically difficult to find the resources to equalize wages for comparable work by public employees, and they have even fewer options for private-sector employees (Sorenson 1994). Instead, as noted in chapter 3, a large pool of women available to work for low wages has been used as a selling point for economic development. Gender disparities in the nonprofit sector, whose employees are predominantly female, are even worse than in the private sector; many nonprofits evidently capitalize on the desires of women to "help others" and to gain experience (Hansen, Ban, and Huggins 2003).

Living-wage laws offer a third strategy for raising workers' wages directly. Such laws mandate wage levels sufficient for a full-time worker to support a family above the federal poverty line; many also have provisions concerning benefits such as health insurance. As of 2004, living-wage ordinances had been enacted in more than seventy localities (Economic Policy Institute 2005). These ordinances usually apply only to companies that have a contract with the city or county government, or have received economic development subsidies; some localities exempt nonprofits. The rationale is that local governments should not subsidize companies that pay poverty-level wages, and that the privatization of public services should not lead to compensation losses for displaced public employees (who tend to be disproportionately female and/or minority).

Obviously, most employers object to being compelled to pay above-market wage rates. Many businesses have reacted to living-wage ordinances by contesting their legality or persuading friendly state governments to preempt them (as Florida's legislature did in 2003). Other cities and counties have rejected living-wage proposals because they feared the result would be a bad business climate, lower business investment, and thus even fewer jobs. However, proponents (including many labor unions and social service agencies) argue that such laws only apply to a small proportion of workers and thus will not have adverse employment effects; Weisbrot and Sforza-Roderick (2003) found no adverse effects in Baltimore. Advocates claim that the result of much state and local economic development policy has been subsidies for low-wage, nonunion firms that offer few benefits (LeRoy and Slocum 1999). Living-wage laws are thus viewed as a fair exchange for the often generous subsidies private companies may receive for moving into a region or for highway or stadium construction. Higher wages for workers would also increase consumer spending, add to tax revenues, and reduce the need for social services, thus helping balance local government budgets (Luce 2004).

A fourth strategy is to use the tax code to raise incomes for the working poor. The Earned Income Tax Credit (EITC) was initiated in 1975 and expanded during the Reagan years with strong bipartisan support. As of 2004, fourteen states with personal income taxes had adopted EITCs as well.[3] Most families qualifying for EITCs make too little to owe income taxes. They may be eligible for a cash grant (a refundable tax credit) if the amount of the EITC exceeds their income tax obligation. At the lowest income levels, the tax credit increases with every dollar a worker earns. The Center for Budget and Policy Priorities estimated that more than 4 million people have been lifted above the poverty level by EITCs (Johnson 2001).

The political appeal of EITCs is twofold. First, because they are administered by the Internal Revenue Service (IRS) (or by state revenue officials), no additional bureaucracy is required to determine eligibility or provide services. And second, unlike welfare payments, they benefit people who are already working. Benefits are on a sliding scale and are much more generous to families with dependent children. Current regulations offer higher benefits for married couples than for nonmarried partners with exactly the same incomes—part of the Bush administration's ongoing efforts to encourage marriage.

However, under the Bush administration, the IRS has stepped up its audits of people qualifying for EITC. One in forty-seven EITC recipients is audited by the IRS, compared with 1 in 145 of people making over $100,000, even though overpayments may only be a few hundred dollars and are usually due to administrative error rather than fraud (Mitchell 2002). Further Republican proposals for a national sales tax, or for a flat-rate income tax with fewer deductions or exemptions, would also do away with EITCs at the federal level (Rosenbaum 2004). The result of either of these proposals would be an even more regressive tax structure without any compensation for the working poor, who already pay far more in sales and Social Security taxes than the wealthy.

Wolff (1994) has proposed a "wealth tax" on assets above $100,000 (excluding houses, pensions, and a maximum amount on cars). Similar taxes are imposed in the Netherlands, Norway, Iceland, and Sweden. Wolff argues that this tax would spur equity by encouraging a switch from consumption of luxuries to more productive, job-creating assets. However, since 1980 states have been reducing rather than increasing tax rates on higher incomes.

Finally, some groups and individuals have initiated private actions to increase the incomes of low-wage workers. In New York City, Greenwich Village residents are urging area retailers to raise wages, provide health coverage, and encourage unions, and they have threatened to boycott retailers that do not participate (Greenhouse 2004a). Students on a number of Ivy League campuses have organized to assist campus service workers; Gordon Lafer dedicated his 2002 book on worker training to the Federation of University Employees Strike Fund. Widespread criticism of Wal-Mart's labor practices by labor unions, the media, and consumers led it to make the June 2004 announcement to its shareholders that it "would make several changes at the corporate and store levels to improve conditions for its workers" (Hays 2004), although it remains to be seen whether higher wages and benefits will result.

CREATING BETTER JOBS

Can public policies create better, higher-paying jobs in either the public or private sector? Federal job-creation programs have been largely discredited (Mucciaroni 1992), and additional federal efforts are highly unlikely under a Republican president and Congress. However, federal tax breaks for American companies incorporating or moving jobs overseas have been subject to partisan debate in Congress and during the 2004 election.

Bartik (2001) argues that states as well as children and families would benefit if states made more of an effort to train former welfare recipients for better-paying, higher-skilled jobs. He also proposes tax credits for public or private employment expansion in high-unemployment areas. The Center for Policy Alternatives (2004b, 40) recommends that states and localities pursue a "high road" economic development strategy, giving government subsidies only to companies that pay a living wage, provide health benefits, and offer job training. They claim that as of 2003, forty-three states, forty-one cities, and five counties had attached "job quality" standards to at least some government contracts or subsidies.

Another way to increase wages is to prevent good jobs from leaving a state or the United States. States have offered tax breaks to try to retain high-wage businesses, despite a lack of evidence that such tax subsidies have been effective (Eisinger 1994). Efforts to restrict companies from outsourcing jobs to India or other lower-wage countries have met with strong political resistance from the business community and from many economists. Their argument is that U.S. profits and long-term growth will benefit from outsourcing, protectionist measures will backfire, and that in the long run better jobs will be created in the United States (Drezner 2004). A number of consulting companies, such as the Outsourcing Institute, have emerged to help businesses move even more jobs and functions offshore. But some rural, low-wage states like North Dakota offer a domestic version of outsourcing, advertising cheaper land and housing to attract companies and workers from high-cost cities (Feller 2005).

Politically, however, public support for outsourcing is hazardous. A firestorm of reaction emerged during the 2004 presidential election after N. Gregory Mankiw, the head of President Bush's Council of Economic Advisers, stated that outsourcing was good for the United States and "just a new way of doing international trade" (cited in Drezner 2004). Some states, faced with such a public outcry when they attempted to outsource government jobs, were forced to keep these service, bookkeeping, or administrative positions within the state. In 2003 Indiana dropped a $15.4 million outsourcing contract for information technology services with an Indian software company. Ironically, the contract was to upgrade a computer system to help the unemployed find jobs in Indiana. Laws have been introduced in Indiana and California to ban the outsourcing of state contracts to companies based abroad. In 2004 the governor of New Jersey signed an executive order banning most state agencies from contracts that would outsource jobs. However, in response to pleas by the state's public institutions of higher learning, the order exempted contracts for academic instruction, educational services, and research services (USWA 2004).

Limiting import competition from low-wage countries is another familiar strategy for job retention. Evidence is mounting that NAFTA and lower tariff barriers with China have cost more American jobs than were created by expanded trade (Economic Policy Institute 2004; Becker 2004). Most economists argue that the United States as a whole benefits from expanded free trade, but many also concede that at least some workers, industries, or regions are harmed thereby (Kletzer 2002; Drezner 2004). However, only a few American workers (mostly in manufacturing) qualify for programs such as Trade Adjustment Assistance (TAA), which supposedly compensates workers displaced by foreign competition. Four sugar-producing states are on record as opposed to the proposed Caribbean free-trade zone, the Central American Free Trade Agreement (CAFTA), because sugar subsidies would end. But other states that export beef, such as Kansas and Missouri, expect to benefit from CAFTA, which passed Congress in 2005 despite union predictions of more job losses (Sanchez 2005).

EUROPEAN ALTERNATIVES TO THE LOW-WAGE STRATEGY

Other industrial democracies have devised methods to spread the burden of international competition more broadly, and to help workers and businesses adjust to the global environment. Do any of these strategies suggest options for the American states? Or will the adoption of measures to maintain wages and living standards end up costing jobs?

One controversial strategy is to limit immigration. Immigrant communities in Europe have been blamed for high crime rates, support for terrorism, downward pressure on wages, and high levels of spending on social services. But Europe also faces a severe decline in birthrates and a rapidly aging population, and it therefore has fewer workers to pay the taxes that finance welfare state benefits. The European Community has struggled to balance its labor market needs and humanitarian concern for refugees against the political appeal of opposition to immigration by politicians on the far right (Wilensky 2002, 652). Germany in particular opposes the harmonization of immigration policy throughout Europe and wants to continue to restrict the influx of foreign laborers to protect its own lucrative but tight labor market. However, the EU has pledged to create a unified immigration policy by 2010 (Bennhold 2004), a major reason working-class voters in France and the Netherlands in 2005 voted against the proposed EU constitution.

A second strategy is to provide greater assistance to workers who lose their jobs because of international competition. Sweden, for example, offers generous tax breaks to encourage foreign investment, but it also provides generous unemployment benefits (Steinmo 1993). Sweden also helps to pay the relocation and retraining expenses of displaced workers to encourage them to move to regions where jobs are more abundant. The "common market" resulting from the euro and the ending of customs barriers will facilitate the movement of workers between EU countries. In the countries other than the United States that belong to the Organization for Economic Cooperation and Development (OECD), health care coverage is universal rather than linked to one's employment, so job loss does not mean loss of health care coverage (except in Hawaii, the only state with publicly funded universal health care).

A third promising strategy is to limit competition for business location and investment. It is official EU policy, backed up by a Commission on Competition with enforcement powers and European Court of Justice rulings, that its member states *cannot* use selective incentives and try to outbid each other to attract mobile capital and footloose firms. A small bureaucracy in Brussels, headed by a commissioner for competition, monitors the extensive reporting requirements and investigates violations. Transparency requirements and the development of a database also provide the commission with solid evidence to use to challenge state aid efforts. The commissioner can demand repayment of any state subsidy found to be in violation of European Community principles (Thomas 2000).

The EU does permit some types of business incentives or state aid. The criterion is whether the EU as a whole will benefit, not the political clout of a particular industry, region, or country. State assistance can also be channeled to lagging regions in an effort to bring employment and gross domestic product closer to EU norms. This contrasts sharply with the North American experience, where (as Bartik 1991 has shown) the people or areas most in need of jobs and new business investment are often the least able to compete for it. Within the EU, "bailouts" of failing industries are not allowed (although exceptions do occur, especially for state-owned firms), but assistance to help industries restructure, improve their use of technology, or expand exports does receive support.

Thomas does note that EU efforts have not all been successful. First of all, agricultural subsidies, as politically sensitive in EU countries as they are in the United States, are not even under the purview of the Commission on Competition. Individual countries do not always provide the required data, and they frequently try to reclassify illegal subsidies into forms that are permitted (e.g., those for research and development). Regions or industries resist being "decertified" as eligible for assistance. The expansion of the EU into Eastern Europe will pose serious additional challenges, because these poorer countries will have a far greater claim on EU assistance than less-developed regions within the current EU.

In Thomas's terms, the development of viable enforcement and monitoring mechanisms is essential to overcoming the prisoners' dilemma problem of states or countries defecting from agreements to limit subsidies. But a *lack* of enforcement has bedeviled efforts in the United States and Canada to counter the ever-increasing escalation of demands by businesses for incentives to locate or expand in a particular jurisdiction. Canada does prohibit local governments from offering incentives, but provinces can still do so. In 1993, the National Governors' Association (NGA) agreed to call a halt to ruinous interstate competition for business. But almost immediately Alabama made a high-stakes and successful bid for the Mercedes-Benz automobile plant, and the NGA agreement was essentially void (Watson, Gardner, and Montjoy 2001). Minnesota and Maine have adopted laws to set strict criteria for the granting of subsidies and to consider their effects on labor markets. But the inexorable logic of interstate competition is that a few states acting on their own will be unable to change the dynamics of subsidies (LeRoy and Slocum 1999).

As Wilensky argues, the impact of globalization has been hardest for the "least skilled, least educated, least trained" workers in Europe as in the United States. But "modern democracies that attend to education, training, job creation, labor standards, and poverty prevention can reduce the pain of their transition to other, often better-paying jobs" (2002, 668). Indeed, Gangl's (2000) research on unemployment policy in Germany and the United States found that more generous benefits did not delay job searches and enabled displaced German workers to find better jobs. But in the United States, expansion or full funding of TAA has met with strong resistance from conservatives who fear that TAA will only delay economic adjustment and the flow of capital into more productive outlets. The American Enterprise Institute argues that "instead of playing political football with jobs, the Senate should make U.S. exporters more competitive by reforming corporate taxation" (Fitzgerald, Kersey, and Owcharenko 2004).

Despite dire warnings concerning the economic impact of globalization, at least some countries have been able to insulate their workers from a "race to the bottom" in wages or social benefits. Has this hurt their economies? Unemployment indeed remains higher in most European countries than in the United States. As the economists Heckman and Pagés (2004) warn, "Policies that may be socially desirable, but that raise labor costs or increase labor market rigidity, have negative consequences for the level of employment." However, Wilensky (2002, 668) strongly disputes arguments that Europe's labor unions and employment protection laws are responsible for unemployment: "Despite their increasing interest in new markets in Asia and Latin America, the multinationals' capital investments are still overwhelmingly targeted to rich, stable democracies. If labor costs were at the center of corporate location decisions, the rich democracies would have emptied out long ago."

A recent OECD study found little or no relationship between employment protection legislation and unemployment rates, especially when other factors that can affect unemployment (age, gender, skill level) are taken into account (OECD 1999). However, the duration of unemployment was somewhat longer and turnover rates were lower, especially for prime-age men, in countries with less labor market flexibility (OECD 1999). And Friedman (2005) attributes Ireland's recent surge in economic growth to its high degree of labor market flexibility.

Many European countries, concerned about high labor costs and high unemployment levels, have made cuts in employment protection and some welfare state benefits. But rather than reducing workers' wages, efforts have been made to increase the number of hours worked (Landler 2004). The OECD has also stepped back from its Jobs Strategy of the 1990s. According to the OECD 2004 *Economic Outlook* (Martin 2004, 12), "Pursuing more and better jobs, however central an objective, needs to be combined with other social objectives, in particular adequate social protection, a better reconciliation of work and family life, and equity outcomes in line with national preferences."

Another comparative indicator of economic performance, the World Economic Forum's *Global Competitiveness Report* (World Economic Forum 2004), ranked Finland first and the United States second. The other Scandinavian welfare states, all with high labor costs, were also ranked in the top ten in their ability to compete internationally.[4] As of 2004, the United States was experiencing a sizable trade deficit with Western Europe. Despite their higher levels of taxes and a higher social wage, European countries are exporting more to the United States than they are importing from it. The Bush administration has decided to let the value of the dollar fall to make U.S. exports more competitive, despite arguments from economists that increasing productivity and reducing the federal deficit would be preferable long-term strategies (Andrews 2004).

THE TRIUMPH OF THE LOW-WAGE STRATEGY?

In a competitive capitalist sysem, it would be foolish to support any and all efforts to increase wages and benefits. Soaring health care costs pose serious problems for private corporations as well as for state governments (Hackey 1998), but they have not increased public health. Millions have also been wasted on poorly designed and weakly regulated worker-training programs. As Lafer (2002) has argued, the better-managed and more effective programs should be expanded and public financial support for the others cut back. Colleges and universities could likewise do a better job of constraining their costs and limiting tuition increases (Ehrenberg 2000).

Strengthening labor unions would certainly increase wages and boost political support for progressive social policies. However, some labor unions have carried rent-seeking behavior to an extreme, alienating the public and earning business enmity. Labor union officials have often acquiesced to employers' demands for layoffs and give-backs because their own jobs were protected by seniority (Golden 1997). Public employees in Philadelphia enjoyed more paid holidays than workers in any other American city until Mayor Edward Rendell used a state oversight board to renegotiate the city's union contracts. Longshoremen have profited greatly from the growth in international trade, with many now earning six-figure salaries; shipping companies have preferred to pay high wages to avoid strikes or slowdowns that could quickly tie up major ports. But New York City's recent resurgence as an entry port for Asian cargo ships was facilitated in part by an agreement with the longshoremen's union to pay newly hired workers at a lower rate (Lipton 2004). Yet most unions are far more economically and politically vulnerable than the longshoremen, and the labor movement as a whole could benefit from a better balance between private gain and the public good. Of course the same logic should apply to business, and the excesses of Enron and WorldCom need to be addressed as well.

For most American workers, the problem is earning too little rather than too much. But the low-wage strategy for economic development is likely to prevail in most of the American states, for several reasons. The first is public concern with unemployment and job creation, which emerge as major state problems in most surveys. State voters are increasingly likely to hold governors responsible for state economic conditions; state unemployment higher than national or regional rates can cost governors both votes and popularity (Wolfers 2002; Hansen 1999b).

Second, governors pressured to create "jobs" often emphasize quantity rather than quality. Governors may actually have little leverage over state economies, compared with the national business cycle, international trends in oil prices, actions of the Federal Reserve, or the impact of defense spending. But governors themselves increasingly campaign on the basis of their economic development strategies, and they pledge to "create jobs" and "boost the state economy" whether or not they can actually do so. Fairly or not, state voters may be holding them to their word (Hansen 1999a, 1999b).

Third, most other state government efforts at economic development have had limited success. Tax cuts seldom have much of an impact on business location or investment decisions, and tax subsidies can reduce the revenue available for public services. My time-series analysis found that higher state/local taxes were associated with *higher* rates of job creation (although they had no effect on unemployment rates). Some innovative attempts at industrial policy and entrepreneurial policies were made in the 1980s. Though these may have compensated to some degree for deindustrialization (Lowery and Gray 1995), most such efforts never attracted sufficient political support or funding to have much of an economic impact.[5]

By contrast, the regulation of state labor costs has been a consistent state strategy ever since the Taft-Hartley Act of 1947. This strategy enjoys strong support from business, and labor unions in most states have become far too weak to provide much of a counterbalance. Despite the many negative social consequences of the low-wage strategy that have been documented, in this analysis and elsewhere, cuts in labor costs (at least before 2000) have indeed been linked to lower unemployment and faster rates of job creation. Constraining labor costs have often been justified as necessary for states to compete in the global economy. With respect to the American states, such an argument represents the triumph of ideology over evidence; the states with higher labor costs are in fact leading in exports and foreign investment.

A fourth reason for the possible triumph of the low-wage strategy is the decline in public investment in education. In the early 1990s, "human capital" became the catchword for state economic development (Snell 1998). But the education share of state budgets has been declining rather than increasing, especially in low-wage states, and the cost of higher education and postsecondary worker training has been shifted from the public sector to individuals. The federal government funds only about 7 percent of education in the United States; state and local governments must provide the rest. Faced with taxpayer resistance and competing demands on state budgets, it has proved easier for states to reduce public investment in human capital.

An earlier report that posed the question "High skills or low wages?" presumed that we had a choice (National Center on Education and the Economy 1990). That may not be the case in future years, especially given the decline in the production of engineers and computer scientists. Scientific research, high-technology production, patents, well-paying jobs, and profits are already moving to countries in Asia or Europe that invest far more in human capital. American companies are outsourcing jobs to places like India, where a large pool of well-trained, English-speaking computer scientists and engineers is available to work at much lower wages.

Fifth, unlike the countries of the EU, the American states have been unable to counter business efforts to obtain costly investment incentives. As Peterson's (1995) analysis predicted, attempts to raise taxes on businesses or the wealthy, to raise wages or worker benefits, to strengthen environmental regulations, or to spend more on social services often lead to credible business threats to relocate or invest elsewhere. This logic may not apply to California; the world's fifth-largest economy may be wealthy and populous enough to forge its own way in investment in higher education, restrictions on automobile emissions, responses to global warming, and public funding for stem cell research.[6] Holt (2004) suggests that because more residents of the "blue" states are likely to benefit from the Bush tax cuts than people in the "red" states who supported Bush, blue-state voters may be more willing to support higher levels of spending on education and other social services. But most states cannot escape the inexorable logic of interstate competition, even if the net result is less attention to investment policies that will pay off in the long run. Instead, short-term "brazen grabs for public resources by well-organized interests" (Brace 2001, 105) are likely to continue.

Sixth and finally, growing Republican dominance in Washington and in a majority of state houses since the 1970s provides little political support for efforts to strengthen labor unions, increase minimum-wage levels, or raise unemployment or TAA benefits. This conservative policy shift may have been possible because of the underrepresentation of workers and the poor among the politically active, a trend exacerbated by the decline in labor union membership and unions' ability to mobilize the less affluent. Low rates of citizen participation, and the class bias of voting and campaign contributions, have led to probusiness, antigovernment policies that do not represent popular preferences (Task Force on Inequality 2004).

In this conservative environment, the emphasis is on the "ownership society" and on tax advantages for the wealthy. The risks of globalization must be borne by individuals, while productivity gains continue to accrue to corporate managers rather than to their employees. However, as Appelbaum, Bernhardt, and Murname argue (2003, 33), "While globalization and technological change are largely beyond our control, the distribution of their burdens and benefits is not." Alternatives to the low-wage strategy do exist, and many have been implemented in other OECD countries. Interstate competition persists, and the United States is unlikely to adopt the measures Thomas (2000) describes, which Europe has pursued to minimize destructive competition for business and investment. Yet even within the liberal market economy of the United States, we see states with higher minimum wages, EITCs, expanded investment in higher education, active labor unions (especially in the public sector), worker protection laws, and increasing voter turnout. Hawaii even has universal health care.

State labor costs have been shown by this analysis to have a significant impact on state economies, independent of federal trends, and a positive effect on international competitiveness. The states have latitude in several areas to capitalize on these positive economic outcomes and to minimize the negative social effects of declining wages, benefits, family incomes, and worker power: Given these results, what are some politically feasible options for state governments?

One option is to find new ways to invest in human capital. A well-educated labor force offers significant economic advantages for income growth, productivity, and exports. This analysis has shown that higher taxes are *not* detrimental to most state economic outcomes, and polls show considerable popular support for investing more in education. Because of widespread resistance to raising property taxes, states need to explore innovations in financing education. Increasing broader-based state taxes would reduce the stark disparities in per-pupil spending across school districts. Some states have dedicated revenues from lotteries to education. Community colleges investment is especially beneficial for both workers' incomes and state or regional economic growth. Many states have also set up "529" tax plans to help parents and grandparents save for future tuition costs.

A second option is to restrain health care costs. Ideally, a federally financed plan would remove health care as an element of interstate (and international) competition, and as I have shown, the business community is increasingly supportive of such options. Federal coverage of "catastrophic" illnesses could make health insurance more affordable for employers, individuals, and state governments. Failing that, however, states can still take steps to reduce health care costs. Reasonable reforms are needed to restrain ongoing cost increases due to medical errors, excess hospital beds, unnecessary duplication of expensive services such as magnetic resonance imaging, pricing strategies of drug companies, and fraud by either providers or claimants. Some states, including California, have already enacted limits on medical liability awards; others have initiated reforms to reduce the burden of workers' compensation on employers. States could also negotiate with drug companies for favorable rates for Medicaid purchases, and many states have been pushing the federal government to assume a greater share of the Medicaid expenses that are draining their budgets.

A third option is that states can raise their minimum wage, even if the federal government fails to act. As of July 2005, eighteen states had adopted minimum wages higher than the federal level. Polls and referendum results consistently show that these measures are popular with the public. In Pennsylvania in 2005, liberal Democratic governor Ed Rendell and conservative Republican senator Rick Santorum, both up for reelection in 2006, joined in support of raising the state's minimum wage (Gaynor 2005b). Also, a higher minimum wage would "create a level playing field for those employers who want to invest in workers' skills and compete on the basis of service and product quality," and would reduce employers' incentives for subcontracting to low-wage suppliers (Appelbaum, Bernhardt, and Murname 2003, 24).

A fourth option is to encourage the creation of high-wage jobs through use of business incentives, targeted investment, and tax subsidies. Many states and cities have already adopted living-wage ordinances or job-quality standards. Other tax and location incentive programs offer greater inducements to employers who create well-paid, permanent jobs with benefits. State support for biotechnology, nanotechnology, and stem cell research should also generate well-paid jobs.

A fifth option is to support coordinating institutions. Appelbaum, Bernhardt, and Murname (2003) report that regional labor market institutions have been beneficial for workers without college degrees in the hosiery, hotel, and hospital industries. Such consortiums can set industry standards, reduce training costs, and encourage cross-firm mobility, thus increasing productivity. But these institutions require state and local governments to provide technical assistance, public training monies, and a viable community college system.

A sixth option is to enact or expand state EITCs. These benefit the working poor and help to counter other regressive state and local taxes. As Gilens (1999) has shown, though most Americans are critical of "lazy, undeserving" welfare recipients, they favor generosity to the "deserving" poor and norms of fairness. So measures to support the working poor have considerable popular support.

A seventh option is to compete vigorously for defense and homeland security spending. As I have shown, federal defense spending has had a sizable positive effect (unemployment excepted) on state economies. And even if some bases must be closed as defense priorities change, Congress has been willing to fund worker training and conversion efforts for these sites; many now house community colleges or industrial parks. The latest variant of federal largesse available to states and localities is funding for homeland security. Such federal monies can benefit first responders (police, fire department, hospitals), as well as companies producing security services or equipment, without burdening local taxpayers. Members of Congress are well aware of the economic benefits of such spending, although unfortunately homeland security has been awarded more on the basis of politics than likely threat levels. Alaska and South Dakota thus receive much more per capita than New York or California (Krugman 2004).

All these measures are likely to generate considerable popular and (except for minimum-wage laws) bipartisan support. But because higher wages and benefits do *not* appear to hurt states' position in the international economy, efforts must be made to counter the rhetoric of globalization as a rationale for cutting wage earners' incomes and opposing labor unions. Over the past few election cycles, Republicans and conservatives have successfully packaged their probusiness agenda in terms of opposition to "big government" and high taxes, support for religious and family values, and commitment to a strong defense. As Frank (2004) argues, this packaging has helped them to gain votes from working-class and minority voters whose economic interests have thereby been harmed.

According to Lakoff (2004), Democrats, liberals, and labor unions must learn to use language and symbols more effectively to dramatize the adverse social effects of reducing labor costs and the benefits of investing in human capital. For instance, how are "family values" supported when both parents must work increasingly long hours to maintain family incomes? Higher rates of crime, divorce, suicide, and births to single mothers in states with declining labor costs likewise do little to help family stability. What is "fair" about a country where executive compensation has reached an all-time high relative to workers' earnings, while the federal minimum wage has not been increased since 1997? How can the United States expect to compete internationally when college (even community college) is increasingly out of reach for working-class families, and U.S. health care costs far exceed those in Europe or Japan?

Rhetoric, however, is only part of the solution. It is certainly striking that low voter turnout emerged as the single best predictor of the decline in state labor costs, as shown by the analysis in chapter 3. Low voter turnout has also contributed to policies more beneficial to business and the wealthy. A revitalized labor movement could help to boost political involvement by lower-class voters, especially if union involvement is not limited to organized workplaces. More liberal churches (both Protestant and Catholic) have also been mobilizing to counter the impact of the religious right and to emphasize the "social gospel" (Wallis 2005). And new forms of political organizations linked to the Internet, such as Moveon.org, proved to be effective in mobilizing younger voters and raising campaign funds in 2004 (Nelson 2005).

The states could do more to facilitate voter turnout by easing registration requirements, upgrading their records of eligible voters, and improv-

What Matters: Policy Recommendations for the States

- Invest more in education and worker training.
- Shift the financing of education and training from individuals and local property taxes to broad-based, less regressive state taxes.
- Preserve free trade, but expand programs like Trade Adjustment Assistance to compensate the individuals and communities most directly harmed by import competition.
- Use state and local tax subsidies and location incentives to encourage the creation of well-paying jobs that provide benefits.
- Find ways to limit the surge in health care costs, and use the savings to expand coverage.
- Raise the minimum wage.
- Adopt or expand state Earned Income Tax Credit programs to assist the working poor.
- Compete vigorously for defense and homeland security spending, now the major forms of federal assistance available to states and localities.
- Use election reform to encourage rather than discourage voter turnout.

ing election day access and vote-counting methods. Several states are repealing the felony disenfranchisement laws that have so adversely affected turnout, especially that of African American males (Texeira 2005). However, other states are implementing laws to require photographic identification at polling places, which could reduce turnout by minorities, the elderly, and urban residents who lack cars and thus driver's licenses (*New York Times* 2005). Voter turnout remains a politically contested issue in the United States, and the outcome of ongoing debates about voter eligibility and access could have far-reaching policy consequences for state labor costs and social programs.

In the 2004 election, Democrats were unable to shift the public agenda away from concerns with terrorism and morality and toward the health care and economic issues where they have a decided advantage (Kristof 2004; Nelson 2005). However, a worsening economy (or a Democratic candidate with greater personal appeal than Kerry in 2004) could lead to a very different result. As the expanded outsourcing of jobs affects more middle-class and well-educated voters, who still vote in sizable numbers, the political salience of declining labor costs may well increase.

I have argued throughout this book that policies concerning the cost of labor represent concrete political choices by the states, not an automatic response to the presumed imperatives of globalization. And political choices can be changed.

Explaining State Differences in Labor Costs

PEARSON CORRELATIONS

The measure underlying tables 3.4 and 3.5 is the Pearson correlation coefficient (designated by r), which can range between -1 and $+1$. If two indicators have no relationship with each other, the correlation coefficient will be close to zero. But if higher values on one indicator are associated with higher values on the other, the value of r will increase; if high values on one indicator are linked to lower values on another, the correlation will be negative rather than positive. For these data on the fifty states, a value of r greater than $+0.20$ or -0.20 suggests a fairly strong relationship that is unlikely to be a random pattern due to chance. Correlations close to zero indicate no linear relationship; correlations higher than ± 0.35 indicate a strong and highly significant relationship. Tables A.1 and A.2 show the actual correlations used for tables 3.4 and 3.5 in the text.

REGRESSION ANALYSIS

The dependent variable used for figures 3.3 and 3.4 was the percent change in state labor cost factor scores, 1980–2000. Total state union membership could not be used as an independent variable, because union density is one of the components of the dependent variable, so public union membership as of 1986 was used. Though this is positively associated with total union membership, the Pearson correlation is modest ($r = 0.24$), and there were no indications of problems with multicollinearity in the regressions. The proportion of public-sector labor union members in earlier or later years produced nearly identical coefficients as the 1986 membership levels; the change since 1986 in this measure has been only 4 percent, and the

Table A.1

Pearson Correlations: Economic and Labor Supply Variables, and State Labor Costs

Variable	Labor Costs (Factor Score), 1980	% Change, 1980–2000
Economic indicators		
Percent of the state labor force employed in manufacturing, 1982	0.24	−0.23
Percent change, 1982–97		
Percent of the state labor force employed in services, 1982	0.11	−0.20
Percent change, 1982–97		
Labor force diversity 1982	−0.04	0.20
Percent change in labor force diversity, 1982–97		
Manufacturing productivity (value added per worker), 1982	0.31	−0.11
Percent change in manufacturing productivity, 1982–97		
Labor supply		
Proportion of foreign-born immigrants in a state, 1980	−0.41	−0.18
Percent change, 1980–2000		
Proportion of women in the labor force, 1980	−0.24	−0.18
Percent change, 1980–2000		
Proportion of high school graduates in the state, 1980	0.33	0.49
Percent change, 1980–2000		
Proportion of college graduates in the state, 1980	0.16	0.03
Percent change, 1980–2000		

Table A.2
Pearson Correlations: State Party Dominance, Ideology, Partisanship, and Change in State Labor Costs, 1980–2000

	Correlations with State Labor Costs		
Variable	All	South	Non-South
Democratic percent of state legislature (N = 49)[a]			
1980	0.20	−0.33	0.26
2000	0.24	−0.69	0.39
Percent change	0.07	−0.51	0.23
State ideology[b]			
1977–88 (N = 48)	0.31	0.35	0.44
1989–99 (N = 50)	0.39	0.48	0.52
Percent change	0.06	0.40	0.08
State partisanship[b]			
1977–88 (N = 48)	−0.01	−0.37	−0.02
1989–99 (N = 50)	−0.10	0.43	−0.15
Percent change	−0.08	0.43	−0.12

[a]Excluding nonpartisan Nebraska.
[b]Measures from Erikson, Wright, and McIver (1993); Wright (2004). Alaska and Hawaii excluded 1977–88.

percent change had no impact on the trend in state labor costs. If overall union density as of 1980 is substituted for public-sector union membership in either model, the sign of the coefficient is negative, although not significant. After controlling for other factors (including the trend in manufacturing jobs), states with strong private-sector unions have experienced significantly slower declines in labor costs. As noted in the text, the indicator of trends in voter turnout was the percent difference in the turnout in gubernatorial elections between 1981–88 and 1996–2002.

METHODOLOGY

Ordinary-least-squares regression analysis (OLS) was used to model the trend in state labor costs. The bar graphs in figures 3.3 and 3.4 are based on standardized regression coefficients, which facilitate the visual comparison of the relative effects of the independent variables. The full regression results, including the unstandardized regression coefficients and standard errors, appear as table A.3. The t-values indicate whether an independent variable had

Table A.3

Predicting the Change in State Labor Costs, 1980–2000: OLS Regression Results

Independent Variable	Model 1			Model 2		
	b	St. Error	t	b	St. Error	t
Percent change in state exports	0.00007	0.000	0.004			
Percent change in FDI	0.00012	0.000	1.36			
Level of state exports, 1985				0.001	0.000	−0.94
Level of FDI, 1985				0.0005	0.000	1.31
Percent change in manufacturing employment	−0.04	0.020	−2.02*	−0.038	0.022	−1.7
Percent change in college graduates	0.001	0.000	2.47*	0.001	0.000	2.53*
Percent public union members, 1986	0.002	0.001	2.31*	0.002	0.001	2.39*
Percent change in voter turnout	0.38	0.110	3.34*	0.33	0.110	3.02*
Percent change in ideology	0.006	0.077	0.84	0.006	0.007	0.91
Constant	−0.33	0.040	−7.56	−0.334	0.044	−7.62
R^2	0.51			0.50		
Adjusted R^2	0.42			0.41		
F-statistic	5.86			5.84		

*Statistically significant ($p < .05$).

Note: OLS = ordinary least squares; St. Error = standard error; FDI = foreign direct investment.

a significant impact on state labor costs. A regression coefficient at least twice its standard error (a t-value of 2 or greater) is considered to be statistically significant; a coefficient that size is likely to be due to chance only 5 times out of 100 ($p < .05$). Model 1, based on trends in exports and FDI, performs marginally better than Model 2 in terms of the F-value test for significance of the model and the percent of the total variance explained.

ALTERNATIVE MODELS CONSIDERED

As Gray and Lowery (1996) stress in their ecological approach to interest groups, relative rather than absolute influence matters. Research on interest groups at both the state and national levels has found sharp increases in the density, resources, and professionalism of organized interests (Gray and Lowery 1996; Thomas and Hrebenar 1999; Heinz et al. 1993). So even in states with high rates of union membership, if opposing groups (business, insurers, tax-cut movements) are highly mobilized and well organized, labor may not be able to fend off efforts to weaken unions or reduce workers' compensation benefits. Labor costs have indeed declined more in states ranking higher on Gray and Lowery's index of the diversity of a state's lobbying environment (Pearson correlation of -0.23). However, the Gray-Lowery index did not meet minimum statistical criteria for inclusion in the regressions in table A.3. Two other labor supply factors (trends in the proportion of women and of immigrants in the state labor force) were also considered, but they likewise failed to meet the minimal criteria for inclusion in these regression equations.

In other regressions, (1) the changes since 1980 in state partisanship and (2) the percent Democratic seats in state legislatures were substituted for ideology, along with a dummy variable for the eleven states of the former Confederacy. None of the coefficients for these indicators proved to be either substantial or significant, although the dummy variable for the South did show some modest impact independent of party on the trend in state labor costs.

In theory, increased party competition should encourage both higher voter turnout and higher state spending on social services. I tried two different measures of party competition in these regressions: the Holbrook and Van Dunk (1993) district-level measure and the Ranney calculations of party competition based on control of state government (described in Bibby and Holbrook 1999). Neither met minimum standards for inclusion. An interaction of voter turnout and party competition likewise had no significant effect in either regression.

Time-Series Analysis of State Economic Outcomes, 1970–2000

The economic analysis of the impact of state labor costs was performed in two stages. The first set of models considers domestic factors only, and it uses state exports and foreign direct investment (FDI) as dependent variables. I then bring in indicators of exports and FDI as independent variables to test whether, and how much, exposure to the international economy affects state employment trends, gross state product (GSP), and growth in personal income. The measure of unemployment used is the *difference* between state and national unemployment rates in a given year, to control for the effects of the national business cycle. And to control for inflation, GSP, exports, FDI, defense spending, and personal income are expressed in constant (1982) dollars.

The basic models of state economic outcomes to be estimated are as follows:

$$DV(1-6) = a + B1^*(SLC) + B2^* (PROD) + B3^* (DEF) + B4^*(TAX) + B5^*(FLC) + e$$

Where:

DV = each of the 6 economic outcomes used as dependent variables (GSP, personal income, unemployment, job growth, value of exports, value of FDI)

$PROD$ = productivity: manufacturing value added per worker (lagged one year)

SLC = factor scores for state labor costs (lagged one year)

FLC = factor score for federal labor costs (lagged one year)

TAX = state/local taxes as a percent of personal income (lagged one year)

DEF = federal defense spending (prime contracts) per year

a = constant term

e = error term

METHODOLOGY

Because labor costs and other dimensions of state economies vary across both states and time, pooled time-series cross-section regression analysis will be used for the fifty states, 1970–2000, to test the hypotheses discussed above. FDI data have been available only since 1978, so the equations for FDI must be interpreted with some caution because we have only 538 cases (state/years since 1978) for foreign investment, compared with 1,050 for the other variables. Pooled analysis combines the advantages of both cross-sectional and time-series analysis, and it provides a much larger N. But since the resulting 1,500 state/years are not independent units, standard regression assumptions such as constant variance and uncorrelated error terms may be violated. Thus the values for California in 1980 and 1981 are likely to be highly correlated, potentially biasing the results. After testing for violations of such assumptions and correcting them as necessary, equations were estimated for the six dependent variables.

These equations were estimated with STATA statistical software using panel-corrected standard errors, as recommended by Beck and Katz (1995) and Beck (2001) to control for heteroskedasticity in time-series cross-sectional data sets. Similar results were found using ordinary-least-squares (OLS) fixed-effects models with dummies for individual states. As noted in the text, Alaska had extreme values for taxation, and the Bureau of Labor Statistics methodology for assessing employment trends was changed after 1994. The equations were therefore reestimated (1) excluding Alaska and (2) with a dummy variable for years after 1994; neither alternative provided results substantively different from those reported in tables B.1, B.2, and B.3 below.

LABOR COSTS AND ECONOMIC OUTCOMES

The equations for the first stage of the analysis (using domestic variables only) are shown in table B.1. The sign and significance of the regression coefficients in these tables are summarized in table 4.2 in chapter 4. The regression coefficients indicate that for every 1 percent increase in labor costs, state unemployment rates will increase by 0.08 percent. Increases in productivity (lagged one year) were associated with modestly lower unemployment; use of three-year lags produced no greater effect. However, the prediction equation for unemployment accounts for only 13 percent of the variance. By contrast, the higher the labor costs in a state, the *greater* the levels of personal income, GSP, and exports (all coefficients are highly significant).

Table B.1
Regression of State Labor Costs on State Economic Outcomes, 1970–2000

Independent Variable	Gross State Product			Growth in Personal Income		
	b	St. Error	t	b	St. Error	t
Productivity	−11.83	353.2	−0.03	38.44	22.81	1.68
Defense spending	4290.2	822.6	17.37	158.3	18.22	8.69
Federal labor costs	−2.83	10.06	−0.28	7.45	1.51	4.92
State labor costs	50.57	5.71	8.85	1.6	0.43	3.79
State/local taxes[a]	171.9	146.6	1.17	47.81	10.41	4.59
Constant	−6998.5	888.3	−7.87	6039	788	7.66
R^2		0.49			0.42	
Wald Chi Square	(1050, 5) 380.78			(1000, 5) 237.2		

Independent Variable	Growth in Labor Force			Unemployment		
	b	St. Error	t	b	St. Error	t
Productivity	0.0093	0.0114	0.82	−0.306	0.81	−0.37
Defense spending	0.071	0.009	7.81	0.248	0.339	0.73
Federal labor costs	0.004	0.0007	5.05	0.038	0.009	4.15
State labor costs	−0.0007	0.00001	−4.26	0.079	0.01	8.25
State/local taxes[a]	0.026	0.005	4.91	0.28	0.303	0.93
Constant	0.966	0.413	2.34	−7.27	5.84	−1.24
R^2		0.46			0.13	
Wald Chi Square	(1000, 5) 101.6			(1050, 5) 143.0		

Independent Variables	Exports			Foreign Direct Investment		
	b	St. Error	t	b	St. Error	t
Productivity	−24.8	25.3	−0.98	−34.5	44.4	−0.78
Defense spending	752.9	106.9	7.05	1182	220	5.37
Federal labor costs	4.19	1.77	2.37	8.85	3.71	2.38
State labor costs	3.19	0.59	5.37	0.65	1.99	0.33
State/local taxes[a]	−29.9	11.5	−2.61	12.48	56.8	0.22
Constant	−1200	1234	−0.97	−427	2912	−0.15
R^2		0.33			0.37	
Wald Chi Square	(1050, 5) 104.2			(537, 5) 119.8		

[a]As % personal income.

According to these models and measures, state labor costs have a significant impact independent of federal labor costs on GSP, personal income, exports, and growth in the labor force. They do not appear to have much impact either way on FDI, but FDI is significantly higher in the presence of higher federal labor costs. Regression tests for longer (three- or five-year) lag times also showed that productivity failed to have a significant effect on any of the dependent variables, although the relationship with personal income growth remained positive.

EXPORTS, FDI, AND STATE ECONOMIC TRENDS

The second stage of the analysis of state economic growth includes estimates for the effects of the international economy. Exports and FDI are now added to the equations for unemployment, GSP, labor force growth, and growth in personal income. Separate equations are estimated for each dependent variable because the number of cases (state/years) is significantly smaller for FDI than for exports. In addition, to test for the combined impact of international economic factors and labor costs, two interaction terms (exports or FDI multiplied by state labor costs) are added to the prediction equations shown in tables B.2 and B.3 (Jaccard, Turrisi, and Wan 1990).

The results for GSP and personal income are shown in table B.2. Both state and federal labor costs by themselves are associated with significantly *lower* GSP when measures of exports or FDI are added to the equation. But exports and FDI by themselves, as well as the interaction terms, are positive and highly significant for GSP; international economic ties in high-labor-cost states are associated with *faster* state economic growth. And the additional of international economic trends improves the prediction; the R^2 values for GSP increase from 0.49 in table B.1 to 0.82 and 0.89 in table B.2. Defense spending is again significantly linked to higher GSP. Higher tax burdens are associated with higher GSP in the equation including the value of state exports, but show no relationship with GSP in the equation including FDI.

The equations for personal income in table B.2 are generally similar to those in table B.1. The coefficients for defense spending and labor costs are all positive and significant; those for state/local taxes are significant only for exports. Productivity shows an even stronger positive association with personal income growth and is now significant at the .10 level. But exports and FDI differ. Higher levels of exports are associated with higher personal income overall, but (as the negative sign for the interaction term indicates) with lower levels in states with high labor costs. By contrast, FDI has a positive impact on personal income in states with high labor costs. But adding exports or FDI to the equations adds little to the amount of variance explained in per capita personal income: R^2 is 0.42 in table B.1 and 0.43 or 0.44 in table B.2.

Table B.2
Combined Impact of Exports, Foreign Direct Investment (FDI), and State Labor Costs (SLC) on Gross State Product and Personal Income

Independent Variable	Gross State Product			Gross State Product		
	b	St. Error	t	b	St. Error	t
Productivity	149.8	179.2	0.84	285.3	249.4	1.14
Defense spending	6344	497	12.92	5735	335	17.09
State/local taxes as % personal income	636.8	108.3	5.88	223.5	656.2	0.34
Federal labor costs	−42.9	10.8	−3.96	−120.6	13.9	−8.67
SLC	−30.2	7.6	−3.99	−23.7	17.7	−1.34
Exports	3.78	1.72	2.20			
FDI				2.35	0.86	2.74
Interact: Exports × SLC	0.028	0.004	6.12			
Interact: FDI × SLC				0.028	0.004	6.52
Constant	−45535	6186	−7.37	−79845	9930	−8.04
R^2		0.82			0.89	
Wald Chi Square		(1050, 7) 2386			(537, 7) 8487	

Independent Variable	Personal Income			Personal Income		
	b	St. Error	t	b	St. Error	t
Productivity	40.47	22.18	1.82	47.16	27.3	1.73
Defense spending	110.44	15.8	6.99	131.3	30.8	4.25
State/local taxes as % personal income	48.64	9.99	4.87	11.21	24.7	0.45
Federal labor costs	7.25	1.42	5.10	10.10	3.42	2.95
SLC	1.87	0.54	3.48	1.61	0.74	2.20
Exports	0.139	0.037	3.73			
FDI				−0.006	0.036	−0.17
Interact: Exports × SLC	−0.0002	0.0001	−2.01			
Interact: FDI × SLC				0.0002	0.0001	1.66
Constant	6042.9	740.7	8.16	7871.2	1775.3	4.43
R^2		0.44			0.43	
Wald Chi Square		(1050, 7) 1490			(590, 7) 1118	

Table B.3 uses the same methodology to analyze trends in state unemployment and labor costs. As before, higher state or federal labor costs are linked to significantly higher state unemployment. The coefficients for defense spending, productivity, and taxes are not significant. Exports, alone or in interaction with state labor costs, also have little impact on

Table B.3

Combined Impact of Exports, Foreign Direct Investment (FDI), and State Labor Costs (SLC) on State Unemployment and Labor Force Growth

Independent Variable	Unemployment			Unemployment		
	b	St. Error	t	b	St. Error	t
Productivity	−0.29	0.83	−0.35	−0.22	0.33	−0.67
Defense spending	−0.36	0.43	−0.84	−1.08	0.49	−2.18
State/local taxes as % personal income	0.31	0.29	1.05	−0.77	0.38	−2.01
Federal labor costs	0.035	0.009	3.97	0.043	0.01	4.15
SLC	0.075	0.009	8.42	0.130	0.018	7.41
Exports	0.0005	0.0006	0.89			
FDI				0.003	0.0006	5.28
Interact: Exports × SLC	0.00019	0.00026	0.45			
Interact: FDI × SLC				−0.0001	0.00006	−3.85
Constant	−5.71	6.03	−0.95	−0.189	5.74	−0.03
R^2		0.14			0.16	
Wald Chi Square	(1050, 7) 150.0			(537, 7) 742.1		

Independent Variable	Labor Force Growth			Labor Force Growth		
	b	St. Error	t	b	St. Error	t
Productivity	0.0096	0.011	0.86	0.0142	0.0089	1.59
Defense spending	0.045	0.009	5.15	0.0345	0.0149	2.33
State/local taxes as % personal income	0.028	0.005	5.08	0.0005	0.007	0.07
Federal labor costs	0.0038	0.0007	5.09	0.057	0.0012	4.43
SLC	−0.0011	0.0002	−5.35	−0.0011	0.0003	−3.87
Exports	−0.0001	0.00001	−0.78			
FDI				−0.00002	0.00001	−2.00
Interact: Exports × SLC	0.00002	0.00008	3.43			
Interact: FDI × SLC				0.00002	0.00006	2.98
Constant	1.08	0.39	2.75	2.37	0.64	3.73
R^2		0.48			0.55	
Wald Chi Square	(1050, 7) 102.23			(537, 7) 84.9		

unemployment rates. However, the results for FDI are striking: higher unemployment rates in states with high levels of foreign investment, but significantly *lower* unemployment in the states that experience both high levels of FDI and high labor costs.

Turning finally to the equations for growth in the labor force (table B.3), we see that higher state labor costs are linked to slower rates of growth in the labor force, but federal labor costs have the opposite effect. The impact of defense spending is positive and significant as before, but to a lesser degree than in table B.1 once the impact of international trade is taken into account. Higher state/local taxes are again linked to increases in the size of the labor force only in the equation including exports. However, the combination of high state labor costs and a high level of either exports or FDI is associated with significantly faster rates of job creation. As in the labor force equation in table B.1, the impact of productivity is positive, and considerably stronger (although still not significant) in the FDI equation. The R^2 values for labor force growth are also improved by adding exports, FDI, and the interaction terms to the predictions.

APPENDIX C

Analysis of Social Consequences of Declining Labor Costs

Pearson correlations for the data in tables 5.2 through 5.5 are shown in table C.1.

REGRESSION ANALYSIS OF CONSEQUENCES OF DECLINING LABOR COSTS

Ordinary-least-squares (OLS) regression was used to compare the impact of state labor costs and job growth on trends in crime rates, voter turnout, and the proportion of children living in poverty. Because of data availability, the years used are slightly different for each dependent variable. Crime rates are based on FBI Uniform Crime Reports data on violent crime. Data on voter turnout for the period 1981–88 are from Gray, Jacob, and Albritten (1990); turnout for the period 1996–2002 was calculated by the author from data on gubernatorial elections in *The Book of the States*. The proportion of children living in poverty (those under eighteen years of age living below the official poverty line) is calculated from Census of Population data reported in the *Statistical Abstract of the United States*.

Each equation also includes several other factors hypothesized to have an impact on the dependent variables, to test whether labor costs had an independent effect. As in figures 3.3 and 3.4, bar graphs based on standardized regression coefficients are used in figures 5.2, 5.3, and 5.4 to provide a visual depiction of the signs and relative contributions of the independent variables. The unstandardized regression coefficients, standard errors, and *t*-values are displayed in table C.2.

The *t*-values show that the impact of trends in state labor costs was statistically significant in each equation, and substantially larger than the impact of trends in job growth. The R^2 values are relatively low; clearly, other factors must be considered to explain these social trends more fully, preferably using time-series data rather than cross-sectional data on rates of change.

Table C.1
Pearson Correlations: State Labor Costs, Job Creation Rates, and State Economic, Social, Demographic, and Policy Trends

Percent Change in	Pearson Correlations with		Interval (if other than 1980–2000)
	Rate of State Labor Cost Growth	Rate of Growth in State Labor Force	
Per capita personal income	0.46*	0.05	
Poverty rate	−0.19	−0.15	1979–99
Child poverty	−0.36*	−0.03	1979–99
Income inequality	−0.22	0.26*	1979–95
Violent crime rate	−0.42*	−0.11	
Divorce rate	0.00	−0.29*	
Suicide rate	−0.32*	0.08	
Births to single mothers	−0.29*	0.10	
Population	0.19	0.80*	
Persons over age 65	−0.03	−0.08	
% foreign born	−0.17	0.23	
Tax regressivity	0.43*	−0.06	1991–2003
Spending on education	0.33*	0.30*	
Spending on welfare	−0.07	0.33*	
Total state/local spending	0.35*	0.29*	
Voter turnout	0.47*	−0.06	1981–2002

*Statistically significant at $p < .05$.

Table C.2

Ordinary Least Squares Regressions: Percent Change in Labor Cost Trends and State Social Outcomes

Independent Variable	Crime Rates, 1980–2000			Voter Turnout, 1981–88 to 1996–2002			Children in Poverty, 1979–99		
	b	St. Err.	t	b	St. Err.	t	b	St. Err.	t
Change in state labor costs, 1980–2000	-0.96	0.45	-2.14	0.52	0.16	3.21	-0.765	0.35	-2.18
Rate of state job growth, 1980–2000	0.026	0.10	0.27	-0.01	0.04	-0.32	-0.04	0.08	-0.46
Abortion rate, 1980	-0.001	0	-3.55				0.001	0.00	2.46
Change, 1980–2000, in % poor children	-0.217	0.18	-1.20						
% Hispanic	-4.56	3.36	-1.35				2.70	2.82	0.96
% over age 65				0.08	0.09	0.93			
% 18–24	-0.20	0.21	-0.12						
% black	0.002	0.004	0.64	0.002	0.002	1.00	0.005	0.004	1.16
% births to single mothers							0.28	0.091	3.06
Voter turnout, 1981–88				0.0003	0.00	0.14			
Party competition, 1980–96				-0.00013	0.00	-1.02			
Constant	-4.48	3.35	-1.34	0.08	0.10	0.83	2.04	2.82	0.72
R²	0.44			0.30			0.31		
Adjusted R²	0.35			0.20			0.22		
F-statistic	4.74			2.97			3.27		

APPENDIX D

Data and Sources

Unless otherwise indicated, all data are from annual editions of the *Statistical Abstract of the United States.*

Abortion rates: The number of abortions performed annually per 1,000 women of childbearing age (15–44 years), as reported by the states to the National Centers for Disease Control.

Births to single mothers: Rate per 1,000 women of child-bearing age (age 15–44 years).

Crime rates: FBI Uniform Crime Statistics for violent crime.

Divorce rates: As reported by states to the National Center for Health Statistics; some include annulments or legal separations as well as legal divorces (see notes to table 111 in the *Statistical Abstract of the United States 2003*).

Exports: Value, in constant (1982) dollars, of manufacturing exports per production worker, based on the *Census of Manufactures.*

Foreign direct investment: Annual value (in 1982 dollars) since 1978, from international surveys by U.S. Department of Commerce.

Gross state product: Total value, in constant (1982) dollars, of the goods and services produced in a state, divided by the number in the labor force.

Ideology/partisanship: Scores based on pooled state surveys by CBS News and the *New York Times*, 1977–99, as described in Erikson, Wright, and McIver 1993 and Wright 2004.

Inequality: Gini indices for income inequality by state, 1969 to 1995 (Langer 1999).

Job growth: Annual percent increase in the size of a state's labor force.

Labor union membership: Private sector: Bureau of Labor Statistics data before 1982, Bureau of National Affairs thereafter (see note 9 to chapter 2). Public sector: Hirsch and MacPherson 1987, 2000.

Manufacturing wages: In 1982 dollars, from the *Census of Manufactures*.

Minimum wage: By federal law, in constant (1982) dollars.

Party competition: Holbrook and Van Dunk (1993) measure calculated at the district level in each state for 1980–88.

Personal income: Annual percent change, in constant (1982) dollars per capita.

Population: Total and by age, ethnicity, and foreign origin, from the Census of Population.

Poverty rates: Overall and child (under 18) poverty data from the U.S. Bureau of the Census, http://www.census.gov/hhes/poverty/histpov/hstpov13.html.

Productivity: Annual rate of changes in value of manufactures per production worker, based on the *Census of Manufactures*.

Right-to-work laws: from *Statistical Abstract* tables on union membership by state.

Social Security benefits: Federal Insurance Contributions Act (FICA) tax rate, as a percent of wages.

State/local spending: Per capita data (overall and on education and welfare) use the broad categories set up by the Census of Government Finance, Classification Manual Function 19, http://www.census.gov/govs/www/classfunc19.html.

Suicide rates: Per 1,000 deaths, as reported by states to the Centers for Disease Control and Prevention.

Tax regressivity: Ratio of taxes on the highest-income group in a state to that of the lowest 20 percent of wage earners (Center for Tax Justice 1991, 2003).

Unemployment: Bureau of Labor Statistics (BLS) data; the difference between official state and federal rates. BLS counts as unemployed only people who were not working but were available for work and engaged in an active job search. The monthly sample for the eleven largest states is used directly; data for the remaining thirty-nine states are estimated by combining current and historical survey data with administrative records on the number of persons applying for unemployment benefits.

Unemployment benefits: State average weekly benefit, in constant (1982) dollars.

Voter turnout: Change in average voter turnout in gubernatorial elections between 1981 and 1988 (Gray, Jacob, and Albritten 1990) and 1996 and 2002 (calculations by the author from *Census of State Governments*, *Book of the States*, and biennial data on gubernatorial elections).

Workers' compensation: Annual state payments, in constant (1982) dollars, divided by the size of the labor force.

Notes

NOTES TO CHAPTER I

1. See Nelson (2005) for an analysis of Ohio's influence on the 2004 presidential election. However, a fall 2005 report by the Government Accountability Office called into question the Ohio results because of the possibility of fraud from electronic voting machines (Fitrakis and Wasserman 2005).

2. See American Council on Education (1998) for an analysis of trends in college tuition relative to family income and the cost of instruction.

3. All data on manufacturing employment, wages, personal income, international trade, and election outcomes are from annual editions of the *Statistical Abstract of the United States*. See appendix D for detailed information on data and sources.

4. Donahue (1997) and Conlan (1998) document the expanding policy and administrative role of the American states.

5. For summaries of the neoliberal arguments, see Casson (1983) and Vedder and Gallaway (1993). Drezner (2001) provides a critical review of this literature.

6. Rifkin (1995) and Tonelson (2002) argue that downward pressure on wages affects all industrialized counties. However, others (Esping-Andersen 1990; Swank 2002; Iverson 1998; Katz and Darbishire 1999; Wallerstein and Western 2000; Hall and Soskice 2000; Kollmeyer 2003) have found very different effects in particular countries or regions, and little evidence of policy convergence. Scruggs and Lange (2002) and Cohen (2001) provide cogent summaries of this burgeoning literature.

7. Essays in Clark and Montjoy (2001) explore several aspects of the growing international role of the states but fail to consider labor costs.

8. These reform efforts are described in Hofstadter, *Age of Reform* (1955), and Skocpol (1992).

9. For overviews of state economic development initiatives, see Brace (1993), Eisinger (1988), Fosler (1988), and Bartik (1991).

10. The seventeen OECD countries are Australia, Austria, Belgium, Canada, Denmark, Finland, France, Germany, Italy, Japan, the Netherlands, Norway, Spain, Sweden, Switzerland, the United Kingdom, and the United States.

11. The slower pace of job creation in the United States after 2000 became a major issue during the 2004 presidential campaign. The problematic war and reconstruction of Iraq, soaring oil prices, the outsourcing of American jobs overseas, and the increasing substitution of technology for labor have all been blamed (Krugman 2004).

12. DiTella and Vogel (2003) survey worldwide trends in equality/inequality in income, wealth, wages, and living standards. In contrast to Wohlers and Weinert (1988), they suggest that greater equality leads to more rather than less economic growth.

NOTES TO CHAPTER 2

1. Only later did feminists succeed in arguing that these "chains of protection" in fact limited women's opportunities for hiring and promotion (Baer 1978). The Equal Rights Amendment would have outlawed most such laws that applied only to women.

2. For detailed accounts of the political process that led to Social Security, see Derthick (1979) and Quadagno (1988). The income limit above which the Social Security payroll tax no longer applies was initially $6,000 and was increased to $83,000 in 2004. In 1993, under President Bill Clinton, the payroll tax was increased 1½ percent to help finance Medicare, and this addition applied to the full range of earned income.

3. Reed (2003) claims that states with right-to-work laws actually pay higher wages, if one considers the cost of living and the very low wages in these states when the laws were adopted.

4. Author's calculation based on *Statistical Abstract of the United States* data on average manufacturing wages by state.

5. Biennial editions of *The Book of the States* have documented these ongoing legislative and regulatory trends. See also Amberg (2003).

6. See Killingsworth (2002) for an analysis of recent trends in adoption of comparable worth. He concludes that it has fostered some modest pay adjustments for government employees in some states, including Washington and Minnesota.

7. As of 2005, seventeen states and the District of Columbia provided EITCs based on a percentage of the federal EITC. See http://www.stateeitc.info/.

8. Political animosity may also have been a factor, since the NEA campaigned against Bush in both 2000 and 2004 (Toppo 2005).

9. For detailed reviews of this extensive literature, see Wilensky (2002), Scruggs and Lange (2002), and Nissen (2002, 2003). Labor union membership data by state were collected by the Bureau of Labor Statistics prior to 1982, and since then have been compiled by the Bureau of National Affairs in Washington

(http://www.bna.com/bnaplus/databook.html). Although the methods used for estimation differ somewhat (see Hirsch and MacPherson 1987, 2000), I found no substantial differences in state percentages or rankings before and after 1982.

10. Heckman and Pagés (2004) rank the United States well below most other OECD countries in both Social Security taxes and employment protection laws that limit an employer's ability to fire a worker.

11. A statistical technique called factor analysis was used to rank the states by overall labor costs. Factor analysis is an appropriate data-reduction technique for combining several hypothetically related indicators into a single overall index (Kim and Mueller 1980). It is similar to a weighted average, but more appropriate when the components are measured in different units. All five indicators loaded on the first (unrotated) factor. The factor loadings are .733 * (manufacturing wages) + .759 * (labor union density) + .702 * (unemployment insurance benefits) + .455 * (workers' compensation benefits) – .769 * right-to-work laws). The Eigenvalue is 2.45; 48 percent of the variance explained. This measure appears to have considerable validity, because the highest-scoring states (New York, Michigan, and Pennsylvania) clearly differ on these dimensions from low-scoring states such as the Carolinas.

12. These three components (Social Security payroll taxes, the federal minimum wage, and dummies for presidential administrations) were subject to factor analysis (principal components). All three loaded on a single factor; the factor loadings are .972 * (Social Security payroll tax rate) – .899 * (minimum-wage rate) + .494 * (presidential administration dummy). The Eigenvalue is 2.0, accounting for 67 percent of the variance.

13. The overall relationship between these measures of state and federal labor costs is negative (with a Pearson correlation of –0.28). To further test whether state labor costs were independent of federal trends, I used multiple regression to analyze the state factor scores, 1970–2000, as a function of these three indicators of federal labor costs, plus a variable for year to pick up any other (unmeasured) national trends. All but the year variable proved to be statistically significant, but together accounted for only about 10 percent of the variance in state labor costs. Some economists have argued that labor costs fluctuate with the business cycle, but I found no relationship between the national unemployment rate and the trend in either state or federal labor costs. Thus labor costs did not decline any faster during recessions than during economic upswings.

NOTES TO CHAPTER 3

1. The International Standards Organization (ISO) identifies standards for quality, ecology, safety, compatibility, efficiency, and effectiveness of products and services required by business, government, and society. It is a federation of the national standards agencies of 149 countries at all levels of development. See http://www.iso.org/iso.

2. *W* is calculated as the standard deviation divided by the mean, and it can range from 0 to 1. It can thus be used to compare variability over time and across a range of items measured in different units, such as dollars or percentages.

3. Data on state and local taxes are from the annual *Census of Government Finance*. States are compared in terms of combined state/local taxes rather than state taxes alone, because the mix of services funded by state versus local governments varies considerably across states.

4. Export data are based on the *Census of Manufactures*, published every five years, and the *Annual Survey of Manufactures*, published during the intervening years by the U.S. Bureau of the Census. All export dollar figures used in this analysis were adjusted for inflation using the implicit price deflator for exports from the National Income and Product Accounts of the United States (*Survey of Current Business*, 1992, 2002).

5. Data on net foreign immigration are from the Census of Population, as reported in annual editions of the *Statistical Abstract of the United States*. North Carolina and Arkansas have experienced the greatest rate of increase in immigration since 1990.

6. These differences between quartiles are statistically significant at the usual level ($p < .05$) only for immigration. This means that differences between quartiles for exports or FDI could be due to chance, and that there is considerable variation among the states within each grouping. See Simon (1999) and Borjas (2001) for review and analysis of the wage and employment effects of immigration. Most economists agree that the employment impact is largest for native-born workers with less than a high school degree, but that the net economic effects of immigration are positive for the states as well as the United States.

7. See Collins (1998) and Krugman and Lawrence (1994) for a review of studies analyzing the impact of foreign trade on American workers. Kletzer (2002) notes considerable variation in job loss due to imports by industrial sector; job loss was highest in textiles, apparel, and footwear, and in regions (such as the Southeast) where these industries are concentrated.

8. The percent of a state's labor force employed in manufacturing and services is calculated from data on state employment by sector in the 1981 and 2002 editions of the *Statistical Abstract of the United States*.

9. People who are working either part time or full time, or unemployed but actively looking for work, are defined as being in the labor force. People who are retired, disabled, homemakers, full-time students, or discouraged workers and thus not seeking employment are not considered to be in the labor force. Male and female wages are compared for people working full time year round, thus excluding part-time or seasonal workers.

10. Productivity in the states, 1970–2000, is measured by the annual rate of change in value added in manufacturing per production worker (annual data from *Statistical Abstract of the United States*, based on the *Census of Manufactures*). The Pearson correlation between this measure of productivity and the proportion of

college graduates in a state is 0.44; the correlation with state educational spending is 0.34.

11. See appendix A for the actual measures (Pearson correlations) on which table 3.4 is based.

12. Klarner (2003) described issues in the measurement of party control of state offices, and he has graciously provided his data from 1970 to 2000 to me and other members of the State Politics and Policy Section of the American Political Science Association.

13. Public employee membership data by state are based on Hirsch and MacPherson (1987, 2000).

14. The Pearson correlations (based on time-series data) between trends in state labor costs and the Democratic percentage of state legislators are 0.27 in the South and –0.04 elsewhere. See table A.2 for correlations between labor costs and percent Democratic by region in 1980 and 2000.

15. According to Gallup Poll data, the high point in support for labor unions (75 percent approval) was in the early 1950s; the low point (55 percent approval) occurred during President Ronald Reagan's firing of the air traffic controllers in 1981. The minimum-wage question was asked on the October 2001 Gallup Poll. The data are available at http://www.brain.gallup.com/topicview.aspx.

16. The Pearson correlation between state scores on the ANES (for forty-one states, 1972–2000), and the decline in state labor costs was –0.23.

17. The EWM data set for 1977–99 was graciously provided to me by Gerald Wright. Mean state ideology scores were –95 in 1977, declined to their lowest (most conservative) point (–171) when Republicans gained control of Congress in 1994, and rose to –132 by 1999.

18. Votes, years of election, and terms of office for governors are listed in the Council of State Governments, *The Book of the States*, biennial editions.

19. Turnout rates for 1981–88 are from Gray, Jacob, and Albritten (1990). Average turnout rates for gubernatorial elections 1996–2002 were calculated by the author based on data in the Council of State Governments, *The Book of the States* (biennial editions). See Carsey (2000) for analysis of factors affecting turnout in gubernatorial elections; open-seat races generally have higher voter turnout than contests involving incumbents, unless an unpopular incumbent governor is facing a strong challenger.

20. See appendix A for discussion of measures of state party competition.

21. Pearson correlations between union density and state voter turnout declined from 0.30 for 1981–88 to only 0.11 after 1996.

NOTES TO CHAPTER 4

1. Fisher (2005) provides an overview and critique of these rankings. Despite their methodological flaws (overemphasis on tax measures, double counting of many variables, antiunion bias), these rankings are widely cited in state capitals,

and they are often used by business groups to justify lower taxes and reductions in labor costs.

2. See Levin-Waldman (2001) for a summary of the ongoing debates over the minimum wage.

3. In 1992, the United States had a trade surplus of almost $9 billion with the fifteen countries in the European Union, but as of June 2004 the twelve-month trade deficit with these countries was $99.8 billion (Norris 2004). European exports are predominantly high-quality goods like machine tools and luxury automobiles.

4. According to *Census of Manufactures* data from the U.S. Department of Commerce, the proportion of the total U.S. labor force employed in manufacturing declined from 24 percent in 1977 to 15 percent in 1997. As of 2000, North Carolina had the highest proportion of its labor force (27 percent) employed in manufacturing.

5. See Winters (1999) for an analysis of trends in state tax revenues, and *The Book of the States* (biennial) for details concerning state corporate tax rates. Data on bids for large manufacturing plants show that the amount of tax subsidy per job generated has increased dramatically since 1990. Only three states (New York, Michigan, and Louisiana) attempt to estimate the dollar value of the tax expenditures they provide to businesses and individuals (Brace 2001).

6. Alesina and Rosenthal (1995) describe the evidence for partisan differences in economic policy for the United States and other industrial democracies.

7. See Anton (1989) for an analysis of the development and demise of most federal regional policies. One survivor has been the Appalachian Regional Commission, which continues to provide financial assistance (largely transportation monies) to the impoverished rural counties in that region (Bradshaw 1992).

8. The source for defense prime contracts by state is the *Statistical Abstract of the United States*, based on data from the U.S. Department of Defense annual *Atlas / Data Abstract for the United States and Selected Areas*. Some of these prime contracts are eventually subcontracted to other states or even abroad, but it is difficult to track the effects of such indirect spending.

9. The political pressure to keep bases open was so strong that in 1988 Congress set up an independent bipartisan commission to recommending closings. The commission's recommendations are voted up or down, to minimize opportunities for amendments or logrolling among members of Congress from the states or districts affected (Deering 1996).

10. The official unemployment rate calculated by the Bureau of Labor Statistics (BLS) is based on the Current Population Survey (CPS), and it counts as unemployed only people who were not working for pay or profit during the week of the survey but were available for work and engaged in an active job search, or who were laid off and expected to be recalled. The monthly sample for the eleven largest states is used directly; data for the remaining thirty-nine states are estimated by combining current and historical survey data with administrative records on the number of persons applying for unemployment benefits. Unemployment rates

are seasonally adjusted by the BLS for factors such as holiday and summer hiring patterns. Details and sampling errors for state estimates are detailed in the BLS monthly periodical *Employment and Earnings*.

The CPS underwent a major redesign beginning in 1986 to reflect a changing labor force (more women and elderly employed, more part-time and temporary workers, more permanent layoffs). Norwood and Tanur (1994) estimate that unemployment had been underestimated by about half a percentage point for several years before the changes were implemented in 1994. Debate continues as to how to count the self-employed and entrepreneurs who work at home. Critics claim that unemployment is underestimated because many of the long-term unemployed are classified as "discouraged workers" and therefore are not officially considered to be in the labor force (Dionne 2004).

11. Data on exports and FDI are from the *Statistical Abstract of the United States*, as described in chapter 3. FDI data by state are available only since 1978; equations including FDI are based on only 578 cases, 1978–2000.

12. GSP is analogous to national gross domestic product (GDP) and represents the gross market value of the goods and services attributable to labor and property located in a state. For a detailed discussion of the composition of GDP and GSP, see the notes to the section titled "Income, Expenditures, and Wealth" in annual editions of the *Statistical Abstract of the United States*. In this analysis, GSP is divided by the size of the state's labor force to control for differences in the size of state economies.

13. The economics profession has long debated the appropriate measures to use in analyzing productivity (Baumol, Blackman, and Wolff 1989; Pilat 1998). The only consistent state measure available for this time-series analysis is manufacturing value added per worker. Productivity, historically lower in the service sector, has increased in recent years due to the use of information technology. No consensus has emerged about how to incorporate service-sector productivity gains into the National Income and Product Accounts (*Economic Report of the President* 1995, 58).

14. Although the most populous states generally receive more prime contracts, the amounts awarded are the product of political factors other than population (Rundquist, Lee, and Rhee 1996), so per capita amounts would not be an appropriate control for state size. The natural log of defense spending will be employed instead, to balance out the very large number of prime contracts awarded to a few states.

15. An alternative indicator of state taxes, the maximum rate of a state's corporate income tax per year, likewise showed negligible effects on state economic outcomes.

16. Defense spending was associated with somewhat lower state unemployment after the Reagan buildup of the 1980s. An alternative measure, defense spending per capita, showed a slightly stronger effect on unemployment than the measure used in tables 4.2 and 4.3 (the log of defense spending), but the per capita measure had less impact on the other dependent variables.

17. Despite strong objections from labor unions, many states have also been making increasing use of prison labor to keep labor costs low (Hansen 2000).

NOTES TO CHAPTER 5

1. The federal minimum wage, in constant (2002) dollars, peaked in 1968 at $7.07, but by 2000 it had fallen to $4.85. During the 1970s, a person working forty hours a week year round could maintain a family of four above the official poverty line, but by 2000, that much work would still leave a family $3,000 below the poverty line (Lafer 2002, 30).

2. State government policies are not immune to political manipulation. Thus tax increases are significantly more likely in the years after a gubernatorial election than in election years (Hansen 1983). See Imbeau and Petry (2004) for an analysis of deficit policies in the United States and other federal countries.

3. See Kelly (1991), Pearce (1985), Mettler (1998), and Um'rani and Lovell (2000) for analyses of gender bias in access to unemployment insurance benefits.

4. Maki and Lichty (2002, 248–55) review the extensive economics literature on this issue. See also Casson (1983) for a discussion of regional trends in employment and population. Though jobs and population flows are interdependent, the consensus is that population inflow spurs job growth because it generates demand for housing and services.

5. For a discussion of measures of the "brain drain" and policy responses to it, see Krieg (1991).

6. The relationships between each of these indicators and trends in labor costs or job growth are summarized by Pearson correlations (table C.1 in appendix C). The correlations are based on the full fifty-state distribution of the measures, not the threefold groupings of states shown in tables 5.2 through 5.5.

7. The federal poverty measure originated in the 1960s, when it was largely based on prices for a Thrifty Food Plan as calculated by the Department of Agriculture. Although families are spending less of their income on food, the costs of housing, transportation, and health care have increased since the 1960s. The alternative poverty measure Lafer (2002) calculates would place a far higher proportion of Americans below the poverty line. Official poverty statistics are from the U.S. Bureau of the Census, http://www.census.gov/hhes/poverty/histpov/hstpov13.html.

8. The Gini index is the size of the area between a line representing perfect equality (distribution of income exactly proportional to the population) and the actual cumulative distribution of income across population groups. Gini ratios range from 0 (perfect equality) to 1 (perfect inequality; one person or household has all the income).

9. The states vary somewhat in the divorce rates they report to the National Center for Health Statistics; some include annulments or legal separations as well as legal divorces (see the footnotes to table 111 in *Statistical Abstract of the United States 2003*). However, the states appear to be consistent over time in how each

calculates divorce rates, so the indicator used here (percent change in reported divorce rates) should not be affected.

10. Publications geared toward retirees (e.g., *Where to Retire* and *Money* magazines) regularly list the "best states to retire to" based in part on the taxation of retirement income.

11. Many industrialized countries now spend far more per capita on public support for higher education than does the United States. China and India are graduating hundreds of thousands of engineers each year, while U.S. production of computer scientists and engineers has declined (Samuelson 2005).

12. The Pearson correlation between trends in labor costs (1980–2000) and voter turnout (1981–88 and 1996–2002) is a robust 0.47. However, the link between trends in state job creation rates and trends in voter turnout is negligible ($r = .04$).

13. The standard for sorting out causal relationships using time-series data is Granger causality (Granger 1969). Given two series, A and B, A is considered to cause B if the forecast of B is improved by incorporating past values of A as well as B in the prediction equation. Such an analysis requires that both A and B include the same units (years, quarters, etc.). Biennial data on state voting patterns cannot establish Granger causality, because turnout fluctuates so much between midterm and presidential elections, and also varies with the competitiveness of races for governor or senator (Carsey 2000).

14. Citizens for Tax Justice has calculated the impact in 1991 and 2003 of major state taxes on different income groups: the lowest to the highest 20 percent of income earners, plus the top 15, 4, and 1 percent of earners. The CTJ measures for 1991 and 2003 differ slightly in the calculations of impact on families. The 1991 data are based on "non-elderly" households, whereas the 2003 data are based on the tax impact on a "family of four." However, state rankings in levels of regressivity in 1991 and 2003 are nearly identical (correlation of 0.90). The same patterns of declining regressivity since 1991 are evident whether the analysis uses state rankings or the actual ratio of taxes on low-versus-high incomes. No consistent measure of state tax progressivity over time exists; Phares's (1980) index has not been replicated.

15. Fifteen states have adopted Earned Income Tax Credit (EITC) laws to exempt the wages of the working poor from state income taxes. However, in recent years, more and more states have relied on revenue from lotteries and casino gambling; most analysts consider these to be highly regressive in impact, further increasing the burden on the poor (Pierce and Miller 2004). Neither gaming revenues nor EITC provisions were included in the CTJ calculations.

16. Data on state/local spending per capita, education, and welfare use categories defined by the *Census of Government Finance*. Federal program monies (Pell grants, veterans' benefits, the federal share of Medicaid) are not included in these measures. See "Classification Manual Function 19" (http://www.census.gov/govs/www/classfunc19.html). State and local spending are combined because the mix of state and local service funding varies considerably across states.

17. State abortion rates are calculated as the number of abortions performed annually per 1,000 women of childbearing age (fifteen to forty-four years). These data are reported by the states to the National Centers for Disease Control and Prevention, and they are published in the *Statistical Abstract of the United States*.

18. The indicator of party competition is the Holbrook and Van Dunk (1993) measure calculated for state legislative districts in each state for 1980–88. Regression equations were also estimated using the Ranney index of state party competition for either 1989–94 (Gray and Jacob 1996) or 1995–98 (Bibby and Holbrook 1999). The Ranney index is based on elections for state offices (governor and legislature) only; bicameral Nebraska is omitted. Ranney's indices show that the states have become more competitive over time (especially in the South), but neither index predicted trends in voter turnout as measured here.

19. Although levels of public employee unionization are positively related to overall union density, tests indicated that multicollinearity was not a problem for this regression analysis. Because union density is the component of labor costs most likely to affect voter turnout, the equations in figure 5.3 were reestimated using the change in labor union membership, 1980–2000, in place of the index of state labor costs. This factor also proved to be positively and significantly associated with higher levels of turnout, although to a lesser degree than combined labor costs.

20. See New (2004) for a recent analysis of factors influencing state abortion rates. Given the strong negative relationship between state labor costs and births to single mothers, the latter variable may pick up some of the impact of labor cost trends on child poverty rates.

NOTES TO CHAPTER 6

1. The Department of Labor's own data show that the wage replacement rates of TAA recipients declined from 87 percent in 2000 to only 73 percent in 2003. Their official goal is 90 percent. See http://www.doleta.gov/tradeact/performance/cfm.

2. In October 2004, a federal judge ruled that the Cannelton Mining Company could be relieved of a provision in its union contract that guaranteed health care benefits to retirees. The company successfully argued that it could no longer compete effectively because of the high cost of retirement health care. Other mining companies were expected to follow suit (Dao 2004). Companies such as Halliburton have also used mergers to divest themselves of pension obligations (Walsh 2004).

3. The states offering EITCs as of 2004 were Illinois, Indiana, Iowa, Kansas, Maine, Maryland, Massachusetts, Minnesota, New Jersey, New York, Oklahoma, Oregon, Rhode Island, Vermont, and Wisconsin, plus the District of Columbia; New Mexico offers a comparable low-income tax rebate. See http://www.taxcreditsources.org. Also see Ventry (2000) for a political history of the use of tax expenditures as an alternative to welfare policy.

4. The World Economic Forum measures "competitiveness" using a combination of surveys of business leaders and hard data on patents, enrollments in higher education, use of technology, macroeconomic stability, the national savings rate, public expenditures on research and development, and the legal system. For details, see http://www.weforum.org/pdf/gcr/Composition_of_Growth_Competitiveness_index and also World Economic Forum (2004).

5. My earlier cross-sectional analysis of the states, for the period 1980–95, found that neither tax incentives nor industrial policy initiatives had a significant impact on state economic trends (Hansen 2001b).

6. American automobile companies filed lawsuits in 2004 to prevent California from setting stricter emission standards than those of the federal government. It remains to be seen how the Rehnquist Court's mixed record of support for state government autonomy will apply in this instance (Conlan and Dudley 2005).

References

AFL-CIO. 2004. Report: Policy Changes Could Stop Manufacturing Job Loss. http://www.aflcio.org/issuespolitics/manufacturing/ns04162004.cfm.

———. 2005. 2004 Trends in CEO Pay. http://www.aflcio.org/corporateamerica/paywatch.

Ahlstrand, Amanda, Laurie Bassi, and Daniel McMurrier. 2003. *Workplace Education for Low Wage Workers.* Kalamazoo, Mich.: Upjohn Institute.

Alesina, Alberto, and Howard Rosenthal. 1995. *Partisan Politics, Divided Government, and the Economy.* New York: Cambridge University Press.

Amberg, Stephen. 2003. Labor Adjustment Policies in the United States: Regional Diversity in National Strategy. Paper presented at the American Political Science Association, Philadelphia, August.

American Council on Education. 1998. *Straight Talk about College Costs and Prices.* Phoenix: Oryx Press.

Andrews, Edmund L. 2004. The Dollar Is Down: Is It a Cause for Concern? *New York Times,* November 16.

Anton, Thomas J. 1989. *American Federalism and Public Policy: How the System Works.* Philadelphia: Temple University Press.

Appelbaum, Eileen, Annette Bernhardt, and Richard J. Murname, eds. 2003. *Low Wage America: How Employers are Reshaping Opportunity.* New York: Russell Sage Foundation.

Asher, Herbert B., Eric S. Heberlig, Randall B. Ripley, and Karen Snyder. 2001. *American Labor Unions in the Electoral Arena.* Lanham, Md.: Rowman & Littlefield.

Avery, James, and Mark Peffley. 2005. Voter Registration Requirements, Turnout, and Welfare Eligibility Policy: Class Bias Matters. *State Politics and Policy Quarterly* 5: 47–67.

Babcock, Linda, and Sara Laschever. 2003. *Women Don't Ask: Negotiation and the Gender Divide.* Princeton, N.J.: Princeton University Press.

Baer, Judith A. 1978. *The Chains of Protection: The Judicial Response to Women's Labor Legislation*. Westport, Conn.: Greenwood Press.

Bailey, Michael A., and Mark Carl Rom. 2004. Interstate Competition across Health and Welfare Programs. *Journal of Politics* 66: 326–47.

Baker, Al. 2004. With Panel's Order to Increase Spending on Schools, Albany's Fiscal Woes Just Got Worse. *New York Times*, December 2.

Ballam, Deborah A. 2000. Employment-at-Will: The Impending Death of a Doctrine. *American Business Law Journal* 37: 1–26.

Barker, David C., and Christopher Jan Carman. 2003. The Spirit of Capitalism? Religious Doctrine, Values, and Economic Attitude Constructs. *Political Behavior* 22: 1–27.

Barrilleaux, Charles, Thomas Holbrook, and Laura Langer. 2002. Electoral Competition, Legislative Composition, and American State Welfare Policy. *American Journal of Political Science* 46: 415–27.

Barro, R. J. and Y. Sala-i-Martín. 1992. Convergence. *Journal of Political Economy* 100: 223–51.

Bartik, Timothy J. 1985. Business Location Decisions in the United States. *Journal of Business and Economic Statistics* 3: 14–22.

———. 1991. *Who Benefits from State and Local Economic Development Policies?* Kalamazoo, Mich.: Upjohn Institute for Employment Research.

———. 1999. Displacement and Wage Effects of Welfare Reform. Kalamazoo, Mich.: Upjohn Institute for Employment Research. http://www.upjohninst.org/brtkppr.

———. 2001. *Jobs for the Poor: Can Labor Demand Policies Help?* New York: Russell Sage Foundation.

Baumol, William J., Sue Ann Blackman, and Edward N. Wolff. 1989. *Productivity and American Leadership: The Long View*. Cambridge, Mass.: MIT Press.

Beck, Nathaniel. 2001. Time-Series Cross-Section Data: What Have We Learned in the Past Few Years? *Annual Review of Political Science* 4: 271–93.

Beck, Nathaniel, and Jonathan N. Katz. 1995. What to Do (and Not to Do) with Time-Series Cross-Section Data. *American Political Science Review* 89: 634–47.

Becker, Elizabeth. 2004. Textile Quotas to End, Punishing Carolina Towns. *New York Times*, November 2.

Bednar, Jenna, William N. Eskridge Jr., and John Ferejohn. 2001. A Political Theory of Federalism. In *Constitutional Culture and Democratic Rule*, ed. John Ferejohn, Jack N. Rakove, and Jonathan Riley. New York: Cambridge University Press.

Belman, Dale. 1992. Unions, the Quality of Labor Relations, and Firm Performance. In *Unions and Economic Competitiveness*, ed. Lawrence Mishel and Paula B. Voos. Armonk, N.Y.: M. E. Sharpe.

Benabou, Roland. 2002. Unequal Societies: Income Distribution and the Social Contract. In *The Economics of Rising Inequalities*, ed. Daniel Cohen, Thomas Piketty, and Giles Saint-Paul. Oxford: Oxford University Press.

Benería, Lourdes. 2003. *Gender, Development, and Globalization*. New York: Routledge.

Bennhold, Katrin. 2004. EU Ministers Set Deadline on Immigration Policy. *International Herald Tribune*, October 26.

Bernat, G. Andrew, Jr. 2001. Convergence in State Per Capita Personal Income, 1950–99. *Survey of Current Business*, June, 36–44.

Berry, Mary F. 1986. *Why ERA Failed: Politics, Women's Rights, and the Amending Process of the Constitution*. Bloomington: Indiana University Press.

Bibby, John F., and Thomas M. Holbrook. 1999. Parties and Elections. In *Politics in the American States: A Comparative Analysis*, 7th edition, ed. Virginia Gray, Russell L. Hanson, and Herbert Jacob. Washington, D.C.: CQ Press.

Bischak, Gregory A. 1999. Demobilization from the Cold War 1990–1998: Lessons of U.S. Conversion Policy. *Peace Economics, Peace Science and Public Policy* 5, article 1. Berkeley, Calif.: Berkeley Electronic Press.

Bjorhus, Jennifer. 2002. U.S. Workers Taking H-1B Visas to Court. *San Jose Mercury News*, September 25.

Black, Earl, and Merle Black. 2002. *The Rise of Southern Republicans*. Cambridge, Mass.: Harvard University Press.

Blank, Rebecca M. 1994. *Social Protection versus Economic Flexibility: Is There a Trade-Off?* Chicago: University of Chicago Press.

Boraas, Stephanie, and William M. Rodgers III. 2003. How Does Gender Play a Role in the Earnings Gap? *Monthly Labor Review* 126: 9–15.

Borjas, George. 2001. *Heaven's Door: Immigration Policy and the American Economy*. Princeton, N.J.: Princeton University Press

Brace, Paul. 1993. *State Government and Economic Performance*. Baltimore: Johns Hopkins University Press.

———. 2001. Economic Development Policy in the American States: Back to an Inglorious Future? In *Globalization's Impact on State-Local Economic Development Policy*, ed. Cal Clark and Robert S. Montjoy. Huntington, N.Y.: Nova Science.

Bradshaw, Michael J. 1992. *The Appalachian Regional Commission: Twenty-Five Years of Government Policy*. Lexington: University of Kentucky Press.

Branigan, William. 1997. The Return of the American Sweatshop. *Washington Post*, national weekly edition, February 24.

Brewer, Mark D. 2003. *Relevant No More? The Catholic/Protestant Divide in American Electoral Politics*. Lanham, Md.: Lexington Books.

Brierly, Allen B., and Richard C. Feiock. 1998. Economic Growth and Unemployment in the American States: The Case of the Missing Multiplier. Paper presented at the Midwest Political Association, Chicago, April.

Bronfenbrenner, Kate. 2003. The American Labour Movement and the Resurgence in Union Organizing. In *Trade Unions in Renewal: A Comparative Study*, ed. Peter Fairbrother and Charlotte A. B. Yates. London: Continuum.

Brown, Philip, Andy Green, and Hugh Lauder. 2001. *High Skills: Globalization, Competitiveness, and Skill Formation*. New York: Oxford University Press.

Cagan, Joanna, and Neil DeMause. 1998. *Field of Schemes: How the Great Stadium Swindle Turns Public Money into Private Profit*. Monroe, Maine: Common Courage Press.

Calzonetti, F. T., and Robert T. Walker. 1991. Factors Affecting Industrial Location Decisions: A Survey Approach. In *Industry Location and Public Policy*, ed. Henry W. Herzog and Alan M. Schottmann. Knoxville: University of Tennessee Press.

Card, David. 2001. The Effect of Unions on Wage Inequality in the U.S. Labor Market. *Industrial and Labor Relations Review* 54: 296–315.

Card, David, and Alan B. Krueger. 1995. *Myth and Measurement: The New Economics of the Minimum Wage*. Princeton, N.J.: Princeton University Press.

Carsey, Thomas. 2000. *Campaign Dynamics: The Race for Governor*. Ann Arbor: University of Michigan Press.

Carsey, Thomas, and Barry Rundquist. 1999. Party and Committee in Distributive Politics: Evidence from Defense Spending. *Journal of Politics* 61: 1156–69.

Casson, Mark. 1983. *Economics of Unemployment: An Historical Perspective*. Oxford: Martin Robertson.

Center for Policy Alternatives. 2004a. Right to Work for Less. http://www.stateaction.org/issues/workforless.

———. 2004b. *Restoring the Promise of America: 2005 Progressive Agenda for the States*. Washington, D.C.: Center for Policy Alternatives.

Clark, Cal, and Robert S. Montjoy, eds. 2001. *Globalization's Impact on State/Local Economic Development Policy*. Huntington, N.Y.: Nova Science.

Clymer, Adam. 1991. Awaiting Congress in Capital. *New York Times*, September 9.

Cohen, Edward S. 2001. *The Politics of Globalization in the United States*. Washington, D.C.: Georgetown University Press.

Cohen, Isaac. 2002. The Caterpillar Labor Dispute and the UAW, 1991–1998. *Labor Studies Journal* 27: 77–99.

Cohen, Jeffrey E., and James D. King. 2004. Relative Unemployment and Gubernatorial Popularity. *Journal of Politics* 66: 1267–82.

Cohen, Roger. 2005. Next Step: Putting Europe Back Together. *New York Times*, June 5.

Collier, Christopher, and James Collier. 1987. *Decision in Philadelphia*. New York: Ballantine Books.

Collins, Susan M., ed. 1998. *Imports, Exports, and the American Worker*. Washington, D.C.: Brookings Institution Press.

Conlan, Timothy. 1998. *From New Federalism to Devolution*. Washington, D.C.: Brookings Institution Press.

Conlan, Timothy J., and Robert L. Dudley. 2005. State Sovereignty and Federal Preemption in the Rehnquist Court. *PS, Political Science & Politics* 38: 363–66.

Consumer Reports. 2000. Workers Comp: Falling Down on the Job. *Consumer Reports* 65, no. 2: 28–49.

Coontz, Stephanie. 2005. *Marriage, A History: From Obedience to Intimacy.* New York: Viking Press.

Council of State Governments. Biennial. *The Book of the States.* Lexington, Ky.: Council of State Governments.

Crain, W. Mark. 2003. *Volatile States: Institutions, Policy, and the Performance of American State Economies.* Ann Arbor: University of Michigan Press.

Crouch, Colin. 1998. Labor Market Regulations, Social Policy, and Job Creation. In *Job Creation: The Role of Labor Market Institutions,* ed. Jordi Gaul. Cheltenham, U.K.: Edward Elgar.

CTJ (Citizens for Tax Justice). 1991. *A Far Cry from Fair.* Washington, D.C.: Institute on Taxation and Economic Policy.

———. 2003. *Who Pays? A Distributional Analysis of the Tax Systems in All 50 States,* 2nd ed. Washington, D.C.: Institute on Taxation and Economic Policy.

Cummings, Stephen D. 1998. *The Dixification of America: The American Odyssey into the Conservative Economic Trap.* Westport, Conn.: Praeger.

Cunningham, James, and Pamela Martz. 1986. *Steel People: Survival and Resistance in Pittsburgh's Mon Valley.* Pittsburgh: River Communities Project, School of Social Work, University of Pittsburgh.

Dao, James. 2001. Dogfight for Dollars on Capitol Hill. *New York Times,* September 2.

———. 2004. Miners' Benefits Vanish with Bankruptcy Ruling. *New York Times,* October 24.

Deering, Christopher J. 1996. Congress, the President, and Automatic Government: The Case of Military Base Closings. In *Rivals for Power: Presidential–Congressional Relations,* ed. James Thurber. Washington, D.C.: CQ Press.

Delaney, John T. 1998. Redefining the Right to Work Debate: Unions and the Dilemma of Free Choice. *Journal of Labor Research* 19: 425–44.

Derthick, Martha. 1979. *Policy-Making for Social Security.* Washington, D.C.: Brookings Institution Press.

Dillon, Sam. 2004. Washington Votes Down New Format for Schools. *New York Times,* November 4.

———. 2005. Students Ace State Tests, but Earn D's from U.S. *New York Times,* November 26.

Dionne, E. J., Jr. 2004. Jobless in Recovery-Land. *Pittsburgh Post-Gazette,* March 9.

DiTella, Rafael, and Ingrid Vogel. 2003. *Inequality and the "American Model."* Case Study 9-703-025. Cambridge, Mass.: Harvard Business School.

Dively, Megan. 2002. Paycheck Protection: Stymied in California, but Still Spreading Roots. *Labor Watch.* http://www.capitalresearch.org/publications/labor_watch/2000/0008b.htm.

Dobbs, Lou. 2004. *Exporting America: Why Corporate Greed Is Shipping American Jobs Overseas.* New York: Warner Business Books.

Donahue, John D. 1997. *Disunited States.* New York: Basic Books.

Donohue, John J., III, and Steven D. Levitt. 2001. The Impact of Legalized Abortion on Crime. *Quarterly Journal of Economics* 116: 379–420.

Doucouliagos, Chris, and Patrice Laroche. 2003. What Do Unions Do to Productivity? A Meta-Analysis. *Industrial Relations* 42: 650–91.

Dreyfuss, Robert. 1998. Paycheck Protection Racket. *Mother Jones*, June, 17–19.

Drezner, Daniel W. 2001. Globalization and Policy Convergence. *International Studies Review* 3: 53–78.

———. 2004. The Outsourcing Bogeyman. *Foreign Affairs*, May/June, 22–34.

Driggs, Don W. 1987. Nevada: Powerful Lobbyists and Conservative Politics. In *Interest Group Politics in the American West*, ed. Ronald J. Hrebenar and Clive S. Thomas. Salt Lake City: University of Utah Press.

Dye, Thomas R. 1980. Taxes, Spending, and Economic Growth in the American States. *Journal of Politics* 42: 1085–1107.

Dyer, Ervin. 2005. Black Males Rare on Nation's Campuses. *Pittsburgh Post-Gazette*, November 14.

Ebbinghaus, Bernhard, and Jelle Visser. 2000. *Trade Unions in Western Europe since 1945.* New York: Grove/Palgrave.

Economic Policy Institute. 2004. Issue Guide on Offshoring. http://www.epi.org/content.cfm/issueguide_offshoring.

———. 2005. EPI Issue Guide: Living Wage. http://www.epi.org/content.cfm/issueguides_livingwage_lwo-table.

Economic Report of the President. 1995. Washington, D.C.: U.S. Government Printing Office.

Edsall, Thomas B. 2005. Bush Suspends Pay Act in Areas Hit by Storm. *Washington Post*, September 9.

Egan, Timothy. 2004. Economic Squeeze Plaguing Middle-Class Families. *New York Times*, August 2.

Ehrenberg, Ronald G. 2000. *Tuition Rising: Why College Costs So Much.* Cambridge, Mass.: Harvard University Press.

Ehrenreich, Barbara. 2001. *Nickel and Dimed: On (Not) Getting By in America.* New York: Metropolitan Books.

Eisinger, Peter K. 1988. *The Rise of the Entrepreneurial State: State and Local Economic Development Policy in the United States.* Madison: University of Wisconsin Press.

———. 1994. State Economic Development in the 1990s: Politics and Policy Learning. *Economic Development Quarterly* 9: 146–58.

Elazar, Daniel. 1984. *American Federalism: A View from the States*, 3rd ed. New York: Harper & Row.

Erikson, Robert S., Gerald C. Wright, and John P. McIver. 1993. *Statehouse Democracy: Public Opinion and Policy in the American States*. New York: Cambridge University Press.

Esping-Andersen, Gotha. 1990. *Three Worlds of Welfare Capitalism*. Cambridge: Cambridge University Press.

Euchner, Charles. 1998. *Playing the Field*. Baltimore: Johns Hopkins University Press.

FAIR (Federation for American Immigration Reform). 2000. Immigration Lowers Wages for American Workers. http://www.fairus.org/html/04148711.

Farber, Henry S., and Bruce Western. 2001. Accounting for the Decline of Unions in the Private Sector, 1973–1998. *Journal of Labor Research* 22: 459–85.

Federal Human Resources Week. 2002. States Find Success in Flexibility. *Federal Human Resources Week*, November 26.

Federation of Concerned Scientists. 2003. Arms Sales Monitoring Project. http://www.fcs.org/asmp.

Feller, Adam. 2005. Outsourcing in the Heartland. *Pittsburgh Post-Gazette*, June 26.

Fiorina, Morris. 1996. *Divided Government*, 2nd ed. Boston: Allyn & Bacon.

Fisher, Peter. 2005. *Grading Places: What Do the Business Climate Rankings Really Tell Us?* Washington, D.C.: Economic Policy Institute.

Fishman, Charles. 2003. The Wal-Mart You Don't Know. *Fast Company Online*. http://www.FastCompany/magazine/77/walmart.htm.

Fitrakis, Bob, and Harvey Wasserman. 2005. Powerful Government Accountability Office Report Confirms Key 2004 Stolen Election Findings. http://www.search.netscape.com/ns/boomframe.jsp?query=GAO+ report+ on+Ohio.

Fitzgerald, Sara, Paul Kersey, and Nina Owcharenko. 2004. More Trade, Less Assistance: Why TAA Should Not Be Expanded. http://www.heritage.org/Research/Labor/wm495.cfm.

Fletcher, Bill, Jr., and Richard W. Hurd. 2000. Is Organizing Enough? Race, Gender, and Union Culture. *New Labor Forum* 6: 58–69.

Florida, Richard. 2004. Creative Class War: How the GOP's Anti-Elitism Could Ruin America's Economy. *Washington Monthly*, January–February. http://www.washingtonmonthly.com/features/2004/0401.florida.htm.

Forger, Gary. 2004. The Power of Outsourcing. http://www.keepmedia.com.

Fosler, R. Scott. 1988. *The New Economic Role of the American States*. New York: Oxford University Press.

Fox, Sharon E., and Jeong Hwa Lee. 1996. Determinants of Foreign Firm Location Decisions in the United States, 1985–1990. *American Politics Quarterly* 24: 81–104.

Frank, Thomas. 2004. *What's the Matter with Kansas?* New York: Metropolitan Books / Henry Holt.

Freeman, Richard B., and James L. Medoff. 1984. *What Do Unions Do?* New York: Basic Books.

Freeman, Richard B., and Joel Rogers. 2002. A Proposal to American Labor. *The Nation*, June 24.

Friedman, Joseph, Daniel A. Gerlowski, and Johnathan Silberman. 1992. What Attracts Foreign Multinational Corporations? *Journal of Regional Science* 32: 403–18.

Friedman, Thomas L. 2005. Follow the Leapin' Leprechaun. *New York Times*, July 1.

Frontline. 2004. Is Wal-Mart Good for America? http://www.pbs.org/wgbh/pages/ frontline/shows/walmart/etc.synopsis.

Galbraith, James K. 1998. *Created Unequal: The Crisis in American Pay*. New York: Free Press.

Gallup Poll. 2001. Labor Unions. http://www.brain.gallup.com/topicview.aspx.

Gangl, Marcus. 2000. A Causal and Distributional Analysis of the Impact of Unemployment Benefits on Reemployment Rates and Reemployment Quality among Unemployed Workers in Germany and the United States. Paper presented at the RC28 Summer Conference on Inequality: Global and Local Perspectives, Berkeley, Calif.

Garrett, Geoffrey. 1998. *Partisan Politics in the Global Economy*. New York: Cambridge University Press.

Garsten, Ed. 2004. GM Health Care Bill Tops $60 Billion. *Detroit News*, March 11.

Gaynor, Pamela. 2005a. Shortage of Math, Science Students Worries Business. *Pittsburgh Post-Gazette,* June 30.

———. 2005b. State Boosts in Minimum Wage Spark Debate. *Pittsburgh Post-Gazette*, July 17.

Geoghegan, Thomas. 1997. The UPS Strike. http://slate.msn.com/id/3656.

Gilens, Martin. 1999. *Why Americans Hate Welfare*. Chicago: University of Chicago Press.

Gillman, Howard. 2002. How Political Parties Can Use the Courts to Advance Their Agendas. *American Political Science Review* 96: 511–24.

Gilmore, D. R. 1960. *Developing the Little Economies*. New York: Committee for Economic Development.

Gimpel, James G. 1999. *Separate Destinations: Migration, Immigration, and the Politics of Places*. Ann Arbor: University of Michigan Press.

Gimpel, James G., and James R. Edwards, Jr. 1999. *The Congressional Politics of Immigration Reform*. Boston: Allyn & Bacon..

Gold, David. 2002. Fewer Jobs, Slower Growth: Military Spending Drains the Economy. *Dollars & Sense*, July–August, 18–21.

Golden, Miriam. 1997. *Heroic Defeats: The Politics of Job Loss*. New York: Cambridge University Press.

Golden, Miriam, and Jonas Pontussen. 1992. *Bargaining for Change: Union Politics in North America and Europe*. Ithaca, N.Y.: Cornell University Press.

Goldin, Claudia. 1990. *Understanding the Gender Gap: An Economic History of American Women.* New York: Oxford University Press.

Goldston, Robert. 1985. *The Great Depression.* Greenwich, Conn.: Fawcett Publications.

Goodman, Robert. 1979. *The Last Entrepreneurs: America's Regional Wars for Jobs and Dollars.* New York: Simon & Schuster.

Gottlieb, Sanford. 1997. *Defense Addiction: Can America Kick the Habit?* Boulder, Colo.: Westview Press.

Grady, Dennis O. 1987. State Economic Development Incentives: Why Do States Compete? *State and Local Government Review* 12: 86–94.

Granger, C. W. J. 1969. Investigating Causal Relations by Econometric Models and Cross-Spectral Methods. *Econometrica* 37: 424–38.

Gray, Virginia, and Herbert Jacob. 1996. *Politics in the American States*, 6th ed. Washington, D.C.: CQ Press.

Gray, Virginia, Herbert Jacob, and Robert Albritten. 1990. *Politics in the American States*, 5th ed. Washington, D.C.: CQ Press.

Gray, Virginia, and David Lowery. 1996. *The Population Ecology of Interest Representation: Lobbying Communities in the American States.* Ann Arbor: University of Michigan Press.

Greenhouse, Steven. 2003. Labor Turns to a Pivotal Organizing Drive. *New York Times*, May 31.

———. 2004a. Customers Take Up the Cause of Higher Pay at Some Stores. *New York Times*, October 18.

———. 2004b. Labor Vows to Change, but Rebel Voices Dissent. *New York Times*, November 11.

Grissmer, David, and Ann Flanagan. 1998. Exploring Rapid Achievement Gains in North Carolina and Texas. Washington, D.C.: National Education Goals Panel.

Hacker, Jacob, Suzanne Mettler, Dianne Pinderhughes, and Theda Skocpol. 2004. *Inequality and Public Policy.* Report of the Task Force on Inequality and American Democracy. Washington, D.C.: American Political Science Association.

Hackey, Robert B. 1998. *Rethinking Health Care Policy: The New Politics of State Regulation.* Washington, D.C.: Georgetown University Press.

Halbfinger, David M. 2004. Kerry Vows Fight for Equal Pay for Women and a $7 Wage. *New York Times*, October 23.

Hall, Peter, and David Soskice, eds. 2000. *Varieties of Capitalism: Institutional Foundations of Comparative Advantage.* Cambridge: Cambridge University Press.

Hall, Robert E. 2000. The Remarkable Prosperity of College Graduates. http://www-hoover.stanford.edu/pubaffairs/we/current/hall_0900.html.

Hallerberg, Mark, and Scott Basinger. 1999. Globalization and Tax Reform: An Updated Case for the Importance of Veto Players. *Politische Vierteljahresschrift* 40: 618–27.

Hansen, Susan B. 1983. *The Politics of Taxation: Revenue without Representation.* Lexington, Mass.: Praeger.

———. 1984. The Effects of Economic Policies on State Economic Growth. Paper presented at the American Political Science Association, Washington, D.C., September.

———. 1996. Popular and Elite Support for Job Creation, 1972–1994. Paper presented at the American Political Science Association, San Francisco, August.

———. 1999a. Governors' Job Performance Ratings and State Unemployment: The Case of California. *State and Local Government Review* 31: 7–17.

———. 1999b. Life Is Not Fair: Gubernatorial Ratings and State Economic Performance. *Political Research Quarterly* 32: 167–88.

———. 2000. The Low-Wage Strategy for State Economic Development. Paper presented at the Western Political Science Association, San Jose, March.

———. 2001a. Accounting for Trends in State Educational Expenditures. Paper presented at the Midwest Political Science Association, Chicago, April 19–22.

———. 2001b. The Impact of a Low-Wage Strategy on State Economic Development. *State Politics and Policy Quarterly* 1: 227–54.

Hansen, Susan B., Carolyn Ban, and Leonard Huggins. 2003. Explaining the Brain Drain from Older Industrial Cities. *Economic Development Quarterly* 17: 132–47.

Hansen, Susan B., Leonard Huggins, and Carolyn Ban. 2003. Explaining Employee Recruitment and Retention By Non-Profit Organizations: A Survey of Pittsburgh-Area University Graduates. Report to the Forbes Fund / Copeland Foundation, Pittsburgh.

Hansen, Susan B., and Stephanie McLean. 2003. Polarization, Partisanship, and Participation: Trends in American Public Opinion, 1972–2000. Paper presented at the American Political Science Association, Philadelphia, August 27–31.

Harlan, Sharon L. 1989. Women and Federal Job Training Policy. In *Job Training for Women: The Promise and Limits of Public Policies*, ed. Sharon L. Harlan and Ronnie J. Steinberg. Philadelphia: Temple University Press.

Hartmann, Heidi. 2004. *Women and the Economy: Recent Trends in Job Loss, Labor Force Participation, and Wages.* Briefing Paper 245. Washington, D.C.: Institute for Women's Policy Research.

Hays, Constance L. 2004. Wal-Mart Plans Changes to Some Labor Practices. *New York Times*, June 5.

Heckman, James J., and Carmen Pagés. 2004. *Law and Employment: Lessons from Latin America and the Caribbean.* Chicago: University of Chicago Press.

Heinz, John P., Edward O. Laumann, Robert L. Nelson, and Robert H. Salisbury. 1993. *The Hollow Core.* Cambridge, Mass.: Harvard University Press.

Helms, L. Jay. 1985. The Effect of State and Local Taxes on Economic Growth: A Time Series-Cross Section Approach. *Review of Economics and Statistics* 67: 574–82.

Helpmann, Elhanan. 1999. The Structure of Foreign Trade. *Journal of Economic Perspectives* 13: 121–44.

Hendrick, Rebecca M., and James C. Garand. 1991. Variation in State Economic Growth: Decomposing State, Regional, and National Effects. *Journal of Politics* 53: 1093–1110.

Herzik, Eric, and Brent W. Brown. 1991. *Gubernatorial Leadership and State Policy.* New York: Greenwood Press.

Hewitt, Paul S. 2002. *Meeting the Challenge of Global Aging.* Washington, D.C.: Center for Strategic and International Studies.

Higgs, Robert. 1990. *Arms, Politics, and the Economy.* New York: Holmes and Meier.

Highton, Benjamin. 2004. Voter Registration and Turnout in the United States. *Perspectives on Politics* 2: 507–16.

Hill, Kim Quaile, Jan Leighley, and Angela Hinton-Anderson. 1995. Lower Class Mobilization and Policy Linkage in the American States. *American Journal of Political Science* 39: 75–86.

Hirsch, Barry T., and D. A. MacPherson. 1987, 2000. *Union Membership and Earnings Data Book.* Washington, D.C.: Bureau of National Affairs.

Hofstadter, Richard. 1955. *The Age of Reform.* New York: Vintage.

Holbrook, Thomas M., and Emily Van Dunk. 1993. Party Competition in the American States. *American Political Science Review* 87: 955–62.

Holt, Jim. 2004. A States-Rights Left? *New York Times Magazine*, November 21, 27–28.

Horin, Adele. 2004. How Poverty Is Pushing Families into Divorce. http://www.smh.com.au/articles/2004/03/24/1079939718989.

Hout, Michael. 1997. Inequality at the Margins: The Effects of Welfare, the Minimum Wage, and Tax Credits on Low-Wage Labor. *Politics and Society* 25: 513–24.

Howard, Christopher. 1997. *The Hidden Welfare State: Tax Expenditures and Social Policy in the United States.* Princeton, N.J.: Princeton University Press.

Howell, David R. 1994. Behind the Numbers: The Skills Myth. *The American Prospect*, Summer, 81–88.

Huckfeldt, R. Robert, and John Sprague. 1995. *Citizens, Politics, and Social Communication.* New York: Cambridge University Press.

Human Rights Watch. 2000. Joint Statement on Human Rights of U.S. Workers. http://www.hrw.org/reports/2000/uslabor/.

Imbeau, Louis M., and Francois Petry. 2004. *Politics, Institutions, and Fiscal Policy: Deficits and Surpluses in Federated States.* Lanham, Md.: Lexington Books.

Institute of International Education. 2004. Open Doors 2004. http://www.opendoors.iienetwork.org.

Iverson, T. 1998. Wage Bargaining, Hard Money and Economic Performance: Theory and Evidence for Organized Market Economies. *British Journal of Political Science* 28: 31–61.

Jaccard, James, Robert Turrisi, and Choi K. Wan. 1990. *Interactive Effects in Multiple Regression*. Newbury Park, Calif.: Sage.

Jackson, John E. 1988. Michigan. In *The New Economic Role of the American States: Strategies in a Competitive World Economy*, ed. R. Scott Fosler. New York: Oxford University Press.

Jacobs, Lawrence R., and Robert Y. Shapiro. 2000. *Politicians Don't Pander*. Chicago: University of Chicago Press.

Jewell, Malcolm E., and Sarah M. Morehouse. 2001. *Political Parties and Elections in the American States*. Washington, D.C.: CQ Press.

Johnson, Nicholas. 2001. A Hand Up: How State-Earned Income Tax Credits Help Working Families Escape Poverty. Washington, D.C.: Center for Budget and Policy Priorities.

Jones, Roland. 2005. After California, More States Eye Stem Cell Research. MSNBC, February 9. http://www.msnbc.msn.com/id/6847933.

Jones-DeWeever, Avis. 2002. *Marriage Promotion and Low-Income Communities: An Examination of Real Needs and Real Solutions*. Report D450. Washington, D.C.: Institute for Women's Policy Research.

Judy, Richard W., and Carol D'Amico. 1997. *Workforce 2020: Work and Workers in the 21st Century*. Indianapolis: Hudson Institute.

Kahlenberg, Richard D. 2000. Unionization as a Civil Right. *The American Prospect*, September 11, 13–15.

Karoly, Lynn A., and Constantijn W. A. Panis. 2004. *The 21st Century at Work*. Report to the U. S. Department of Labor. Washington, D.C.: RAND Corporation.

Katz, H. C., and O. Darbishire. 1999. *Converging Divergences: Worldwide Changes in Employment Systems*. Ithaca, N.Y.: Cornell University Press.

Kaufman, Bruce E. 2004. What Unions Do: Insights from Economic Theory. *Journal of Labor Research* 25: 371–81.

Kaufman, Leslie. 2004. It's A Trend: Births Out of Wedlock Are Falling in New York. *New York Times,* October 2.

Kelly, Rita Mae. 1991. *The Gendered Economy*. Newbury Park, Calif.: Sage.

Key, V. O. 1949. *Southern Politics in State and Nation*. New York: Alfred A. Knopf.

Killingsworth, Mark R. 2002. Comparable Worth and Pay Equity: Recent Developments in the United States. *Canadian Journal of Public Policy* 28: 171–90.

Kim, Jae-On, and Charles W. Mueller. 1980. *Introduction to Factor Analysis*. Thousand Oaks, Calif.: Sage.

Kinsella, David. 1990. Defense Spending and Economic Performance in the United States: A Causal Analysis. *Defence Economics* 1: 295–309.

Klarner, Carl. 2003. The Measurement of the Partisan Balance of State Government. *State Politics and Policy Quarterly* 3: 294–308.

Kletzer, Lori. 1998. International Trade and Job Displacement in U. S. Manufacturing: 1979–1991. In *Imports, Exports, and the American Worker*, ed. Susan M. Collins. Washington, D.C.: Brookings Institution Press.

———. 2002. *Imports, Exports, and Jobs: What Does Trade Mean for Employment and Job Loss?* Kalamazoo, Mich.: Upjohn Institute for Employment Research.

Kollmeyer, Christopher J. 2003. Globalization, Class Compromise, and American Exceptionalism: Political Change in 16 Advanced Capitalist Countries. *Critical Sociology* 29: 369–91.

Korpi, Walter, and Joakim Palme. 2003. New Politics and Class Politics in the Context of Austerity and Globalization: Welfare State Regress in 18 Countries, 1975–1995. *American Political Science Review* 97: 425–46.

Kreig, Randall G. 1991. Human Capital Selectivity in Interstate Migration. *Growth and Change,* Winter, 68–76.

Kristof, Nicholas D. 2004. Living Poor, Voting Rich. *New York Times,* November 33.

Krueger, Alan B. 2004. Economic Scene: The Most Cost-Effective Way to Encourage People to Turn Out to Vote. *New York Times,* October 14.

Krugman, Paul. 2004. *The Great Unraveling: Losing Our Way in the New Century.* New York: W. W. Norton.

Krugman, Paul, and Robert Z. Lawrence. 1994. Trade, Jobs, and Wages. *Scientific American,* April, 44–49.

Lafer, Gordon. 2002. *The Job Training Charade.* Ithaca, N.Y.: Cornell University Press.

Lakoff, George. 2004. *Don't Think of an Elephant: Know Your Values and Frame the Debate—The Essential Guide for Progressives.* White River Junction, Vt.: Chelsea Green.

Landler, Mark. 2004. Europe Reluctantly Deciding It Has Less Time for Time Off. *New York Times,* July 7.

Langer, Laura. 1999. Measuring Income Distribution across Space and Time in the American States. *Social Science Quarterly* 80: 55–67.

Lee, Christopher, and Stephen Barr. 2002. Unions Fear Bush Will Abuse Freedom from Civil Service Rules. *Pittsburgh Post-Gazette,* November 13.

Lee, R. Alton. 1966. *Truman and Taft-Hartley: A Question of Mandate.* Lexington: University of Kentucky Press.

Leichenko, Robin. 2000. Exports, Employment and Production: A Causal Assessment of U.S. States and Regions. *Economic Geography* 76: 303–25.

Leighley, Jan, and Jonathan Nagler. 2004. Unions as Mobilizing Institutions in the U. S., 1964–2000. Draft manuscript, Texas A&M University, College Station.

Lemov, Penelope. 1997. The Workers' Comp Tug of War. *Governing,* January, 24–25.

Lerner, Stephen. 2003. The Cliff Notes Version of Reorganizing and Rebuilding the Labor Movement. Washington, D.C.: AFL-CIO.

LeRoy, Greg, and Tyson Slocum. 1999. *Economic Development in Minnesota: High Subsidies, Low Wages, Absent Standards.* Washington, D.C.: Good Jobs First.

Levi, Margaret. 2003. Organizing Power: The Prospects for an American Labor Movement. *Perspectives on Politics* 1: 45–68.

Levin-Waldman, Oren M. 2001. *The Case of the Minimum Wage: Competing Policy Models.* Albany: State University of New York Press.

Lindbeck, Assar, and Dennis J. Snower. 1988. *The Insider-Outsider Theory of Employment and Unemployment.* Cambridge, Mass.: MIT Press.

Lipset, Seymour Martin, and Gary Marks. 2000. *It Didn't Happen Here: Why Socialism Failed in the United States.* New York: W. W. Norton.

Lipset, Seymour Martin, and William Schneider. 1987. *The Confidence Gap: Business, Labor, and Government in the Public Mind.* Baltimore: Johns Hopkins University Press.

Lipton, Eric. 2004. New York Hums Again with Asian Trade. *New York Times,* November 22.

Lohr, Steve. 2004. Debate over Exporting Jobs Raises Questions on Policies. *New York Times,* February 23.

Long, Larry. 1991. Residential Mobility Differences among Developed Countries. *International Regional Science Review* 12: 133–47.

Lowery, David, and Virginia Gray. 1995. The Compensatory Impact of State Industrial Policy: An Empirical Assessment of Midterm Effects. *Social Science Quarterly* 76: 438–46.

Luce, Stephanie. 2004. *Fighting for the Living Wage.* Ithaca, N.Y.: Cornell University Press.

Luker, Kristin. 1996. *Dubious Conceptions: The Politics of Teenage Pregnancy.* Cambridge, Mass.: Harvard University Press.

Lyter, Deanna, Melissa Sills, and Gi-Taik Oh. 2003. *Children Left Behind: America's Poorest Children Left in Deeper Poverty after Welfare Reform.* Report D456. Washington, D.C.: Institute for Women's Policy Research.

MacKenzie, Donald. 2005. Wal-Mart Escalates the War on Workers. *Canadian Press,* February 9. http://www.reclaimdemocracy.org/walmart/quebec_canada_store_closed.php.

Maki, Wilbur R., and Richard W. Lichty. 2000. *Urban Regional Economics: Concepts, Tools, and Applications.* Ames: Iowa State University Press.

Maranto, Robert. 1999. Turkey Farm. *Washington Monthly,* November, 26–29.

Mares, Isabela. 2000. Strategic Alliances and Social Policy Reform: Unemployment Insurance in Comparative Perspective. *Politics and Society* 28: 223–44.

Markusen, Ann, Peter Hall, Sabina Dietrick, and Scott Campbell. 1991. *The Rise of the Gunbelt.* New York: Oxford University Press.

Marshall, Scott. 2004. Union on Demand. http://www.politicalaffairs.net/article/view/298/1/36/.

Martin, Cathie Jo. 1995. Nature or Nurture? Sources of Firm Preferences for National Health Reform. *American Political Science Review* 89: 898–913.

Martin, John P. 2004. Editorial: Reassessing the OECD Jobs Strategy. *OECD Economic Outlook.* Paris: Organization for Economic Cooperation and Development.

Massey, Steve. 2004. Bush Likely to Have Much to Crow About in Four Years, No Thanks to Him. *Pittsburgh Post-Gazette,* November 7.

Mayer, Kenneth. 1991. *The Political Economy of Defense Contracting*. New Haven, Conn.: Yale University Press.

McCrate, Elaine. 1997. Welfare and Women's Earnings after AFDC: Reshaping the Anti-Poverty Agenda. *Politics and Society* 25: 417–53.

McGee, Joseph J. 1993. Recapturing Jobs. *State Government News*, May, 10–12.

Melman, S. 1974. *The Permanent War Economy: American Capitalism in Decline*. New York: Simon & Schuster.

Mettler, Suzanne. 1998. *Dividing Citizens: Gender and Federalism in New Deal Public Policy*. Ithaca, N.Y.: Cornell University Press.

Mitchell, Daniel J. 2002. Tax Reform—Not More Audits. http://www.heritage.org/Press/Commentary/ed051602.cfm.

Mitchell, John G. 2004. The Late Great Plains. *National Geographic*, May, 2–29.

Mucciaroni, Gary. 1992. *The Political Failure of Employment Policy, 1945–1982*. Pittsburgh: University of Pittsburgh Press.

National Center on Education and the Economy. 1990. *America's Choice: High Skills or Low Wages?* Washington, D.C.: National Center on Education and the Economy.

National Institute for Labor Relations Research. 1997. Big Labor's Massive Political Machine, September 9. http://www.nrtw.org/d/political_spending.html.

National Public Radio. 2004. California Eyes Change in Workers' Comp. http://www.npr.org/templates/story/story.php?storyId=1804690.

NEA (National Education Association). 2004. Financing Higher Education: A Crisis in State Funding. http://www.nea.org/he/fiscalcrisis/.

Nelson, Michael. 2005. *The Election of 2004*. Washington, D.C.: CQ Press.

New, Michael J. 2004. Analyzing the Effects of State Legislation on the Incidence of Abortion during the 1990s. Heritage Center for Data Analysis. http://www.heritage.org/Research/Family/CDA04-01.cfm.

Newman, Robert J. 1983. Industry Migration and Growth in the South. *Review of Economics and Statistics* 65: 440–49.

New York Times. 2004. As the Dollar Declines [editorial]. November 13.

———. 2005. Georgia's Undemocratic Voter Law [editorial]. July 20.

Nissen, Bruce. 2002. *Unions in a Globalized Environment: Changing Borders, Organizational Boundaries, and Social Roles*. Armonk, N.Y.: M. E. Sharpe.

———. 2003. The Recent Past and Future of Private Sector Unionism in the U. S.: An Appraisal. *Journal of Labor Research* 24: 323–39.

Nordlund, Willis J. 1998. *Silent Skies: The Air Traffic Controllers' Strike*. Westport, Conn.: Praeger.

Norris, Floyd. 2004. Campaign Tactic: Blame Foreigners and Ignore the Trade Deficit. *New York Times*, August 20.

North, Douglass C. 1983. *Growth and Welfare in the United States*. Englewood Cliffs, N.J.: Prentice-Hall.

Norwood, Janet L., and Judith Tanur. 1994. Measuring Unemployment in the Nineties. *Public Opinion Quarterly* 58: 277–94.

OECD (Organization for Economic Cooperation and Development). 1995. *The OECD Jobs Study: Taxation, Employment, and Unemployment*. Paris: OECD.

———. 1999. *Employment Protection and Labour Market Performance*. OECD Employment Outlook. Paris: OECD.

Pantuosco, Lou, Darrell Parker, and Gary Stone. 2001. The Effect of Unions on Labor Markets and Economic Growth: An Analysis of State Data. *Journal of Labor Research* 22: 180–202.

Partridge, Mark D., and Dan S. Rickman. 1995. Differences in State Unemployment Rates: The Role of Labor and Product Market Structure Shifts. *Southern Economic Journal* 62: 89–106.

Paulsen, George E. 1996. *A Living Wage for the Forgotten Man: The Quest for Fair Labor Standards, 1933–1941*. Selinsgrove, Pa.: Susquehanna University Press.

Pearce, Diana M. 1985. Toil and Trouble: Women Workers and Unemployment Compensation. *Signs* 10: 439–60.

Peterson, Paul E. 1995. *The Price of Federalism*. Washington, D.C.: Brookings Institution Press.

Peterson, Paul E., and Mark C. Rom. 1990. *Welfare Magnets: A New Case for a National Standard*. Washington, D.C.: Brookings Institution Press.

Phares, Donald. 1980. *Who Pays State and Local Taxes?* Cambridge, Mass.: Oelgeschlager, Gunn, and Hann.

Pierce, Patrick A., and Donald E. Miller. 2004. *Gambling Politics: State Government and the Business of Betting*. Boulder, Colo.: Lynne Rienner.

Pilat, Dirk. 1998. What Drives Productivity Growth? OECD Science, Technology and Industry Outlook. http://1998/scripts/publications/bookshop/redirect.asp?921998061P1.

Polsby, Nelson W., and Aaron Wildavsky. 2004. *Presidential Elections*, 11th ed. Lanham, Md.: Rowman & Littlefield.

Porter, Michael E. 1985. *The Competitive Advantage of Nations*. New York: Free Press.

———. 2002. Enhancing the Microeconomic Foundations of Prosperity: The Current Competitiveness Index. In *The Global Competitiveness Report 2002*, ed. Peter K. Cornelius and John W. McArthur. New York: Oxford University Press.

Portz, John. 1990. *The Politics of Plant Closings*. Lawrence: University of Kansas Press.

Posner, Paul L. 1998. *The Politics of Unfunded Mandates: Whither Federalism?* Washington, D.C.: Georgetown University Press.

Potoski, Matthew. 2001. Clean Air Federalism: Do States Race to the Bottom? *Public Administration Review* 61: 335–42.

Potoski, Matthew, and Aseem Prakash. 2004. Regulatory Convergence in Nongovernmental Regimes? Cross-National Adoption of ISO 14001 Certification. *Journal of Politics* 66: 885–905.

Progressive Policy Institute. 2000. *The State New Economy Index*. http://www.neweconomyindex.org/states/.

Pryor, Frederic C., and David J. Schaffer. 1999. *Who's Not Working and Why; Employment, Cognitive Skills, Wages, and the Changing U.S. Labor Market.* New York: Cambridge University Press.

Putnam, Robert D. 2000. *Bowling Alone: The Collapse and Revival of American Community.* New York: Simon & Schuster.

Quadagno, Jill S. 1988. *The Transformation of Old Age Security: Class and Politics in the American Welfare State.* Chicago: University of Chicago Press.

Radcliff, Benjamin, and Martin Saiz. 1998. Labor Organization and Public Policy in the American States. *Journal of Politics* 60: 113–25.

Raley, R. Kelly, and Larry Bumpass. 2003. The Topography of the Divorce Plateau: Levels and Trends in Union Stability in the United States after 1980. *Demographic Research* 8: 246–59.

RAND Corporation. 1997. Breaking the Social Contract: The Fiscal Crisis in Higher Education. http://www.rand.org/publications/CAE/CAE100/index.html.

Reed, W. Robert. 2003. How Right-To-Work Laws Affect Wages. *Journal of Labor Research* 24: 713–30.

Reich, Robert. 1991. *The Work of Nations.* New York: Vintage Books.

Rifkin, Jeremy. 1995. *The End of Work: Decline of the Global Labor Force.* New York: G. P. Putnam's Sons.

Rivlin, Alice M. 1992. *Reviving the American Dream: The Economy, the States, and the Federal Government.* Washington, D.C.: Brookings Institution Press.

Rochelle, Dudley, and Hans von Spakovsky. 2003. Paycheck Protection: Union Dues, Political Spending, and Employee Freedom of Choice. http://www.gppf.org/pubs/analyses/paycheckprot.html.

Rosenbaum, David E. 2004. If a Tax Overhaul Has Winners, It Will Also Have Losers. *New York Times,* November 14.

Royster, Deirdre. 2003. *Race and the Invisible Hand.* Berkeley: University of California Press.

Rozhon, Tracie. 2005. Wal-Mart Lags but Target Hits Sales Goal. *New York Times,* May 13.

Rundquist, Barry, Jeong-Hwa Lee, and Jungho Rhee. 1996. The Distributive Politics of Cold War Spending: Some-State Level Evidence. *Legislative Studies Quarterly* 21: 265–79.

Ryscavage, Paul. 1999. *Income Inequality in America: An Analysis of Trends.* Armonk, N.Y.: M. E. Sharpe.

Saal, David S. 2001. The Impact of Procurement-Driven Technological Change on U. S. Manufacturing Productivity Growth. *Defence and Peace Economics* 12: 537–68.

Samuelson, Robert. 2005. America Shouldn't Fear Rise of China, India. *Business Times,* May 26.

Sanchez, Mary. 2005. Ranchers, Sugar Makers, Labor Wrangle over Trade Agreement. http://www.truthout.org/issues_05/061505LA.shtml.

Sbragia, Alberta. 2005. The US and the EU: Comparing Two "Sui Generis" Systems. In *Comparing the U.S. and the E.U.,* ed. Sergio Fabbrini. New York: Routledge.

Schor, Juliet B. 1991. *The Overworked American*. New York: Basic Books.

Schram, Sanford P., and Gary Krueger. 1995. *Welfare Magnets and Benefit Decline: Symbolic Problems and Substantive Consequences*. Madison, Wis.: Institute for Research on Poverty.

Schulman, Bruce J. 1991. *From Cotton Belt to Sunbelt: Federal Policy, Economic Development, and the Transformation of the South*, 1938–1980. New York: Oxford University Press.

Schwarz, Joel. 1988. *America's Hidden Success: A Reassessment of Public Policy from Kennedy to Reagan*, 2nd ed. New York: W. W. Norton.

Scott, Janny. 2002. Foreign Born in U. S. at Record High. *New York Times*, February 7.

Scott, Janny, and David Leonhardt. 2005. Class in America: Shadowy Lines That Still Divide. *New York Times*, May 15.

Scruggs, Lyle, and Peter Lange. 2002. Where Have All the Members Gone? Globalization, Institutions, and Union Density. *Journal of Politics* 64: 126–53.

Sennott, Charles M. 1996. Armed for Profit: The Selling of U. S. Weapons. *Boston Globe*, February 11.

Sexton, Patricia C. 1991. *The War on Labor and the Left*. Boulder, Colo.: Westview Press.

Shanker, Thom, and James Dao. 2002. Defense Secretary Wants Cuts in Weapons Systems. *New York Times,* April 16.

Shaughnessy, Timothy J. 2003. How State Exceptions to Employment-at-Will Affect Wages. *Journal of Labor Research* 24: 447–57.

Siebert, Horst. 1997. Labor Market Rigidities: At the Root of Unemployment in Europe. *Journal of Economic Perspectives* 11: 37–54.

Simon, Julian. 1999. *The Economic Effects of Immigration*, 2nd ed. Ann Arbor: University of Michigan Press.

Skocpol, Theda. 1992. *Protecting Soldiers and Mothers*. Cambridge, Mass.: Harvard University Press.

———. 1997. *Boomerang: Health Care Reform and the Turn against Government*. New York: W. W. Norton.

Skocpol, Theda, and Morris P. Fiorina. 1999. *Civic Engagement and American Democracy*. Washington, D.C.: Brookings Institution Press.

Slater, Robert. 2003. *The Wal-Mart Triumph*. New York: Penguin.

Smith, Kevin B. 1997. Explaining Variation in State-Level Homicide Rates: Does Crime Policy Pay? *Journal of Politics* 59: 350–67.

Snell, Ronald. 1998. *A Review of State Economic Development Policy*. Denver: National Conference of State Legislatures.

Sorenson, Elaine. 1994. *Comparable Worth: Is It a Worthy Policy?* Princeton, N.J.: Princeton University Press.

Stein, Herbert. 1996. *The Fiscal Revolution in America*, 2nd ed. Washington, D.C.: AEI Press.

Steinmo, Sven. 1993. *Taxation and Democracy: Swedish, British, and American Approaches to Financing the Modern State*. New Haven, Conn.: Yale University Press.

Stetson, Dorothy M. 1997. *Women's Rights in the USA*, 2nd ed. New York: Garland.

Stieber, Jack. 1984. Most U.S. Workers Still May Be Fired under the Employment-at-Will Doctrine. *Monthly Labor Review*, May, 34–38.

Stiglitz, Joseph. 2002. *Globalization and Its Discontents*. New York: Basic Books.

Stone, Deborah A. 1984. *The Disabled State*. Philadelphia: Temple University Press.

Stull, Donald D., and Michael J. Broadway. 2004. *Slaughterhouse Blues: The Meat and Poultry Industry in North America*. Belmont, Calif.: Wadsworth.

Swank, Duane. 2002. *Global Capital, Political Institutions, and Policy Change in Developed Welfare States*. New York: Cambridge University Press.

Sweeney, John. 1996. *America Needs a Raise: Fighting for Economic Security and Social Justice*. Boston: Houghton Mifflin.

Task Force on Inequality. 2004. *American Democracy in an Age of Rising Inequality*. Washington, D.C.: American Political Science Association. http://www.apsanet.org/inequality/taskforcereport.pdf.

Texeira, Erin. 2005. Felon Disenfranchisement Is Being Rolled Back. http://www.onenationnews.com/fullstory.asp?newsid=60.

Thomas, Clive S., and Ronald J. Hrebenar. 1999. Interest Groups in the States. In *Politics in the American States: A Comparative Analysis*, 7th edition, ed. Virginia Gray, Russell L. Hanson, and Herbert Jacob. Washington, D.C.: CQ Press.

Thomas, Kenneth P. 2000. *Competing for Capital: Europe and North America in a Global Age*. Washington, D.C.: Georgetown University Press.

Thompson, Lyke. 1983. New Jobs versus Net Jobs: Measuring the Results of an Economic Development Program. *Policy Studies Journal* 12: 365–75.

Thurow, Lester. 1980. *The Zero-Sum Society: Distribution and the Possibilities for Economic Change*. New York: Basic Books.

———. 1999. *Building Wealth: New Rules for Individuals, Companies, and Nations in a Knowledge-Based Economy*. New York: HarperCollins.

Tiebout, Charles. 1956. A Pure Theory of Local Expenditures. *Journal of Political Economy* 64: 416–24.

Tonelson, Alan. 2002. *The Race to the Bottom*. Boulder, Colo.: Westview Press.

Toner, Robin. 2004. Southern Democrats' Decline Is Eroding the Political Center. *New York Times*, November 15.

Toppo, Greg. 2005. NEA, School Districts Sue over "No Child" Law. *USA Today*, April 20.

Uchitelle, Louis. 2003. A Missing Statistic: U.S. Jobs That Went Overseas. *New York Times*, October 5.

Um'Rani, Annisah, and Vicky Lovell. 2000. *Unemployment Insurance and Welfare Reform*. Report D441c. Washington, D.C.: Institute for Women's Policy Research.

USWA (United Steel Workers of America). 2004. New Jersey Stops Most Outsourcing. http://www.uswa.org/uswa/program/content/1589.php.

Uchitelle, Louis. 2006. *The Disposable American: Layoffs and Their Consequences.* New York: Alfred A. Knopf.

Vedder, Richard K., and Lowell Gallaway. 1993. *Out of Work: Unemployment and Government in 20th Century America.* New York: Holmes & Meier.

Ventry, Dennis. 2000. Political History of the EITC. In *Making Work Pay: The Earned Income Tax Credit and Its Impact on America's Families,* ed. Bruce D. Meyer and Douglas Holtz-Eakin. New York: Russell Sage Foundation.

Verba, Sidney. 2003. Would the Dream of Political Equality Turn Out to Be a Nightmare? *Perspectives on Politics* 1: 663–80.

Verba, Sidney, Kay Lehman Schlozman, and Henry E. Brady. 1995. *Voice and Equality: Civic Voluntarism in American Politics.* Cambridge, Mass.: Harvard University Press.

Volgy, Thomas, John E. Schwarz, and Lawrence Imwalle. 1996. In Search of Economic Well-Being: Worker Power and the Effects of Productivity, Inflation, Unemployment, and Global Trade on Wages in Ten Wealthy Countries. *American Journal of Political Science* 40: 1233–52.

Walker, Susan C. 2004. U. S. Consumer Credit Card Debt May Crash Economy. Fox News, December 31. http://www.foxnews.com/0,3566,143037.html.

Wallack, Todd. 2004. Where the Candidates Stand on Health Care. *San Francisco Chronicle,* October 11. http://sfgate.com/cgi-bin/article.cgi?f=/c/a/2004/10/11/MNGII96D031.DTL.

Wallerstein, Michael, and Bruce Western. 2000. Unions in Decline? What Has Changed and Why? *Annual Reviews of Political Science* 3: 355–77.

Wallis, Jim. 2005. *God's Politics: Why the Right Gets It Wrong and the Left Doesn't Get It.* New York: HarperCollins.

Walsh, David J., and Joshua L. Schwarz. 1996. State Common Law Wrongful Discharge Doctrines. *American Business Law Journal* 33: 645–99.

Walsh, Mary Williams. 2004. A Hard-to-Swallow Lesson on Pensions. *New York Times,* October 4.

Warren, Elizabeth, and Amelia Warren Tyagi. 2003. *The Two-Income Trap: Why Middle-Class Mothers and Fathers Are Going Broke.* New York: Basic Books.

Watson, Douglas, Edwin I. Gardner, and Robert S. Montjoy. 2001. Moving into the Global Economy: A Case Study of Alabama's Recruitment of Mercedes-Benz. In *Globalization's Impact on State-Local Economic Development Policy,* ed. Cal Clark and Robert S. Montjoy. Huntington, N.Y.: Nova Science.

Wattenberg, Benjamin, and Richard Scammon. 1970. *The Real Majority:* New York: Coward-McCann.

WCRI (Workers' Compensation Research Institute). 2001. *CompScope Benchmarks: Multistate Comparisons, 1994–1999.* http://www.insurancejournal.com/news/south/2001/09/04/14952.html.

Webber, Alan M. 2004. Reverse Brain Drain Threatens U.S. Economy. *USA Today,* February 23. http://www.usatoday.com/news/opinion/editorials/2004-02-23-econ.

Weber, Ronald E., and Paul Brace, eds. 1999. *American State and Local Politics: Directions for the 21st Century.* New York: Chatham House.

Weingast, Barry R. 1994. The Economic Role of Political Institutions: Federalism, Markets, and Economic Development. *Journal of Law, Economics, and Organization* 11: 1–31.

Weisbrot, Mark, and Michelle Sforza-Roderick. 2003. *Baltimore's Living Wage Law.* Washington, D.C.: Preamble Center.

Weiss, Linda, and John M. Hudson. 1995. *States and Economic Development: A Comparative Historical Analysis.* Cambridge: Polity Press.

White, Sammis B. 1987. Reservation Wages: Your Community May Be Competitive. *Economic Development Quarterly* 1: 18–29.

Wibbles, Erik. 2000. Federalism and the Politics of Macroeconomic Policy. *American Journal of Political Science* 44: 687–702.

Wilensky, Harold. 2002. *Rich Democracies: Economics, Public Policy, and Performance.* Berkeley: University of California Press.

Wilson, Graham K. 1998. *Only in America? The Politics of the United States in Comparative Perspective.* Chatham, N.J.: Chatham House.

Wilson, Kenneth G. 1995. *The Impact of Unions on United States Economy-Wide Productivity.* New York: Garland.

Wilson, William Julius. 1997. *When Work Disappears: The World of the New Urban Poor.* New York: Alfred A. Knopf.

Winters, Richard F. 1999. The Politics of Taxing and Spending. In *Politics in the American States: A Comparative Analysis,* 7th edition, ed. Virginia Gray, Russell L. Hanson, and Herbert Jacob. Washington, D.C.: CQ Press.

Wise, Lois R. 1989. *Labor Market Policies and Employment Patterns in the United States.* Boulder, Colo.: Westview Press.

Wohlers, Eckhardt, and Gunter Weinert. 1988. *Employment Trends in the United States, Japan, and the European Community.* New Brunswick, N.J.: Transaction Books.

Wolfers, Justin. 2002. Are Voters Rational? Evidence from Gubernatorial Elections. Working Paper 1730, Stanford Graduate School of Business, Stanford University, Stanford, Calif.

Wolff, Edward N. 1994. *Top Heavy: A Study of the Increasing Inequality of Wealth in America.* Washington, D.C.: Brookings Institution Press.

Wood, Peter. 1986. *Southern Capitalism.* Durham, N.C.: Duke University Press.

World Economic Forum. 2004. *Global Competitiveness Report 2004–2005.* http://www.weforum.org/site/homepublic.nsf/Content/Global+Competitiveness.

Wright, Gerald. 2004. CBS / *New York Times* National Polls, Ideology, Partisanship, 1976–2003 (Zip file). http://www.mypage.iu.edu/~wright1.

Yanarella, Ernest J., and William C. Green, eds. 1990. *The Politics of Industrial Recruitment.* Westport, Conn.: Greenwood Press.

Yeomans, Barry. 2001. Silence in the Fields. *Mother Jones,* January–February, 40–47.

Young, Rebecca. 1998. Cheap Tricks: When Employers Cheat on Their Workers' Comp Insurance, Everybody Pays. *Washington Monthly,* September, 34–38.

Zernike, Kate, and John M. Broder. 2004. War? Jobs? No, Character Counted Most to Voters. *New York Times,* November 4.

Index

abortion rates, 127–28, 130, 181, 183, 194n17
AFL-CIO, 3, 16, 18, 19, 21, 40, 43, 44, 46, 61, 69, 73, 74, 144
African Americans, blacks, 29, 31, 34, 35, 72, 73, 81, 115, 120, 128–30, 140, 142, 163
age structure of population, 115, 122, 127–29, 153, 193n10
agriculture, 8, 22, 28, 29, 31–34, 42, 94, 110, 115, 154, 192n7
Ahlstrand, Amanda, 142
aircraft manufacturing, 4, 95, 100–101, 111
Alabama, 22, 36, 40, 52, 89, 95, 98, 155
Alaska, 40, 68, 79, 98, 100, 162, 172
Alesina, Alberto, 190n6
Amberg, Stephen, 186n5
American Council on Education, 185n2
American Federation of Labor (AFL), xvi, 14, 17, 32, 33, 73, 145
American Federation of Labor-Congress of Industrial Organizations. See AFL-CIO
American National Election Studies (ANES), xvi, 78–80, 189n16

Americans with Disabilities Act, 47, 50
Andrews, Edmund L., 156
ANES. See American National Election Studies
Anton, Thomas J., 190n7
Appalachian Regional Commission, 23, 190n7
Appelbaum, Eileen, 131, 159, 161
Arizona, 22, 63, 69, 72, 79, 82, 122
Arkansas, 3–5, 36, 67, 69, 74, 79, 122–23, 188n5
Asher, Herbert B., 81, 115
Asia, 8, 20, 21, 32, 155, 158
automobile manufacturing, 2, 8, 15, 21, 34, 67, 89, 95, 146, 155
Avery, James, 116

Babcock, Linda, 148
Baer, Judith A., 16, 186n1
Bailey, Michael A., 61
Baker, Al, 140
Ballam, Deborah A., 17, 46
Barker, David C., 86
Barrilleaux, Charles, 88
Barro, R. J., 59
Bartik, Timothy J., 42, 68, 92, 93, 110, 151, 154, 185n9

Sbragia, Alberta, xvi, 10
Schor, Juliet B., 3
Schram, Sanford P., 23, 89
Schulman, Bruce J., 35
Schwarz, Joel, 7, 8, 11, 22, 69, 108, 138
Schwarzenegger, Arnold, 75
Scott, Janny, 63, 118
Scruggs, Lyle, 15, 185n6, 186n9
Sennott, Charles M., 100, 102
Sexton, Patricia C., 15, 32, 33, 35, 44, 69, 95
Shanker, Thom, 100
Shaughnessy, Timothy J., 47
Sherman Antitrust Act, 32, 33
Siebert, Horst, 12
Simon, Julian, 19, 94, 188n6
single mothers, births to, 115–16, 120, 127–28, 130, 132–33, 137, 162, 183, 194n20
Skocpol, Theda, 16, 17, 30–34, 49, 116, 146–47, 185n8
slavery, 1, 7, 28, 29
Smith, Kevin B., 120, 127, 129
Snell, Ronald, 158
social capital, 115–16, 132
social gospel, 20, 73, 86, 162
Social Security, 7, 9, 17, 24, 27, 28, 34, 42, 50, 52, 53, 56, 57, 104, 145, 150, 184, 186n2, 187n10, 187n12
social wage, xv, 6, 7, 11, 19, 20, 52, 93, 95, 97, 136, 156
socialists, socialism, 8, 14, 15, 31, 33, 34
Sorenson, Elaine, 149
South Carolina, 40, 43, 53, 82, 95, 125
South Dakota, 39, 69, 72, 162
southern states, 2, 4, 7, 8, 20, 27, 29–31, 34, 38, 43, 46, 52, 68, 72, 74, 75, 77, 79–82, 88, 90, 92, 94, 104, 118, 122, 129, 169, 188n7, 189n14, 194n18
state-local spending, 125–26, 140,

142, 184, 193n16
Stein, Herbert, 34
Steinmo, Sven, 14, 153
Stetson, Dorothy M., 18, 30, 148
Stieber, Jack, 17
Stiglitz, Joseph, 60, 95
Stone, Deborah A., 50
strikes, xiii, 15–17, 32–35, 38, 40, 45, 56, 93, 145, 157, 189n15
Stull, Donald D., 69, 129
subsidies to business, xiii, xiv, 23, 38, 89, 92, 97, 142, 149–50, 152, 154–55, 157, 190n5
suicide rates, 9, 25, 114, 120, 132–33, 137, 184
Sunbelt, xv, 3, 22, 40, 89, 93, 101
Supreme Court, 16, 17, 23, 30, 45
Swank, Duane, 8, 14, 185n6
sweatshops, 31, 61, 68
Sweden, 14, 151, 153, 186n10
Sweeney, John, 16, 19, 21, 144

Taft-Hartley Act (1947), 17, 27, 36, 57, 144, 158
tariffs, 28, 29, 33, 152
Task Force on Inequality, 81, 86, 87, 132, 159
tax burden, state/local, 4, 11, 62, 65, 98, 99, 104, 108, 110, 125
taxes
impact on economic growth, 5, 10, 27, 91–92, 97–99, 104–11, 136
regressivity of, 98, 116, 125–26, 132–33, 150, 184, 193nn14–15
state, xiii, xv, 3–7, 10–12, 14, 20, 22, 24, 42, 59–63, 65, 72, 81, 87, 89, 115, 120, 122, 136, 142, 151, 153, 156–58, 160–63, 171, 174, 176–77, 188n3, 190n1, 190n5, 191n15, 193n14
Tennessee, 35, 40
Texas, 43, 63, 82, 98, 100, 122
Texeira, Erin, 163